THE GREAT
OLYMPIC
SWINDLE

THE GREAT OLYMPIC SWINDLE

When the World Wanted its Games Back

Andrew Jennings

and

Clare Sambrook

SIMON & SCHUSTER
A VIACOM COMPANY

First published in Great Britain by Simon & Schuster UK Ltd, 2000
A Viacom company

1 3 5 7 9 10 8 6 4 2

Simon & Schuster UK Ltd
Africa House
64-78 Kingsway
London WC2B 6AH

Simon & Schuster Australia
Sydney

A CIP catalogue record for this book
is available from the British Library

ISBN 0-684-86677-3

Typeset in Fairfield by SX Composing DTP, Rayleigh, Essex
Printed and bound in Australia by
Griffin Press Pty Ltd.

For Sophie McMillan

Contents

Chapter 1

Anita's Bad Hair Day

When Anita DeFrantz strode through the government halls that bright, gusty spring day in 1999, it was obvious to anyone watching that she was special. You could see it in her powerful physique. She looked taller than her five foot eleven inches, broad-shouldered and vigorous, younger than her forty-seven years.

You only had to look at the way people gathered around her, smiling and eager, as she made her entrance into the spacious hearing room, just across the street from the Capitol. Resplendent in peacock blue, she turned her large, handsome head and beamed back at them, took a hand here, a hand there, meeting and greeting like a member of royalty.

Anita belongs to that most regal of families, the Olympic family. On the world body that governs the games, the International Olympic Committee, she is one of few women and the only African American. Anita is a royal with a difference. The daughter of a civil rights activist, she takes inspiration from the life of Harriet Tubman, an escaped slave who led three hundred more to freedom.

Anita DeFrantz would need inspiration in Washington that day. The Olympic family was in peril and she'd been sent to defend it. Members of the IOC, handpicked by their leader, Juan Antonio, Marqués de Samaranch, to select the cities that host the Olympic Games, had been caught behaving badly. They chose Salt Lake City, Utah, for the winter games of

1

2002, and, it turned out, some of them had traded their votes for jobs and scholarships for their children, sometimes scholarships for other people's children or kids who did not exist at all. Some members dispensed with the scholarship malarkey and settled for plain old cash.

In Utah Olympic people took free ski holidays and sleigh rides and shopping trips and massage. Yes, massage. Back home they greeted delivery men who strained under the weight of free bicycles and sports goods and all sorts of things that had nothing legal to do with deciding which city might put on the best games.

There was no problem until people outside the Olympic family found out, and that wrecked Christmas 1998. The world's press united in disgust at the notion that bribery should taint the near-sacred Olympics, and the family set about defending what credibility it had left.

When scandal broke, the family's American branch, the United States Olympic Committee, had the Salt Lake bidding team investigated by tough-minded outsiders, owned up to mistakes and pledged to change.

Across the globe in Switzerland, in his splendid Lausanne compound, IOC President Samaranch took a different tack. He called up a world-class group of spin doctors. He personally selected five trusty IOC members to investigate their peers. The five made some inquiries and reported back.

There was bad behaviour, they said, and the hosts were the culprits. Those people were so insistent, and persistent, and, well, so darned friendly down in Utah that some vulnerable members thought those lovely gifts were about personal friendship, nothing to do with the business of getting the games. A few Olympic heads rolled.

That wasn't good enough for most people. In Washington,

DC, Senator John McCain felt agitated. As chairman of the Senate's commerce committee, which supervises Olympic affairs, he knew that more than half of the IOC's budget comes from US tax breaks, American television companies and sponsors. He knew that many thousands of ordinary sports fans could be relied upon to send cheques and cash to support their Olympic team. He didn't like to see his country being taken for a ride. McCain invited Samaranch to come and talk to the committee – in April, a gorgeous time of year in Washington, when cherry trees begin to flower.

Perhaps he had a blossom allergy. Offering no excuses, Samaranch snubbed the invitation. A frequent traveller to the United States, he knew that Americans hold athletes in very high regard. Anita DeFrantz had won an Olympic bronze in rowing. Perhaps Samaranch calculated that senators might go easy on a fellow American, a woman of colour, a medal winner. He sent her in his place.

Anita dressed with particular care that day. Over black silky trousers and T shirt she wore a garment designed and made especially for her, a loose-fitting peacock-blue velour jacket with a rowing motif hand-stitched in satin. Six oars of alternating bright purple, black and vivid pink, with green blades, danced across the jacket's front. Six more on the back sang out: here is an athlete, an oarswoman, a medal winner.

John McCain is not easily impressed. He has won a few medals of his own. As a young navy pilot he was shot down over Hanoi, held prisoner for five and a half years, and tortured repeatedly. He won the Silver Star, the Bronze Star, the Legion of Merit, the Purple Heart and the Distinguished Flying Cross. However revered Olympians may be in the American psyche, war heroes stand above them.

A famously maverick politician with a notorious temper,

McCain has attacked the tobacco industry, fought to limit the many millions of dollars spent courting electors, and tried and failed to end free parking for politicians at Washington airport. He also brought in a bill to protect young boxers from being exploited, and named it after Muhammad Ali.

McCain had every reason to put on a good show when Anita and her friends came to town. The senator wanted to be the Republican candidate for the presidential elections of late 2000. Soon he'd be touring the country in a battle-bus called the Straight Talk Express. The hearings, on a subject so close to American hearts, would be broadcast on television across the nation.

The friendly chatter under the broad, high ceiling of hearing room 106 died down. Reporters gathered at their table, arranged their tape machines and notebooks, tested their pens. Anita's entourage, fellow athletes, Olympic bureaucrats and spin doctors, took their seats at the front of the house and waited.

These people are accustomed to a sense of occasion. When President Samaranch does make an appearance he is announced with all due ceremony. It wasn't like that when American democracy kicked into action. One minute the senators' dais was empty. The next minute there they were, and snowy-haired John McCain had got to what he called, 'the heart of the matter', integrity and trust, and he was talking about one great Olympic athlete he knew, 'who represents a human ideal we all dream of', Muhammad Ali.

Who could forget Ali? The eighteen-year-old-boy who flew to Rome for the 1960 Olympics wearing a parachute because he feared flying, who won a Gold medal and wore it day and night, slept on his back for the first time in his life so it would not cut his skin. Ali had sacrificed his title for a principle. And, as McCain reminded his audience, Ali, one hot summer night in Atlanta in 1996, stepped out from the shadows, in front of three billion people watching television around the world and, trembling from exertion, excitement and from his own crippling disease, held up the heavy Olympic torch and opened the games.

What had the Olympics come to? asked McCain. 'A culture of corruption, with lavish travel and gift-giving, bribe-taking and exploitation,' he went on in his clenched-jaw way of speaking. 'At its core, this issue is about the integrity of an institution and the public trust. In a democracy, our institutions rise and fall according to the level of public trust. In a free world, trust is the foundation on which we build the institutions of our culture and our society.'

Anita and her entourage sat still and silent in their seats.

'I look forward to hearing from the IOC representatives regarding what the organisation plans to do about the culture of corruption so evident in the Olympic bid process,' said McCain in a tone all the more menacing because it gave no emotion away.

Then other senators joined in.

What stuck in Senator Ron Wyden's throat was the secrecy of the Olympic family. Richard Bryan from Nevada wanted Samaranch to go: 'I do not believe that any credible reform can be undertaken at the international level until he steps down.'

Senator Ben Nighthorse Campbell, a Native American who led the US judo team at the 1964 Tokyo Games, was the mildest critic, and he was angry too. He was angry that America was not allowed to elect its own IOC members, but had them picked by Samaranch, instead.

'Can you imagine NATO calling over here and telling us who

they want to be our representative on NATO, rather than us picking a representative?' asked the senator with the long grey pigtail. He remembered the tens of thousands of Americans, 'who send in ten dollars or twenty dollars or whatever they can afford to support this team'.

And then the attack really got started.

Senator McCain had invited along Senator George Mitchell, who had headed the independent inquiry commissioned by the American Olympic family into Salt Lake. Having spent a long, hard time negotiating in the political hell of Northern Ireland, fresh-faced, bespectacled George, you might think, would be unshockable. He and his team took their seats at the witnesses' table in front of the senators, and Mitchell began.

'Sadly,' he said, 'members of the International Olympic Committee were the recipients of a total of between four million dollars and seven million dollars in gifts and services.'

It did not start in Salt Lake. 'Indeed we learned that as far back as 1991 the city of Toronto, Canada, had delivered to the IOC a report of its experiences of the gift-giving culture,' Mitchell said. The IOC told Toronto it could take no action without culprits' names, even though Toronto had identified structural flaws in the bidding process that invited corruption. Toronto, planning to bid again, was reluctant to jeopardise future votes by naming names, so the IOC did nothing. The Toronto people told Mitchell's team that they were gravely disappointed about that.

Mitchell wasn't convinced by Samaranch's in-house Inquiry, which blamed the Salt Lake givers of the improper gifts, 'suggesting that IOC members were victims of predator cities'. The record did not support such a conclusion, he said.

'In the absence of swift and meaningful reform, the

Olympic movement runs the risk of becoming a testimonial to excess, to elitism, to money,' said Mitchell. 'The Olympics deserves better. The public deserves better. The Olympics should be an ideal to competition, to excellence, to integrity, and we are confident that with proper action for reform it once again will be.'

George Mitchell, it turned out, was half of a Mr Nice and Mr Nasty team. If Anita hoped that Mr Nasty had just spoken she was wrong. George was the nice guy.

'We recommend strong medicine,' said Mr Nasty, a thick, squat man, wriggling in his seat, anchoring himself more firmly for the attack. 'The IOC seems to be trying to get a second opinion more to its liking. They want to take an aspirin and call a doctor in the morning, some time in the year 2000.'

Mr Nasty was Mitchell's deputy Ken Duberstein, who had made his name as President Reagan's no-nonsense chief of staff. 'Expelling a few rank-and-file members, allowing a handful to resign but leaving the two most prominent culprits who sit on the executive board to escape with a gentle slap on the wrist is not encouraging,' he said, delivering every word firmly, as if each one were a smart smack across the backside for President Samaranch.

Blaming the Salt Lake City bidding team 'for entrapment of so-called hapless IOC members says some still do not get it', he said. 'In short, the IOC to date has not cleaned house. They have just begun to air out one small room.'

Mr Nasty was not through.

'We did not recommend President Samaranch's resignation, but he must demonstrate urgent, serious and comprehensive action, not mere words or a PR offensive, to reform the Olympic movement. Fundamental systemic reform from financial transparency to real accountability, from term limits to more athletes' participation in open governance must be the prescription taken at the top of the IOC to cure its culture of corruption.'

The 'marvellous athletes and the viewing public deserve no less', said Mr Duberstein who has a way of expressing scorn that penetrates human bone.

By the time Anita's turn came to walk the few yards to the witnesses' table, she seemed to have lost a few inches in height. Perhaps it had dawned on her that things were not going her way. Head up, shoulders back, she had a brave smile for the senators, and things didn't seem too dreadful, until she started talking.

'I am testifying in my capacity as a vice-president of the International Olympic Committee,' said Anita. You could almost see cartoon thought bubbles floating above the senators' heads. ('Okay, so they're the funsters who sold their votes for a ski holiday in Salt Lake. Hmmm.')

'And I am a member of both the United States Olympic Committee and the Salt Lake Organising Committee Executive Boards,' said Anita. ('Okay, so she's with the funsters *and* the USOC – weren't they supposed to ensure Salt Lake played fair? And Jeez, she's in bed with Salt Lake people too. Can she be serious?')

She didn't mention yet another Olympic job of hers, the $230,000-a-year presidency of a charitable foundation, built on profits from the Los Angeles Games, that funds community sports in the region.

'I am a US Olympian, who won a bronze medal in the 1976 games, and a member of the 1980 team,' said Anita, and bronze never sounded more like third.

Then she trotted out a good news story, about, 'a little-known aspect and function of the IOC . . . to fund training programs in support of athletes around the world', and she reeled off the steps the IOC had taken to clean house so far. She told them she'd been 'touched by the magic of the Olympics', and a stern-faced John McCain muttered, 'Thank you very much.'

Anita had an ally at her side, and it was his turn to speak. It might have helped if he'd been a plain-speaking, affable fellow with a thoroughly altruistic commitment to sport.

This wasn't Anita's lucky day. Her right-hand man was Jim Easton, a multimillionaire manufacturer of aluminium sports goods – baseball bats, hockey and archery equipment – that Olympic athletes tend to use. He's an IOC member and before Samaranch chose him Jim donated a brace of $900 bicycles to Samaranch and his secretary. When baseball won its place in the Olympics in 1992, Jim's business got a boost because Olympic baseball players used aluminium bats. Since then, they've noticed that big men hitting small balls with aluminium bats can hit them a long, long way at murderous speeds, so for the Sydney games, they decided on wooden bats.

Jim attended meetings with the Salt Lake bidding people but never noticed that jobs were being traded for votes. Imagine his surprise, when, walking the floor of his Salt Lake factory one day, he bumped into a new employee called Sibu Sibandze, son of Swaziland's IOC member! What with one thing and another Jim was not the ideal man for Anita to have at her side when she faced the cool, hard gaze of McCain. And that was the good news.

The bad news was that Jim had chatted with a reporter a few days before the Senate meeting and here's what he said about McCain and his colleagues: 'You talk about people in glass houses. Here we have our politicians who live daily with conflicts of interest criticising us on the way we run our business. I think it's out of line.'

That wasn't all.

'What I'm afraid is that they're doing it for political advantage and not for the benefit of anybody except for themselves,' Jim went on. 'They just get on a soap box and preach their righteousness. I think they've got to look at themselves a bit too. They don't understand what's going on with the Olympic movement. They take a few sound-bites and move out on those.' Well, Jim had a few days to mull over the wisdom of his words and the senators had all the time they needed to work up a rage and hit on the most withering way of expressing it. Before the start of the session two cheerful young men set about building something with bits of wood in front of the senators' dais. Could it be – no, surely not – a scaffold for Jim Easton?

It almost was.

The men had soon erected four easels, and on each one they set a big board. On each board, and at mind-numbing length, were laid out the rules that govern senators' behaviour, on travel arrangements, receiving gifts, on conflicts of interest. They stood there, all four of them, all through that day, as clear as if McCain had hired an aeroplane to tow a banner across Washington's wide blue sky bearing the message: 'JIM EASTON, YOU'RE AN IDIOT!'

Grey-haired, thin-lipped and guarded, it wasn't Jim's fault that he possessed the manner of a man who enjoys tearing wings off butterflies. He had an apology to make and it didn't look as though the multimillionaire was accustomed to that.

'I would like to apologise, and I have apologised publicly, in the press and in a letter to you,' he said. His head turned to his right, his eyes to the left. An unfortunate choice of posture: it made him look shifty. 'And I would like to do it now personally to you and the committee for these statements that I made in Lausanne, which were spontaneous and certainly personalised more than they should have been.'

There. That was it. It was over. And he'd managed to get through it without saying, 'Sorry.'

'We will not mention that subject again,' said McCain.

The laws of physics might suggest that things couldn't go downhill from there. But that was where I came in.

When I first heard of John McCain's interest in the Olympics I sent him a copy of my book *The New Lords of the Rings*. He invited me along to share with the senators some of what I knew about the Olympic family. I felt honoured to be asked.

'Will you pay my expenses?' I asked McCain's people.

'Er, no, I'm afraid we can't do that,' they said.

I took my best Marks & Spencer jacket to the dry-cleaners, had a hair-cut, brushed my shoes, packed my rucksack and off I went, economy class, to Washington.

'Er, do you happen to have a tie?' asked McCain's people. I did not.

Sitting a yard or two away from Anita, I told the senators how the IOC had tried to jail me a few years back, for saying what everyone now accepted as the truth: that there was a culture of corruption in the Olympics. I told them how astonished I had been to learn that the Olympics are controlled by a man who joined Spain's youth fascists in 1936 and kept on doing that right-arm salute until the dictator General Franco died in 1975. I introduced them to some of the characters Samaranch has chosen to run the world's biggest festival of goodwill – the man who destroys rainforests for a living, the man who served as Idi Amin's defence minister, and some other nice guys.

When McCain thanked me, he was smiling. Then he turned to Anita.

'How much of the money raised by the IOC is used to fund programmes that provide direct support for the athletes?'

It seemed like an easy starter for her. Didn't Samaranch always say, 'Everything we do is for the athletes?'

It wasn't as easy as all that. Anita burbled. Anita rambled. The senator asked her again. Anita burbled. Anita rambled. 'We do not know how the funds are used. I suppose that is your question, sir.'

'Ms DeFrantz, I do not mean to appear as if I am subjecting you to any kind of unfair questioning,' said McCain. He sighed, he steadied himself. 'My question was – and I am going to ask it for the third time – how much of the money raised by the IOC – I am familiar with many of the very wonderful programmes – how much of the money raised by the IOC is used to fund programmes that provide direct support for the athletes?'

Anita couldn't say.

Then McCain asked an obvious question. It didn't sound clever. He asked if Anita and Jim supported George Mitchell's conclusions about how the Olympic family should reform itself, and he went through them, one by one.

Term limits. That was an easy one. Surely only dictators believe it's all right to stay in power for ever.

Anita looked stumped. McCain waited. Anita appeared to be listening for something, perhaps a message from Lausanne. Were those long, dangling earrings of hers really radio receivers, taking coded orders from Samaranch in his Swiss compound?

Anita stared. McCain looked worried. It doesn't do to have a witness turn catatonic on the stand.

'Ms DeFrantz?'

'Yes, sir, I am thinking.'

'Oh, sorry,' said the senator.

Anita thought some more.

'Excuse me, Mr Senator. Yes, Sir, I do.'

Jim thought so too. Term limits, that was the thing.

How about letting national Olympic committees choose their own international members, instead of having them handpicked by Samaranch?

Anita explained that she was one of six people recommended by the United States Olympic Committee and Samaranch had picked her. That was OK, wasn't it?

Which reminded me. Someone once told me how Anita beat the favourite, Donna de Varona, the Olympic swimmer, ABC commentator and long-time athlete's advocate, to win that IOC slot. Robert Helmick, who used to be a senior member of the American and world Olympic family, discussed the two candidates with Samaranch in his suite at the Lausanne Palace Hotel and he told me what passed. 'Samaranch was afraid Donna would be too strong. He said, "Anita won't give us any problems," and it was right after talking about Donna and the fact that we were not going to be able to control her.'

While I was thinking about that, Jim wittered on and on and it was hard to tell what he thought about the idea of letting countries choose their own IOC members. McCain assumed he disagreed with it. Jim conceded that he did, and the senator went on to the next of Mitchell's modest proposals for reform. Did they agree that countries should be allowed to bid for the games only if their anti-bribery laws encompassed the IOC?

Anita and Jim had reservations about that one.

And how about the IOC moving away from the worrisome 'interlocking directorates', which meant the same person could, like Anita, serve on the IOC, the national committee and the organising committee of the city hosting the games.

'Mr Chairman, that is one that specifically confuses me,' said Anita. Jim didn't like it either.

McCain did his arithmetic.

'So, of the four recommendations that I asked you about, three of them you have, quote, reservations about, or outright oppose. That is very interesting.' It came out slow and gravelly: innerresting.

Then McCain asked Anita about the IOC's rule that minutes of its meetings should be kept secret for as long as twenty years. Anita supported it: 'Some of the discussions would put at jeopardy some of the members and their positions in their own country,' she said.

'In what way, Ms DeFrantz?' McCain almost squeaked.

Anita couldn't say, exactly.

McCain dropped his head stiffly into his hands. He rubbed his face. He sighed. When he was ready, he spoke. There was a quiver in his voice and you could believe what people say about McCain throwing tantrums. He seemed to be taking a grip on himself.

'Well, Ms DeFrantz, I have to tell you that this is an organisation with sixty per cent or seventy per cent of its funding coming from the United States of America. The American people, I am sure – I am absolutely convinced – deserve to know what goes on in those meetings. And to assume a position or a thought that these kinds of deliberations, which have such a profound impact would be kept in secret for ten or twenty years flies in the face of everything I have ever known in my life.'

John McCain had a message for Samaranch. He explained how things are done in America when scandal breaks. We investigate, he said. 'We find the best minds we can who are willing to serve in an independent status.' Then he spoke so clearly that it seemed his words might reach the IOC President right that minute, crouched over a radio receiver in his Swiss bunker, picking up the signal from Anita's earrings. 'The appearance of independence, of course, is very difficult to maintain if the person who heads the organisation that is being investigated has control of the commission doing the investigating.'

McCain ended with as little ceremony as he had begun. He sounded pessimistic, but the parlous state of the Olympics was still more dire than he could know. I'd seen those secret minutes among stacks of IOC documents which told the true story of the Olympics. I knew their blunders did not stop at taking gifts. I flew back to London and over the next few months I'd hear my doorbell ring and pound downstairs to greet the postman bearing a fresh bundle of confidential documents from inside President Samaranch's compound.

I learned about how they plotted to resist the reformers, to tell the world that change was happening when it wasn't. I discovered, and at first I found it hard to grasp, that Olympic corruption had gone further than any outsider knew. What I found out made the Salt Lake shenanigans seem almost quaint. Organised crime was moving in on the Olympics, and some of the Olympic family welcomed the gangsters with open arms.

But we're running ahead of ourselves. That's all to come. This is Anita's story.

Two things mark rowers out from other athletes, besides the awesome way they absorb physical pain. One is their ability to propel themselves backwards at speed and put their faith in someone else to do the steering. The other is a capacity to surrender the self to the team. A rower like Anita isn't one of eight individuals, she is one eighth of the crew, one vital part of a machine. And the team, in turn, surrenders itself – totally – to the coach. 'It's the ultimate team sport,' Anita once said. 'You're not supposed to say anything when you're rowing. You're supposed to listen and become part of the boat.'

Perhaps Samaranch saw Anita's fine qualities, looked at the woman who as a teenager played clarinet for her high school marching band, saw her enthusiasm, her loyalty to the team, her trusting nature, saw it all and judged that here was a person he could use. Whatever, Anita was defending him to the end.

She'd backed her way towards the far end of the hall and the exit. She was looking smaller, a little crumpled, you could see the dry ends in her hair. Half a dozen reporters crowded around her asking questions, like, 'Why isn't President Samaranch here?'

'There are three basic reasons. Firstly, I'm vice-president and I serve in the United States. It's my duty to represent the IOC here. Actually, maybe there are two. Secondly, English is his fourth language, and it's the one he's least facile in.'

Millions of people across the United States who'd watched Samaranch on HBO's *Real Sport*, telling a stunned Frank Deford about his admiration for the Romanian dictator, Nicolae Ceauşescu, might have been concerned to learn that Samaranch's English had deteriorated so dramatically.

'This is a whole different league from being interviewed by journalists,' Anita told the journalists.

One reporter asked, what do you think of his fascism?

'What he always says is go back to Spain and ask them,' said Anita. Reporters shuffled their feet. No-one dared ask the question that hung in the air: 'But Anita, you're an African American. Your old man was in the civil rights movement. Samaranch was a fascist, a blue-shirt for God's sake. Don't you feel, well, don't you wonder sometimes, "Have I accidentally joined the wrong team?"'

Usually when important people are sparring with the press and not obviously winning, their minders step forward and whisk them away. 'Your next meeting Ms DeFrantz' – that would do the trick. 'The car is waiting' is always a good one. Anything will do, so long as it looks as if the minders are doing the running, and the speaker would gladly stay all day shooting the breeze if she had half a chance and didn't have some tedious old meeting to dash to. Anita's minders stood talking among themselves. Anita kept on yammering.

'We're not having a crisis in leadership with people jostling for position,' she said, wildly casting about for the bright side. Then she started explaining why she'd run into trouble when McCain asked her the easy-peasy question 'What are the IOC's annual revenues?'

'My problem, and I apologise, is that I am not facile with numbers,' said Anita, who sits on boards from Lausanne to Los Angeles making decisions about money, and lots of numbers, many of them big ones. Any half-decent minder might have bundled her off and urged her to lie down in a dark room until the urge to blabber subsided. 'If I had known I was going to be asked I could have looked it up on the website,' said Anita. Then it seemed to strike her that it might be wise to withdraw.

'I'm being backed out. I'm being backed out,' she said, smiling apologetically at the reporters. No-one was backing her out. The minders failed to take their cue. Anita exited room 106, as is her way, moving backwards and smiling.

Chapter 2

The Raiders Are Coming!

Who was bored with his wife? Who had a wife who loved to shop, but didn't like to pay the bills? Patricia knew all of them: who was on the lookout for sweetheart business deals, who had expensive kids to get through college, the 'good time Charlie', the man with a weakness for gold trinkets, the dowager who liked attentive young men, Patricia made it her business to know all of them.

At first she watched and listened over cocktails and canapés on the Olympic stops around the world. Before long, the Olympic family came to like the slim blonde Australian who was such a good listener. Patricia felt confident enough to schmooze; she made fast, easy friendships, traded confidences, disappearing now and then to a private place to write her secret notes on them, the people who decide where to stage the games.

Patricia learned what anyone trying to get the Olympic Games needed to know. In Utah, as Christmas 1990 drew near, some businessmen badly wanted the games, and in time they would need Patricia's help.

Utah's businessmen had kept their eye on the games for decades. They said it would lift their state out of economic decline. Some of the finest powder snow in the world falls on the upland meadows of the Wasatch Mountains, which end high and majestic in a giddy view of Salt Lake City, the Great Basin and the Great Salt Lake.

A Mormon walking through Salt Lake's downtown can look up and see the opening to Emigration Canyon where one hundred and fifty years ago Brigham Young led his wagon train of pioneers fleeing persecution down from the savage mountains into their promised land. 'This is the place,' he told them. They settled, polygamy produced large families and today 70 per cent of the population call themselves Latter Day Saints and their missionaries claim to have recruited ten million adherents across the world.

At the federal government's demand they traded one core belief – polygamy – for the right to convert the Utah Territory into a State. Their revered prophet Brigham Young spoke candidly of bribing federal officials 'to grease the wheels' and Utah has been living with such contradictions ever since.

The members-only Mormon Temple dominates the city skyline, it can be hard to get a drink, women think twice about wearing skirts above the knee, and the education board banned all high-school clubs to stamp out gay ones. Visitors are struck by a culture of deference towards Church elders and Mormon businessmen.

For all its piety, some say there is another side to Salt Lake. A federal task force labelled the city 'the penny-stock sewer of America'. Utah prides itself on the 'Western values' of self-reliance, sturdy independence and freedom to walk the streets with a gun under your coat. It's always been known that Utah's polygamists harbour child-abusers and wife-beaters and protect them from the law. The polygamists say they're wilfully misunderstood. The Mormon Church says, they're nothing to do with us.

The Church saw bidding for the Games as a chance to refresh the image of a much-mocked way of life. Success might also divert international attention from recent embarrassments, like the 'breakthrough' on cold fusion at the University of Utah and a Waco-style shootout between local religious zealots and the Feds.

Early efforts had foundered on taxpayers' reluctance to subsidise the event. This time, with big bucks expected from television and sponsors, the voters agreed to lend the Olympic boosters around $60 million to help construct sports facilities. The money would be paid back after a profitable and scandal-free games. It cost plenty of effort to win that one in a political culture inclined to feel that paying taxes should be outlawed. Soon they were to find that it cost a lot more to get audiences with the IOC members, the ones who had the games in their gift.

Tom Welch, beefy, piggy-eyed and touchy-feely, was a grocery-chain lawyer who dreamed of becoming something greater. A one-time Mormon bishop who sometimes came on a little strong, a family man with family troubles, he quit his job in 1990 to concentrate full-time on his dream, leading Utah's hunt for the Olympics.

At his side was his old friend Dave Johnson. A fellow churchgoer and former Saab dealer, dishy Dave was known for being persuasive; his boss said he 'doted on customers'. Dave took his talents into sport in the mid-eighties, and joined the public payroll trying to attract events to Utah.

Even in the early days Dave could be too keen. He headed a private foundation chasing the Olympics which was criti-cised for misusing public funds for entertainment, hotel rooms, dinners and airfares. 'They were doing things we don't think they should have been doing,' said legislative auditor-general Wayne Welsh. 'They were paying too high a cost for the Olympics.'

Dave enjoyed his life. With four young children, a home in an upscale suburb and a talented wife who anchored a local television news programme, Dave had everything going for him.

Tom and Dave became a team, Tom 'n' Dave, two accomplished schmoozers, bound together by their hunger for the games. Like all good salesmen they understood that to win people over you had to get to know them, their likes and dislikes, you had to flatter them, become their friend – fast. Surreptitiously – it cost him tens of thousands of dollars – Tom hired the international relations director of the US Olympic Committee, based in Colorado Springs on the other side of the Rockies, to get him confidential information on IOC members in Latin America. Dave soon became known to the concierge of every fabulous hotel in Europe as he tracked members to their lairs.

Samoa's Paul Wallwork couldn't be more isolated, out there in the middle of the Pacific. It was important to get him and other members to inspect the splendid facilities Utah was preparing for the games. Who cared if it cost $38,500 to fly Paul, his wife Julia and two children to Utah for a week's holiday at Christmas 1990? That's what you had to do if you wanted to win.

For Paul and Julia that Christmas was such fun that they did it again a couple of years later, costing Tom 'n' Dave's budget a further $17,000. Paul couldn't get enough of Utah and eighteen months later he was back; this time he brought his brother Jerry for a refreshing break.

Julia, spending some time one winter in Boulder, Colorado, became agitated. She sent a telegram to Tom. 'I seek your assistance. I need to help friend in serious situation but resources limited in NZ. Urgently require thirty thousand. Would you kindly remit today via telegraphic transfer.'

Uh oh. This meant trouble.

'Nothing to do with Paul or bid city but regard as business arrangement between you and me, therefore appreciate your absolute confidence,' she went on, although it was a funny kind of business loan, with no mention of interest.

'Please forgive imposition on friendship,' she wrote. 'Repayment in period of 3 months. Warm regards and thanks. Julia.'

If Tom said no, he risked losing a crucial vote. He dug into the trust fund set up for his kids' education and dispatched the money to Julia's personal account in New Zealand.

One month after the promised repayment date, Julia was writing to Tom asking for sixty days' grace. 'There is extreme devastation here at home,' she told him. 'My heartfelt appreciation for your kindness and friendship.'

More than two months after the repayment date, Tom faxed Julia, asking for his money back and Julia faxed back, straight away.

'As that number was the office number it practically went through the whole office,' she shrieked. 'AS EXPECTED ALL HELL HAS BROKEN LOOSE. There is much pain and heartache at this time, but hopefully it will heal for all concerned, with special thought of you and your family. The saddest part is I did move heaven and earth to honour my commitment, which you will receive very soon.'

Not soon enough. Another month went by, and Tom told Julia he needed the money urgently to pay his kids' fees, or they would lose their school places. Tom says he did, eventually, get his money back.

Salt Lake recalls Paul Wallwork as a jovial fellow. They say he joked that friends back home had never seen snow. Too bad, laughed Salt Lake's jokers, and it's said they gave him some snow to take home, and a freezer unit to keep it fresh on the flight. Buried in the accounts of the Salt Lake team is a receipt for a refrigerator.

Tom 'n' Dave had heard all about David Sibandze, a Don King lookalike from Swaziland who had spent years encouraging bidding cities to share their wealth with him. He flew in to Salt Lake and brought his son Sibu along. They headed straight for the facility they wanted most to inspect. Not an ice rink or a ski-jump, not a sports facility at all: the Sibandzes were most interested in the University of Utah's business school. Sibandze doesn't like to pay for his children's education if someone else will write a cheque. He bombarded Tom with faxes until Sibu had a university place.

What more could Tom 'n' Dave achieve in the few months before the IOC met in June 1991, in Birmingham, England, to elect a host city for the winter games of 1998? Salt Lake, they all knew, was strong on the fundamentals – perhaps the best powder snow in the world, close to the downtown, and impressive facilities under construction. Its main rival, Nagano in the Japanese Alps, had barely laid a brick.

There was one last chance to impress the IOC President. He was coming to Salt Lake and they'd make it a trip to remember. Ian Cumming, a billionaire who could expect to be a little richer after the Olympics, offered his jet. The National Guard sent its marching band and performed a water-cannon salute at the airport for the imperial visit. President Samaranch's gift, on this occasion, was a handmade quilt to go with the Indian head-dress they'd given him the previous year. Later, there'd be guns as well. Samaranch hinted that Salt Lake's time had come and Tom 'n' Dave looked forward, with rising confidence, to the vote.

Birmingham was a nightmare. Twice Tom 'n' Dave were hit by

shakedown artists wanting to sell IOC votes for cash. The son of one prominent member demanded $35,000 for four votes. One agent wanted just as much cash for a single vote. What could the Mormon team do? Pay up, or blow the whistle on the extortionists? They didn't pay and they didn't blow the whistle. They couldn't afford to risk spoiling their chances.

The IOC's voting system is hell on bid cities' nerves. Members cast their votes, and the least favoured city drops out. They vote again, and again, until one city remains. Tom 'n' Dave weren't too worried about the first round. With all Salt Lake's fine attributes, naturally they would romp through the early stages. They did not. The first-round results came through and Salt Lake hearts sank. They were tied at the bottom with Aosta, the lightweight candidate from Italy. Was the IOC serious about choosing the best candidate? One vote less and Tom 'n' Dave would have been on the next plane home.

They beat the Italians in a run-off vote and things started looking up. Three rounds later they faced Nagano, and lost by the respectable margin of forty-six votes to forty-two. Tom 'n' Dave were back in business, front runners for the next vote in four years' time for 2002. In Birmingham Tom 'n' Dave learned what really matters. The Japanese had swamped members with gifts and geishas and drummed up an incredible $27 million contribution to help Samaranch build a monument to himself, the IOC's magnificent museum in Switzerland. Tom 'n' Dave had got the message.

Even as the Salt Lake boys recovered from their defeat, their quarry was off around the world again, visiting the contenders for the summer games of 2000, their demands and expectations rising by the day. Just imagine what those Chinese were getting up to in Beijing, far from the gaze of spoilsport auditors and nosy reporters. Manchester was gouged on the ticket racket, Berlin splashed out so much they had to shred the paperwork. Salt Lake would need to offer something really special next time around.

The trouble with bribery is that, once you've developed a taste for it, more of the same is never enough. Appetites grow if you feed them, and the IOC had gorged and gorged again. The appetite that hit Salt Lake would be truly voracious. Tom 'n' Dave needed some expert advice on how to feed the monster.

Phil's life was good. He'd made Australia's canoeing team for three consecutive games and was delighted to join the IOC in 1982. For the former plumber from Bondi it was now Mr Coles, the car is waiting, Mr Coles, would you like your champagne now, Mr Coles you are a great Olympian. Things weren't so good at home between Phil and his wife Georgina but now he was away much of the time – and boy, how nice it was in his early fifties to be so appreciated around the world.

Phil was not one of the IOC's gougers, but he understood the Olympic way. He got friendly with the Salt Lake boys and just before Christmas 1990 Tom invited him on a New Year's skiing trip to Salt Lake. 'Fresh snow will be ordered and a good time planned for all,' joked Tom, but it wasn't going to be all downhill racing and après-ski. 'I NEED YOUR HELP!' he pleaded. 'Please advise as to your preference of either having me make your flight reservations or reimbursing you the cost.'

Phil was part of the campaign to bring the summer games to Sydney. Phil knew his stuff and so did his girlfriend. He left his wife and set up home with Patricia Rosenbrock, a stylish, blonde mother of two, who had an easy manner which made people want to confide in her. She'd worked in public relations, and she was good.

In early 1993 Phil left Australia for a six-month stay in Paris, wooing European IOC members on behalf of Sydney. With him went Pat, now on the Australian Olympic Committee's payroll. On their way they stopped off in Utah for a week's skiing, as guests of Tom. Lessons on the slopes, a car, lodging, whatever they wanted, Tom was paying. Of an evening the talk turned to business; Phil 'n' Pat had been at the Barcelona games, where Pat filled out her dossiers on every member and how to procure their vote. Their campaign would end in Monte Carlo in the autumn. Tom's would run another twenty-eight months. He needed to learn what Pat had learned.

Oh, the joy of Patricia's fat file. That Greek chap, what had she written about him? He's very excitable and unpredictable, likes to be the centre of attention. 'Very temperamental,' she wrote, 'emphasis on *Mental*.' And how about the new wife of the wealthy banker from the Caribbean? Pat first met her in Switzerland and noted, 'She was *very* new, bubbly and enthusiastic. She confided that she wanted Sydney but her husband wanted Beijing.' Later, Pat detected a change in the marriage. The banker was, 'obviously besotted', but 'a little of the new had worn off and her extrovert Latin ways were not so acceptable'.

A real sucker for the Pat effect was the lady from Venezuela. The fragrant Flor Isava Fonseca practised her favourite sport, showjumping and dressage, from her favourite home, the Shangri-La Country Club on the outskirts of Caracas. The men on the Sydney bidding team said it was 'difficult to assess her sincerity'. Pat worked her over and soon she was writing, 'Get on very well.' So well that Pat could add, 'Has passed on her beauty secrets to me.' How should the Utah bidders approach her? Pat had a suggestion. 'Flor loves men, especially good-looking attentive ones. They keep her young.'

Everybody wanted to confide in Pat. The wife of one member was a magpie. 'She quite likes to receive small gifts and complained to me that she had missed out on some things.'

If Tom had his way, nobody with a vote would miss out on anything. He'd got $13 million to spend and the only problem was how best to apply it. He was not short of suggestions. After the Birmingham defeat, Swaziland's David Sibandze sent Tom a consolation letter. 'I want to assure you that the friendship developed between us has surpassed the results of the IOC vote . . . and I shall continue to be in contact with you.' Tom wasn't consoled. Sibandze had eight children, and that's an awful lot of college fees. One down and seven to go!

Soon Sibu Sibandze flew into Salt Lake to begin his studies at the University of Utah. Staff in the bidding office recall Sibu's regular drop-ins, heralded with the cheery cry of 'Where's my cheque?' He wasn't through until late 1996, by which time he'd cost more than $110,000.

That wasn't all. Sibu was given a job at City Hall. Mayor Deedee Corradini said later that nobody told her about it. When Tom's side-kick Dave Johnson wanted to lay off some of the burden, another job was found at a local factory owned by IOC member Jim Easton. Jim was so busy running the rest of his business empire, world archery and the IOC franchise in America that, he says, he didn't find out until just after Salt Lake won the games. And that was an accident.

Sons and daughters. That was the key to victory, Tom thought. Look at our scholarship programme, he said. We're rich folk here in America and we must share our blessings with others less fortunate. We're running a humanitarian aid programme. We invite national Olympic committees to nominate the finest youngsters in their countries and we'll pay their way through college. Tom 'n' Dave set themselves up as an academic selection committee. But try as they might, the best candidate was always the offspring of an IOC member. It must be something in the Olympic genes.

Pat quickly spotted that special something. 'Not to be trusted,' she wrote after bumping into IOC member Lamine Keita from one of the world's poorest countries, arid, landlocked Mali in western Africa, with its one in ten infant mortality rate, its creeping desert and recurring droughts. Lamine had made his way up through basketball and was 'more than prepared to take advantage of any expense account'. That wasn't all. He was 'a very difficult customer', he wanted a job, and his wife could be a problem. Why? 'Likes to shop!!!'

The Keitas went shopping for their son Moriba, and Tom 'n' Dave obliged with nearly $100,000 for him to attend Washington's Howard University for four years. He was given a summer internship at Utah's First Security Bank, where the boss was good old Spence Eccles, way up in the state's business elite and naturally a member of the bidding team. Moriba looks back fondly on those days. 'They were really nice to me,' he says. 'They would call me and send me postcards . . . I didn't think it had anything to do with my dad. They just liked me.'

Tom 'n' Dave liked Sonia too. Sonia was special. Her dad, René Essomba, a surgeon in one of Africa's poorer countries, Cameroon, was a big wheel in the continent's Olympic movement. Pat schmoozed René in Sydney. 'I would not rely on him *at all*. I believe he is quite devious,' she said. Oh, and as for the wife, Julienne, Pat's word for her: 'grasping'.

After fifteen years on the IOC René had learned how to procure Christmas any time of year, so that made the real thing a bit of a challenge. Tom 'n' Dave were persuaded to pay for the Essomba family to spend four nights in the Paris Intercontinental in early December 1994. It was such fun that they came back for another five days over the Christmas holiday, and the next year they did it all over again.

Tom 'n' Dave also paid Mr and Mrs Essomba's first-class round-trip airfare from Cameroon to Paris and then on to New York, Atlanta and Salt Lake City for more fun. One day Tom and René had a private chat and then clerks in the bidding office were instructed to write René a cheque for $15,000. It was such a pleasant way to express the friendship and Olympic solidarity between Utah and Cameroon that they did it another three times.

Tom 'n' Dave liked Sonia so much that they came across with $108,000 for her to spend a few years at the American University in Washington.

They invited only one local African American on to the bidding team, and they had a special job for him. Bennie Smith, who'd played football for Brigham Young University and then built a successful construction company, became their point man in Africa, making dozens of visits.

'He went way above and beyond in trying to do the right thing for the bid committee and city,' said a friend. One thing Bennie did, on the eve of the second vote in 1995 when Salt Lake's dream came true, was hand $5,000 in cash to Louis Guirandou-N'Diaye, the IOC's man in Abidjan, Ivory Coast. There was a little trouble about this later – until an Olympic official in Abidjan remembered that the money was destined for 'sports development'.

Phil 'n' Pat had been tracking Louis, a retired diplomat, for months. 'He expects service and ambassadorial type treatment,' Pat noted. 'Enjoys flattery – especially about his elegant dress. Smokes Monte Cristo No 1 cigars. Enjoys having a female take care of him.' And enjoys shopping, she might have added. Louis flew into Salt Lake with his daughter Gazelle in the spring of 1995 and went home a few days later clutching nearly $1,000 worth of gifts.

Patricia knew that the IOC's Charles Mukora, a former Kenyan runner, was now director of external affairs for Coca-Cola in Africa and her private opinion was 'difficult to know how much to trust him'.

Charles was also a senior official of international track and field, and one of the privileges was business-class travel. So there was surprise in Berlin when in 1993 Charles wrote out of the blue to their team chasing the Millennium Games and said, Look, fellows, when I flew to the world athletics championships in Stuttgart the other week I and my wife had to fly tourist. That's not good enough, especially when I was your guest, so don't mess about, send me $4,371, the price of an upgrade from tourist to first class.

By this time the Berlin bidding team were as punch drunk as Salt Lake would become – they sent the money immediately. Emboldened, Charles hit Tom 'n' Dave for cash time and again, and within eighteen months he'd amassed $34,000. You just had to give him the money. 'I am so depressed that I may develop ulcers,' he once mourned. Another time, he claimed he'd lost a court case and needed cash because, 'we are continuously threatened with death'. It worked. The money rolled in.

And out. Tom 'n' Dave couldn't say no. They'd hired a fixer

in the Middle-East, Muttaleb Ahmad, the Kuwait-based director-general of the Olympic Council of Asia. They paid him $62,400 to advise them for twelve months and, trustingly, they did what he told them. Muttaleb considered the situation and offered them wise counsel: pay more money. And they did – to his friends. One was General Zein Gadir, the IOC's man in Sudan, a noted drunk. To keep him sweet, they paid $17,000 to his son Zuhair who was studying in Mississippi.

Once the General got the taste for free cash, he wanted more. 'Dear Dave,' wrote Muttaleb Ahmad in October 1994, 'On a personal level: he has a daughter in UK. Help may be extended. He expect $1,000 only a month to ZEMA GADIR.' Without waiting for a reply, Muttaleb passed on Zema's account number at the National Westminster Bank in London's Brompton Square.

Consider it done, said Dave. Zema was sent seven consecutive payments of $1,000. There was never a word of thanks from her, but you can't blame Zema for that. She didn't exist.

Phil 'n' Pat recommended another fixer who'd worked for Sydney, Nagano and Toronto. Mahmoud el-Farnawani claimed he knew how to get Arab votes and he urged Tom 'n' Dave to send money to Raouf Scally, who he said was a grandson of the Algerian member, Mohamed Zerguini. Over the next few months Raouf received a total of $14,500. Mr Zerguini was unimpressed, perhaps because he'd never heard of Raouf, who, it turned out, was related to the member from Morocco.

Another suggestion from Farnawani was giving a scholarship to the son of the Libyan member, Bashir Mohamed Attarabulsi. A few thousand dollars went immediately on an English-language course for young Suhel and by the time he'd

32

finished his studies at Utah colleges the bill topped $62,000.

Money for nothing became Tom 'n' Dave's theme. It was great to hear that Chile's Sergio Santander was running for mayor of his home town and $20,000 was wired to his campaign.

And there was the ever-present problem of what to do about Bjarne, the husband of Finland's Pirjo Haggman. He is 'demanding', wrote Pat in her confidential files, 'he is desperate to get a job'. Bjarne was a forester who seemed unable to find work in the vast woodlands of Finland. To keep them happy the Toronto team that later lost to Atlanta installed Bjarne and Pirjo and their family in a cottage in Canada and paid Bjarne $36,000 to count trees.

Could Tom 'n' Dave find a job for Bjarne among their friends in the lumber industry of the Pacific North West? They sent begging letters as far as the giant Weyerhaeuser forestry group up in Tacoma in Washington State but the résumé Bjarne sent them impressed nobody.

Tom came up with a solution. The good folk of Utah had lived too long without a reliable study, 'defining the re-foresting practices existing in the country of Finland, and its impact on timber production projected to the years 2004 and 2014'. Please, please, would Bjarne oblige? He did, and every-body pretended he'd been hired by a local company. His $33,750 fee, for a report which is lost without trace, was slipped out of the back door of the bidding team. Asked later about the propriety of this deal, Ms Haggman said, 'We are divorced. I knew nothing of this.'

What could Tom deliver to satisfy the Arroyos? Pat had written a special memo about Agustín, the dapper former diplomat from Ecuador, and IOC member of three decades' standing, and his wife, Raquel, 'a cross between a nun and a beauty queen'. A nun? That gave Tom a whiz of an idea. The Mormon God was onside and contributing money to the bid but it would be wise to schmooze the Catholic God as well.

When you come and visit, wrote Tom to Agustín, would Raquel please invoke divine grace for Salt Lake's bid by leaving a basket of thirteen eggs – one egg apiece for Jesus and the twelve apostles – at a local nunnery? 'As you know, I have great faith in Raquel's feelings and promptings,' said Tom, 'and would love to accompany her to the convent.'

It was a brief interruption to the splendid two-week 1994 Christmas and New Year vacation the Arroyo family helped themselves to in Park City, close to the ski slopes. The bill was $7,000 and Arroyo's son-in-law, managing director of Chase Manhattan Bank's branch in Venezuela, was beaten to the draw by Tom, who insisted. 'No, no, no, this is my invitation.' The family weren't short of walk-about money on their holiday. Tom thoughtfully made arrangements for Agustín to pick up $3,000 at First Security Bank.

Would this be enough? Pat had warned in one of her briefing notes, 'Would not trust either of them to deliver. They love the people of Salt Lake – they also loved the people of almost all 2000 [bidding] cities!! and visited all, some more than once.'

When Arroyo's stepdaughter ran into marriage difficulties and 'personal problems', Tom brought her to Salt Lake, paid her rent, her American Express bill and gave her a job. At the end of it all she found a home in Atlanta.

Jean-Claude Ganga was clear winner of the IOC in-house competition to see who could squeeze the most from the Utah boys. He'd led the 1976 African boycott of the Montreal Games and was now the boss of all Africa's national Olympic committees. This man could make or break Tom 'n' Dave's support from Africa. And don't forget to call him 'Your Excellency'. A former trade-union official, Jean-Claude had briefly been the Congo's ambassador to Beijing and, now back in Brazzaville, still expected due homage. And cash. And trips. And free hospital treatment. And sweetheart business deals. And scholarships for his ten children. And free sports equipment. And vacations, loads of free car parts, and more cash and more cash.

Jean-Claude's final total was well in excess of $250,000. Tom Welch confided to colleagues that he had agreed with Jean-Claude that the best way to help African sport was to pay tens of thousands of dollars direct to his new account at First Security Bank, but Tom wasn't hurrying. This was to 'deter' Jean-Claude from soliciting extra contributions.

Tom admitted he was being 'squeezed' for money, yet went on down the slippery path of placating Jean-Claude, even setting up a business partnership to exploit property deals. When in town, and never it seemed at his own expense, Jean-Claude would ask bid staff to walk envelopes of cash to his bank. Once, someone peeped. One hundred $100 bills!

Despite this nest-egg Jean-Claude wangled free medical treatment for himself and free knee-replacement surgery for his mother-in-law. Not to be left out, his wife Eugénie demanded and received cosmetic surgery on her eyelids. And then a holiday in Las Vegas.

Bennie Smith, who'd led the bid into Africa, couldn't escape Jean-Claude in Utah and ended up introducing him to the sort of no-risk business deal we'd all like a part of. Three plots of land overlooking the Great Salt Lake could be bought for $75,000 and, after a road and utilities were put in, they'd be sold for a good mark-up. 'It will be pure profit for you,' wrote a Tom 'n' Dave aide to Jean-Claude. And so it was. Another $60,000 for His Excellency.

We'll never know about all the bribes taken during the five years the IOC sent raiding parties to Utah. Setting an example to the footsoldiers, Samaranch took expensively engraved shotguns and a rifle from Tom 'n' Dave. The Utah boys spent nearly $10,000 on lethal weapons for members of an organisation that says it deserves the Nobel Peace Prize.

They are adamant that sex was one inducement never used. Terri, the lady from Snow White Escorts, who performs strip-tease for you in the privacy of your hotel bedroom, says that's not true. Terri told a local reporter she did her best to help persuade a couple of IOC members to give Salt Lake the Olympics. She won't identify them, 'I really respect their privacy,' she says. Terri says that they liked her best for her conversation and personality.

Phil 'n' Pat couldn't stay away and their next trip began at Sunesta Beach Resort in Key Biscayne, Florida. They were there for something many Americans want but will never have. Tom got them tickets for the Superbowl, staged in Miami. Then they headed up to the Utah slopes. Just as they left, Phil's daughter and son-in-law arrived for their week's skiing. When Tom heard they were in town, he made sure their bills were paid.

Tom 'n' Dave had done almost everything that could be done to win Olympic votes, providing every comfort and removing all possible irritation. Each year the city's ten-year-olds get together to debate an issue of their choice. They picked the Olympic bid. That might turn dicey – you know how ten-year-olds can be. So the bidding team heaved in with all its weight against the children until the debate was cancelled.

The Raiders Are Coming!

The last move was secretly to lay out thousands more dollars paying the fares of seven members' wives to the jolly week of the IOC meeting in June 1995 in Budapest which culminated in the vote. Quebec City, Östersund in Sweden and Sion in Switzerland stood against them. Tom 'n' Dave triumphed, taking fifty-four out of eighty-nine votes. They'd done it. Now it was time for business.

Chapter 3

There's Jim and Earl and Frank and Nick and Spence and Bob and all those Fellows doing Deals down in Salt Lake

It doesn't get much more beautiful in the Rockies, but Snowbasin is changing. Looking across from Mount Ogden you can see the construction crews hacking out the Olympic downhill and super-giant slalom runs that will plunge nearly three thousand stomach-churning vertical feet to the valley floor.

This was unspoiled forest until the heavy machinery came crawling up the slopes in 1998. There's been a day-trip skiing area here for decades, good enough, said the Salt Lake bidders, to stage Olympic events. The forest land surrounding it, publicly owned, was off limits to developers.

In the 1930s the federal government took over these hills, then ravaged by floods and over-grazing. The taxpayer re-planted them, returning them to sylvan condition. Now the very best of the valley belongs to R. Earl Holding, a man who has lived his American dream. Earl, in his early seventies and shy of the press, is putting the final touches to one of the more profitable deals of a stellar business career.

Beneath the ski runs and chairlifts being carved from the public forests up in the Wasatch Mountains, Earl has taken possession of 1,300 acres of prime land and he's developing a luxury four-season resort with golf, tennis, swimming, winter sports, shops, hotels, six hundred luxury homes and eight hundred condominiums

Under the looming mountains, the classic nineteenth-century Western storefronts in old Ogden City will soon be renovated to cater for the new tourists. The government is paying $15 million for a new road cut through the wilderness and, when the games are over, visitors will be able to fly into Salt Lake's airport, pick up a rental car, connect to Interstate 15 heading north and check in at one of Earl's hotels in the hills within forty-five minutes.

The Olympic organisers will pay Earl around $14 million to use his new ski runs for less than a week, two thirds of what it's costing him to construct them.

The business magazines say Earl is worth getting on for $1 billion but it wasn't always like that. The legend is that his Mormon parents lost everything in the Crash of 1929 and by the 1950s Earl was managing a motel with some gas pumps up in Wyoming. He saw his chance, scraped up the money to buy out his boss, added more pumps and cheekily advertised it as the world's largest gas station.

That grew into the Little America hotel chain in the Western states and in the seventies he acquired America's best-known ski resort, Sun Valley in Idaho, and Sinclair Oil with refineries, oil pipelines and hundreds of gas stations scattered across the Rockies.

Between times Earl became one of the country's biggest ranchers with 450,000 acres sprawling across Wyoming and Montana, and Salt Lake City's biggest landowner, after the Mormon Church. He flies around his empire in his two jets, one bought from the Sultan of Brunei.

Earl donated $100,000 to the Olympic effort, and the

Olympic elite would stay in his $185 million Grand America hotel, close to the Mormon Temple. Earl says the ugly twenty-four-storey block is, 'inspired by the world's grand hotels of the past', and will be opulent, sumptuous, plush, ornate and exquisite. And tasteful.

From the time he purchased Snowbasin in 1984, Earl wanted to expand, to imitate Sun Valley and create another world-class adult playground. But that needed more land, land the government owned. Give me 2,000 acres, said Earl. No, said Forest Supervisor Arthur J. Carroll. 'We feel it would not be prudent to support the exchange of National Forest lands for commercial real estate development.'

Earl tried again in 1990. New supervisor Dale N. Bosworth wouldn't budge. 'I cannot in good conscience dispose of public land for that purpose,' he said. Earl wouldn't stop badgering and eventually he was offered a deal. He could have 220 acres of public land if he traded it for land he owned elsewhere. That wasn't good enough and Earl had some powerful friends who'd say so. Utah's Senator Orrin Hatch called the offer a 'dumb-assed, boneheaded decision'. If anyone backed this miserly offer, 'I'll kill them,' said Orrin, who is a powerful fellow. Among other things, he chairs the Senate Judiciary Committee.

The public guardians upped the offer to 700 acres. Earl wanted more. No deal. No progress. Then the Republicans won control of Congress in 1994, Salt Lake won the winter Olympics seven months later and Snowbasin was put back into play.

When the Salt Lake boosters had laid out their plans for staging the games they boasted that nothing more need be built at Snowbasin. 'All alpine and cross-country venues are ready,' they insisted. It was one of their aces in the battle against Nagano in 1991. So great was their commitment that they had most of the facilities ready to go. Howard Peterson, then head of US Skiing recalls, 'We were given complete assurance that there was no land swap or any other activity necessary for these events to be held.'

Suddenly the successful Salt Lake organisers discovered that Snowbasin wasn't up to scratch and their rich donor friend Earl had a point after all. The Forest Service must be forced to give him the land he wanted. Right away!

That was it, no more negotiations. Orrin introduced a bill in the Senate to force the Forest Service to submit to Earl. To ram the point home, Ogden congressman and fellow-Republican Jim Hansen promoted a similar bill in the House. Jim was the newly installed chairman of the House sub-committee overseeing the Forest Service. Their message was urgent: 'Forest Service lands are necessary to facilitate certain events of the Olympic Games.'

'You bet I've got the votes,' exclaimed Jim Hansen. 'It's going to pass. Will the president veto it? I hope he does. I could care less, because we could override that veto very easily.' The bill gave Earl's grandiose construction plans at Snowbasin protection from those interfering people at the Environmental Protection Agency and from appeals and lawsuits by environmentalists.

The bill became law, Earl got 1,370 acres of prime Snowbasin land for his new resort and environmentalists were left with little to do but tot up how much the politicians had pocketed from him over the years. Earl, recently ranked as the 237th richest man in America, is a generous chap when it comes to politicians. Utah's Republican governor, Mike Leavitt, who'd lobbied Congress to support the bill, got $20,000 from Earl for his 1996 re-election campaign. More money went on public dinners for other local politicians. When Utah's state legislators meet in Salt Lake, one of Earl's hotels gives them a discounted rate.

Earl's money seemed especially well targeted while the bill giving him Snowbasin's best acres was under discussion in the Congress. His generosity caught the eye of the Center for Responsive Politics, a non-profit, non-partisan group. They looked at three particular days in March 1996. On the 11th, Congressman Jim Hansen received $1,000 from Earl Holding and his wife Carol. The next day the couple gave $2,000 to Orrin Hatch's political action committee. In less than twenty-four hours Orrin's committee gave $5,000 to Jim's campaign funds. That was on March 13, the day the House Resources Committee passed the Snowbasin bill along party lines, with one lawmaker reportedly calling Jim's efforts 'heavy-handed'.

Three months later and two days before Jim reintroduced the Snowbasin bill, Orrin's committee pushed another $5,000 his way. The bill became law three months later. When the Center for Responsive Politics released their study, one of Jim's aides became most upset. It was offensive, far-fetched and a smear, he said. Orrin's man put it down to 'coincidence'.

Earl's Sinclair Oil, high on *Forbes*'s list of America's top five hundred private companies, is a long-time contributor to Orrin's campaigns for the Senate. And Earl's family were absolute bricks when Orrin did something foolish and needed bailing out. After the Bank of Credit & Commerce International was convicted of money-laundering, Orrin was persuaded to make a speech defending the bank. He didn't have to write it; BCCI took care of that. The Justice Department had a poke around and the Holdings philanthropically contributed $30,000 to Orrin's legal bills.

'Earl is soft-spoken, friendly, comes across as very sweet,' says one of the few reporters who have talked to him. 'He's so rich now it's not so much about making more money, it's about the legacy he leaves.'

As a rich local citizen who would get even richer out of the games, Earl sat on the unfortunate sounding SLOC, the Salt Lake Organising Committee. He was among friends. In the president's chair, and pocketing $280,000 a year for his services, was Frank Joklik, a gnomelike geologist out of Austria via Australia, who had run the massive Kennecott copper mine up at Bingham Canyon. After he retired, he went to work for MK Gold. That's a mining company linked to the Park City ski resort, where Olympic snowboarding and giant slalom would be staged.

The gold company and the resort business were both owned by Ian Cumming's Leucadia Corporation which sells insurance and financial services out of New York and Salt Lake City. Ian is a billionaire who supported the bid from its early days. He took control of MK Gold in mid-1995 and five months later hired Frank, at a salary of $150,000, to run it.

There was surprise when the snowboarding events were awarded to Park City, a resort that had never welcomed the irreverent youngsters who'd broken away from what they saw as stuffy skiing. 'A small and different element has made snowboarding bad,' complained a Park City spokesman back in 1994. 'Why should we deal with something other resorts call a problem?' Those were the thoughts of sports-loving Nick Badami, boss of the Park City resort, partner of Ian Cumming and, naturally, a member of the SLOC Board of Trustees.

Another resort, The Canyons, popular with snowboarders,

tried to bid to the SLOC for the Olympic events but got nowhere. 'It was the good old boy network,' said proprietor Kenny Griswald. 'It was really covert.'

Frank, asked if he saw any conflicts of interest, replied, 'MK Gold is a mining company. There is no connection. Snowboarding details are [something] I don't know anything about.'

Frank Joklik also put time in as a director of First Security Bank and the bank's boss, Spence Eccles, returned the courtesy by joining Frank at the SLOC. Spence gets to see a lot of Jim – Jim Beardall, that is – because First Security Bank owns Anderson Lumber, whose boss, Jim, is also a director of the bank, and, you guessed, another member of the SLOC.

Spence is always bumping into SLOC's chairman Bob Garff when they attend board meetings of the huge Intermountain Health Care company which has the multimillion-dollar contract with the SLOC to provide health care for the games.

Spence's bank lends the SLOC the money it needs to fund Olympic construction. One project, the $24 million contract to remodel the Olympic speed-skating rink, has gone to Alan Layton's construction business. Alan finds it easy to make progress reports to the SLOC because he's a member – alongside Earl, Frank, Nick, Spence, Jim and Bob. And Gordon Strachan, the lawyer, who represents Nick. Gordon got some unwelcome attention during the Watergate scandal when he was an assistant to Nixon's aide H. R. Haldeman.

In its first few years the SLOC gave out contracts worth $68.3 million. Around $50 million of that went to businesses controlled by individuals closely associated with . . . the SLOC.

These apparent conflicts of interest disturbed some local

citizens. They complained to the SLOC's ethics panel that Earl Holding sat on the committee that had awarded him $14 million for his involvement in the Olympics. Local business-man and IOC member Jim Easton, who sat alongside Earl, Frank, Nick, Spence, Jim, Bob, Alan and Gordon, dismissed the complaint as 'bullshit', adding. 'You've got to keep these things as businesslike as possible.' The ethics panel took a similar, albeit more courteous, view and business went on as usual.

The citizenry were diverted by the antics of another SLOC member, Salt Lake's dashing blonde mayor, Deedee Corradini. Deedee made her world debut at the closing ceremony of the Nagano winter games, breathlessly taking the Olympic flag into safe custody to be hoisted again in 2002. It was a pleasant break from problems back home, where Deedee was selling her lovely home up at Federal Heights, with its stunning view over the Great Salt Lake, vaulted ceilings, hot tub and sauna, to help pay off investors in a failed company she'd founded.

Half a dozen of her fellow executives were charged with criminal offences but Deedee struck a deal with the court and had to raise $800,000 fast for the investors. She didn't have it but her friends, some of whom did business with the city, had lots of money. Deedee held private conversations with twenty-five of them, who agreed to donate more than $200,000 in cash and stocks to settle with bilked creditors. The twenty-sixth, a local sports promoter, handed over his $20,000 cheque in a parking lot.

Deedee stayed out of jail but had to go looking for a home to rent. The thirteen-room house she moved into belonged to Frank Joklik, president of the SLOC. They were all good people and she couldn't but be grateful to Earl who, looking for his

way to help, chipped in $12,000, the biggest single contri-
bution, to her mayoral campaign.

Spring 1997, Los Angeles, and the Olympic family is doing
what it does best, meeting and greeting its revered seventy-six-
year-old leader, President Samaranch. Anita DeFrantz, the
IOC's senior member in America, stands tall on the tarmac, her
Olympic colleague Jim Easton by her side. Also standing to
attention is SLOC chairman Frank, accompanied by Tom 'n'
Dave.

Standing by is Earl's private jet, ready to fly them to Utah.
Arriving at the Mormon capital they're driven straight to Tom's
home where his wife, Alma, prepares dinner, and her special
home-made banana cream pie. 'I only make it about once every
decade,' Alma tells the local paper. 'Tom has begged me for it.
And I said, "For you and the president, I'll do it." ' The highlight
of the night, Alma adds, will be enjoying her ten-year-old son
David play the piano for President Samaranch before he's
swept off to spend a pampered night at an Earl Holding-owned
hotel.

Within six months this picture of Olympic family
harmony is shattered. Tom is battering Alma in their garage
in a row about his girlfriend. Little David calls the cops, Tom
moves out and is soon an ex-Olympic official. He loses his
annual salary of $325,000 but secures a $2 million pay-off to
ease his pain.

The Australians, Phil and Pat, had been back vacationing,
a few weeks before Samaranch's visit. They paid their own
fares this time and Tom 'n' Dave found a delightful condo in
Deer Valley, a snip at $785 a night, with ski passes thrown in.
When the couple came back a year later for a two-week skiing
break, they were met by Dave but not Tom. The SLOC gave

them a car and two gold passes to the slopes and Jim Easton donated his beautiful Deer Valley home. In between, in September 1997, there was a story in the feisty *Salt Lake Weekly* disclosing that the SLOC had a special line in its budget for college scholarships for relatives of IOC members. Nothing happened.

Fifteen months later local television station KTVX promised a big story on its late-evening news. Reporter Chris Vanocur waved a piece of paper saying, 'This is a letter Olympic folks probably didn't want us to get.' Come 10 p.m. Vanocur screened what he claimed was a 1996 letter from Dave Johnson to Sonia Essomba, whose father had been so influential at the IOC, telling her that her latest tuition cheque, for her studies at American University in Washington, would be the last.

The two-and-a-half minute report made fewer ripples than Vanocur expected. A couple of days later the SLOC chairman, Bob Garff, dismissed Sonia's $108,000 payment: 'I wouldn't characterise it as a bribe . . . it was humanitarian aid.' He was quickly backed up by the US Olympic Committee on the other side of the mountains in Colorado Springs. 'The situation is a lot more complex than calling something a shoddy bribe,' said their mouthpiece, Mike Moran. The SLOC reluctantly revealed that several more 'students' had been assisted. Tom weighed in from exile in Park City: 'Family helps family, that's what the Olympics is all about.'

Is that so? wondered National Public Radio reporter Howard Berkes. He sat up until the early hours of 9 December, 1998 in Salt Lake City and then called a lawyer's office in Bern, Switzerland to ask senior IOC member Marc Hodler what he thought about the payments. His president, Juan Antonio Samaranch, turns a deaf ear to suggestions that members are less than perfect. If you were a gambler you might have considered it safe to bet that Marc Hodler would hear Howard out and forget him. But Marc was about to do the unexpected.

Chapter 4

The Corruption-Hunter, *or* Blind Man's Buff

It was two in the morning in Salt Lake City when Howard
Berkes got through to Marc Hodler in his law office in Bern. It
might have been another routine call. A reporter contacting a
public figure seeking his opinion, trying to develop a local story
that was going round in small circles. The SLOC people were
digging in, calling the scholarships 'humanitarian aid to the
developing world'; their critics called them bribes to members.
'I wanted to see if someone from the IOC thought it was a
problem,' says Berkes, 'and I knew that Hodler had written the
rules governing gift giving.'

Hodler declined to be recorded on tape, a setback for
Berkes, who wanted an interview for National Public Radio,
but he didn't turn the reporter away. 'Hodler listened to the
sketchy information revealed by SLOC and gave me an
interview that turned into the biggest ethics scandal in the
history of the Olympic movement,' recalls Berkes.

'This is the information we need,' declared Hodler as he
rumbled what Berkes was telling him. 'That is not legitimate.
Salt Lake City paid because they lost twice and wanted to win.
I think it helped get votes.' Hodler went on to call the payments clear violations of the rules. He would use the
information, he said, to identify and punish 'corrupt' members,
and to reform the process used to choose Olympic cities. 'Why
hasn't the IOC cracked down on allegations of corruption
before?' Berkes asked.

'We never had the proof,' Hodler replied.

Howard got his report on to coast-to-coast radio later in the day and talked to a colleague, Mike Carter, in the Salt Lake bureau of Associated Press. Carter kept on writing stories about the scandal but his bosses kept spiking them. 'I was being told repeatedly by the people in New York that this was small potatoes, a local story. It wasn't until Howard got in touch with Hodler that it became a big damn deal.' This time the man in New York had to say Yes, and Carter's story, headlined, 'IOC Official Criticizes SLOC For Scholarships,' instantly circled the globe, flashing up on screens in newsrooms everywhere: a thousand reporters dialled Bern. Sorry, they said, you can't speak to Marc; he's out of contact for a few hours, travelling to Lausanne for the executive board meeting. Some dialled Lausanne, others grabbed their bags and jumped on planes.

Over the years, Marc Hodler has become a sort of Olympic policeman-cum-regulator. He hasn't made any arrests but he has a shrewd idea of what's gone on. In January 2000, months after the storm has passed, he's on his way to the bridge world championships in Bermuda, stops over in London and we meet in the Intercontinental overlooking Park Lane. (He is about to be elected Bridge Personality of the Year.) He's an affable fellow, not the wily, suspicious kind you'd expect to find in a regulator's job. Marc sits by the window and the weak wintry sunshine illuminates his kindly face. He's not tall but even in his eighty-second year there's a robustness about his stocky frame and limbs that tells you he was very strong once and it's not hard to believe that he was a Swiss skiing champion a very long time ago.

He can't remember how many times reporters have called him, chased him, cornered him, followed him in packs this last twelve months. Marc embodies modesty and Swiss bourgeois caution. In two hours of softly talking he never names a name. 'You can't risk a libel or defamation action,' he says over and over again – he's a very cautious lawyer.

Marc was one hell of a skier in the 1930s. After a horrible accident with the sharp end of a ski pole which had the lifeblood pumping from his thigh, he insisted on going back to racing, but his future in sport was going to be as an administrator. And such longevity! We thought Brazil's autocratic João Havelange held the record for running an international federation: twenty-four years in soccer's driving seat at FIFA.

'In 1951 they elected me president of the International Ski Federation and until last year, for forty-seven years, nobody challenged me,' Marc says softly. 'I decided I would like to have my general secretary as my successor in order to continue my ideas.' Marc was co-opted into the IOC gentlemen's club in 1963 and was soon both an insider, taking over finances and half a dozen commissions, and an outsider, fighting to protect his winter sports athletes from the blazer brigade trying to exclude skiers who earned their living as instructors.

Long before Berkes called, Hodler knew how corruption worked. He'd wrestled with it in his own ski federation. Winter sports resorts competed hard to host ski championships. It brought in the money and later the tourists. 'In 1991 I found out that a lawyer had gathered together about twenty votes out of a total of eighty or eighty-five. He asked for many millions of Swiss francs, selling those votes as a package,' Hodler tells me. Forcing through rule changes, Hodler removed the right to vote on venues from the majority of his delegates.

In the same year he heard stories of IOC members on the

take. 'I knew that things happened, particularly in Africa, somebody collected votes and of course had to offer something for that, sometimes there were scholarships, sometimes there were gifts.' Hodler tried to take the right to vote on host cities away from the rank and file and vest it in the executive board. 'At a certain moment in Lausanne there was an unofficial meeting of members where they said we are not going to give up any of our rights.' So who were the leaders of that group? 'I wasn't there in the room,' he says, closing the matter.

In private, the allegations continued. Samaranch suggested that after each vote for Olympic hosts Hodler should call in all the bidders and ask them what had happened. 'For several years I invited people and said, "Can you give me some information?" And they said, "No, we can't, we don't really have any proof which would be sufficient if we are asked in court because of defamation." On such occasions the most I got was "Yes, if I get millions of dollars guarantee from the IOC, I will take the risk."'

The jig was up. Here at last was the evidence they said they'd been waiting for. The delegation from Toronto, led by the mayor, Norm Seagram, presented themselves at Lausanne on the afternoon of 9 January 1991. 'Ladies and gentlemen, good afternoon,' said Norm. 'Over the next few minutes we wish to recount some of the experiences we gained during Toronto's five-year quest to host the 1996 summer Olympic Games.'

Norm took his time laying out those experiences. They'd been defeated by Atlanta four months earlier at the IOC's session in Tokyo. Their bid had cost $14 million and they'd been supported by the efforts of three thousand volunteers. In total, the Toronto team reckoned, the six bidders, themselves, Atlanta and Melbourne, Belgrade, Manchester and Athens, had spent around $85 million, chasing the votes that would give them the games.

'The pursuit is without doubt riddled with extraordinary and serious problems,' said Norm, warming up. What was the biggest challenge? 'The city must demonstrate why it is in each IOC member's personal interest to vote for, and award, the games to that city.' Hell, we'd all been told the members were dedicated to choosing the best city for the games; what was this about 'personal interests'? Here was some more. 'The integrity and image of the IOC is often put at risk by the conduct of various parties during the course of the bidding cycle.'

Norm told the executive board their rules for bid cities were 'ambiguous or poorly enforced' and that 'the process does not appear to lead in all cases to the selection of the best candidate city'. Then he handed over to Paul Henderson, who was rising up the ladder of the yachting federation and might have hopes for an IOC seat one day. He'd led the Toronto bid and, ever since, has not rushed to talk about corruption. But he did that day in January 1991. He told the Lords of the Rings about Olympic freeloaders who plundered their hosts while spouting idealistic humbug about athletes. Sixty-nine members had visited Toronto. Thirty had found it essential to bring their wives. Twenty-one had brought other guests. Twenty-six of the visitors had broken the rules.

'The most blatant abuse,' said Henderson, 'was the misappropriation of travel expenses and airline tickets or passes.' Henderson reckoned that eighteen members and their companions had been racketeering. There were so many opportunities. Some had bought their own cheap tickets and then demanded that the Canadians reimburse them for first class. Another swindle – and this should have had the Mounties called in – was to buy a cheap round-trip ticket taking in several bidding cities and then bill each city, separately, for a pair of first-class return flights. Finally, there were the muggers; they demanded full-fare first-class tickets but never turned up. They cashed them in and stole Toronto's money.

These Olympic thefts – or 'abuses', as Henderson called them – totted up to $800,000. And when members did show up, 'on more than one shopping trip the bid city host was expected to pay for all the purchases made by not only the member, but the guests as well'. And, added Henderson, 'Unfortunately, many IOC members expect to receive gifts above and beyond what anyone would judge to be courteous and gracious . . . Cash, jewellery or other items easily converted to cash were hinted on several occasions.'

And there was another level of shakedowns. They'd been hit by the self-styled consultants, 'a great number of people on the fringe who claim they are capable of exerting considerable influence on the IOC itself and its members'. Who were they? Some were 'members of the IOC organisation'.

Henderson and his Toronto team hadn't just turned up to be negative. They wanted to help the IOC climb out of the slime and urged them to set up a review board that could hear complaints from bidding cities during the process and make recommendations to the executive board about punishments.

This dismal list of disgraceful – and sometimes criminal – activities by their colleagues was received by the executive board with Samaranch in the chair. On the board were Judge Mbaye of Senegal, head of the IOC judicial commission, Dick Pound, a lawyer and businessman, Australia's Kevan Gosper, a senior executive with the Shell Oil Company, businessman Chiharu 'Chick' Igaya from Japan, Korea's Kim Un-Yong, the fragrant Flor Isava, and lawyer Marc Hodler.

They loved to compare the IOC to a business operation, but any business with their kind of resources, any organisation which held the public's trust, would, at the very least, have called in private investigators or forensic accountants, ripped through Toronto's accounts, interviewed the bid leaders and gathered some evidence. Armed with the evidence, the IOC could have confronted the villains and told them to go . . . unless they'd prefer to make this a police matter. Even without an investigation, the IOC had learned enough from Toronto to change the system and make shakedowns more difficult.

What did they do? They did nothing.

The report was buried and these great sports leaders sat back and allowed their leader to declare, whenever challenged, that his members were 'one hundred per cent clean'.

That sent a signal to the marauders: carry on boys. You have a licence to do whatever you want, abuse and rip off our 'Olympic family'. They knew the rules that mattered. Always follow the Leader. Never speak against him in public, just deliver the winning cities he wants. It was just like the old days in Spain: you could plunder away as long as you stayed loyal to the Leader.

'I've been robbed! A burglar's been in my room! Twenty thousand dollars is missing!' It was Sunday morning in Manchester's Midland hotel and the distinguished IOC member was distraught. Local bid team officials rushed to his assistance. 'We'll call the police,' they said. 'No, no,' he replied. 'I don't want the police to get involved. I just want my money back.' The officials inspected his room and one recalls, 'There was no sign of a break-in. After that, it was, well, dropped,' and the member caught his plane home. Another vote lost in Manchester's efforts to win the games of 2000.

The same man tried the same deception in Melbourne and Toronto and was rebuffed. Once he claimed to have lost cash, the other time it was jewellery but always the loss was a round $20,000. The stories – and his name – are well known to reporters and IOC officials. But his activities have never been investigated by the IOC and he remains an honoured Olympian, a member of the 'reformed' IOC with a guarantee of the best seats at future games.

Another member – let's call him Mr Greedy – had a stab at the ticket racket. He flew into Manchester in 1993 from his faraway home with his equally grasping wife, flourished a receipt which said he'd paid for two first-class return tickets and was given around £8,000. One of the officials in the bid office told me, 'The procedure was that members had the choice to book through the IOC and we reimbursed Lausanne, or they showed us their tickets and we paid them direct.

'After we'd lost the vote and were closing the books, in came a demand from the IOC to pay this chap's fares. We knew we'd paid him and we told them so, but they said, "No, you owe us £8,000. Get the money back from him." François Carrard, the IOC's director general, or one of his deputies wrote to him, and in the end he paid up. We'd never have got the money back if Lausanne hadn't put the pressure on.'

Mr and Mrs Greedy proceeded on their merry way for another six years before he was caught over his rip-offs in Salt Lake and had to be expelled. The IOC buried the case back in 1993. It was so inconvenient, and taking action against him would have undermined the Leader's robotic claims about his members' pristine honesty.

On and on the scams and shakedowns went; the Olympians

spread corruption wherever they travelled. The Greeks, who'd
also lost to Atlanta, had their own 'experience' of the IOC and
in private they were happy to share it. A few weeks after the
Athenians had been rudely rejected for the 1996 games they
entertained a visitor from the Berlin team cranking up their
pursuit of the games of 2000. Hard luck, chaps, he said, but
can you tell me, how do we win IOC votes? This is what you
have to know, the Greeks told him.

The secret emissary was Dr Manfred Lämmer, a professor
at the Sports University in Cologne and a leading light in
awarding Europe's Fair Play sporting honours. He asked a lot
of questions, listened diligently, then wrote a detailed report
for the Berlin team and, rather melodramatically, assigned
himself the codename 'Astrid' and disguised his sources in
Athens as 'Icarus' and 'Daedalus'. Icarus was especially helpful
– he'd been in charge of 'personal lobbying' – and he gave
Astrid several hours of his time. He was blunt about the
Olympians: 'The success or failure of an Olympic application
depends exclusively on the extent to which one succeeds,
using methods of personal lobbying, to win the votes of IOC
members.'

Are you sure? asked Astrid. 'Large-scale public opinion
campaigns, saturation PR activities at sporting events and
conferences are of minor significance,' Icarus assured him.
Much more important was setting up 'a database of all IOC
members listing precise personal circumstances . . . personal
preferences, values and weaknesses.' You've got to believe it,
said Icarus, the self-importance and vanity of most IOC members is extraordinary. Then the Athenians claimed that some
East European members, 'numerous ones,' from South
America as well as 'some' from Africa and Asia were 'venal in
principle'.

One member resolutely worked the air-ticket racket, another promised his vote to Athens if the contract for the city's new Metro went to his company. A female member entertained discussions about a 'lucrative university position' for her husband. One was labelled a 'playboy', another, a 'drunk'.

For all Astrid's secrecy, his report leaked and was screened on German television in June 1992. The local Associated Press office put it on the wire, but the regular beat reporters packing their bags for the Barcelona Olympics couldn't see a story that might be of interest to the public.

There was so much more, if only they'd looked. The Berlin team took Astrid's 1991 report to heart and spent the next two years squandering money on IOC members who had trained exhaustively for the next round of challenges, from Barcelona to Atlanta to Toronto and, as we'll see, other eager cities. And they'd been given the tacit 'carry on grabbing all you can carry away' signal from the leadership when they shelved Paul Henderson's evidence.

But they hit a new low – or high, if you happen to be one of them – when they helped the Berlin 2000 team run up one of the biggest-ever bid budgets. I devoted a chapter of *New Lords of the Rings* to the Berlin scams but it's worth looking back. Sixty-two members visited and most violated their own rules, all but a dozen staying longer than they should have in the host city. Flor Isava spent much of her week in town checking out restaurants, provoking one local MP to ask, 'Did Flor Isava come to Berlin as a representative of the IOC or the *Guide Michelin*?'

About thirty members took free medical check-ups and dental work. One had his dog vaccinated, another made off with a camera. The rules said that members shouldn't visit a bidding country more than once but at least thirty-one – and their hangers-on – accepted the bidding team's invitation to attend the world track and field championships in Stuttgart, six weeks before the crucial vote in Monaco. Some ageing arteries must have been rejuvenated when they got the invitation telling them, 'You will not be asked to present a credit card.'

When government auditors announced they were going to sequester the bidding team's archives, the shredders went to work and little was left to investigate. Every file dealing with the hospitality enjoyed by the IOC was destroyed. Without the shredders, this might have been a scandal of Salt Lake proportions.

An assiduous local investigative journalist, Matthew Rose, tracked down former employees and recovered documents they'd removed for their own protection. Rose went on to advise the Berlin state parliament, who set up their investigation in early 1995. Despite wide coverage in the German press, it was blanked out on the Lausanne radar, and, along with other compelling evidence they had already seen, ignored. One phone call would have given the IOC enough evidence for a bloodletting.

The Salt Lake dam had broken and telephones were ringing all over the building. President Samaranch had pressing work to do and nothing would deflect him from it. Was he planning a rigorous clean up of his disgraced organisation? Deciding whose heads would have to roll? It was far more important than that. Samaranch was composing his latest missive in his campaign to win the Nobel Peace Prize, for which he'd authorised a secret budget back in April 1987.

This is what he wanted the world to know.

Lausanne, 10 December 1998:
The Olympic Movement commemorated this morning in Lausanne the 50th anniversary of the Universal Declaration of Human Rights with a solemn meeting of the Juridical Commission of the International Olympic Committee. The IOC President recalled the importance of respecting the rights of all humankind within the national and international communities.

There was some guff from Judge Mbaye, who opined, 'Sport is both an individual and a collective right, the foundation of which is the same as that of human rights, namely humanism.'

And there was a line about 'universal ethical principles' – the very thing the world's reporters were phoning about.

'To my knowledge, there has always, always, been a certain part of the vote given to corruption,' said Hodler, just down the corridor that same day. The reporters scratched on their pads again. Every hour that passed more hacks arrived to find Hodler was available – and still quoting! The dam had broken. The sunlight was shining in. The metaphors were running amok. Hodler wasn't stopping now. Every time he stepped out of the board meeting he had something to say. Losing cities had told him, 'There is a list of IOC members who can be bought.' The reporters scratched some more. 'Don't forget that about fifty members are not interested in winter games,' he said, 'They ask their wives where they want to spend holidays in the winter.' His estimate was that 'Five to seven per cent of members are susceptible to bribes.' He talked on for two days.

There had been 'irregularities' in the system for as long as he had followed the bidding process closely. It had grown from individual members taking back-handers. Now, he believed, it was organised. 'There are four agents making a living out of this. They charge them around three to five million dollars if they win. There is one agent who boasts, no city has ever won the Olympic Games without his help,' Hodler said. 'It could be possible.' One agent, he added, 'is an IOC member.'

As the damaging quotes flowed, reporters painted their pictures. The *Deseret News*'s Lisa Riley Roche described for her readers in Utah the sight of this spry old chap standing in the marble lobby of the gleaming Olympic headquarters near the shores of Lake Geneva, 'making extraordinary allegations'. She had some solace for shamed Utah: 'He went so far as to suggest that in the past 10 years the Games have never gone to a city that didn't pay up . . . Salt Lake City was a victim of blackmail and not a villain, he said. Salt Lake City had been forced by blackmail to give financial favors.' Besides wanting to rid the IOC of crooks, Hodler said his actions of the past few days were motivated by his respect and liking for businessman Earl Holding and the people of Utah.

The *Salt Lake Tribune*'s Mike Gorrell said Hodler's concern 'was that a tarnished image would hurt the SLOC's ability to balance the $1.45 billion budget. He said it could sour Holding's willingness to finish upgrading Snowbasin Ski Area for the Olympic downhill race and expanding Little America Hotel in downtown Salt Lake City.'

Inside the boardroom, as Hodler's monologue stretched on through a weekend, there was rage. 'Samaranch, who told Hodler on Sunday not to talk anymore about the case was visibly annoyed to see one of his oldest lieutenants still holding court,' reported the Associated Press. 'He grimaced, gave a dismissive wave and stalked off.'

Hodler was getting out of hand. 'After talking openly Saturday,' wrote *US Today*'s Mike Dodd, 'he answered reporters' questions in two separate 20-minutes sessions and three times took to a dais to clarify statements as stunned IOC officials looked on.' Then came the guillotine. 'I'm not to say anything. By presidential orders. I'm muzzled,' he said, putting both hands to his mouth.

The London *Daily Telegraph*'s Mihir Bose reported: 'When Hodler was talking to the press at one stage, Françoise Zweifel, the IOC secretary-general, came on to the rostrum and shepherded him away as if he was a sick man.' There were even rumours in the corridors that Hodler might be expelled from the IOC.

'These allegations come as a surprise to us,' said François Carrard, the director-general, who'd held that position when the Toronto team presented their report. When the board consented to hold a press conference, Samaranch said through gritted teeth, 'The spokesmen for the IOC executive board are Carrard and myself. All the other comments are personal comments, not official comments.'

Around the Olympic family, people were getting twitchy about Hodler. What would the old man say next? He had hinted that the selection of Sydney might have had its problems. Phil Coles jumped up to say the slur was unfounded and demanded an apology. Coles said he had never been offered bribes for his votes. 'If I have been offered anything, I've been asleep and missed it completely.'

Kevan Gosper recalled those days in his autobiography. 'Hodler seemed to be behaving out of character,' he wrote, gently twisting the knife. 'Emotionally, he did not seem to be his normal self . . . We just couldn't control him . . . A few of us told the President, who till now had been unbelievably patient with Hodler, that he had to do something about him. A couple of us said: "You've just got to make him aware of the damage he's causing."'

Hodler whipped up such a storm that Samaranch had to say the IOC would investigate the Salt Lake allegations. Hodler was relieved: 'For two days last weekend I had the feeling the IOC wanted to push everything under the carpet.' Judge Mbaye wasn't sure there was evidence. 'Only on the third day, when he got a copy of the file and saw many African members were there, did he agree.' The investigation, said Samaranch, would be led not by an independent firm of professional investigators, but by vice-president Dick Pound.

Chapter 5

Detective Dick, Salesman Dick

Dick Pound has the safest pair of hands at the IOC. Samaranch's invitation to take control of the exploding scandal wasn't the first time he'd been asked to intervene when members were behaving badly. Detective Dick solves problems. That's what he's good at. There was one embarrassing problem after the Olympic raiders descended on Sweden in the spring of 1985. They were supposed to be inspecting facilities for a winter games bid by the Swedish city of Falun. Some came only for the golf, two popped over for dinner with the royal family and one took it as his Olympic right to have sex with the Swedish hostesses. Wasn't that what they were there for?

One Saturday night he hit on the first hostess he encountered at a hotel reception. She turned him away so he tried another woman. Getting desperate, he cornered a third in the lift. It was his last chance that night and he got to the point fast in their few moments alone. She had a choice: strip off and be nice, or lose Sweden a vote. He got a succinct answer. Mr Wandering Hands stalked off to his room and his quarry was still weeping the next morning when bidding team leader Lars Eggertz found her, disconsolate that she might be responsible for losing a precious vote, and shocked to be the victim of sexual blackmail.

Falun never stood a chance, defeated in a complex Olympic power-game that delivered the summer games of 1992 to Samaranch's home city, Barcelona. Eggertz reported the incident privately to a senior IOC member who did nothing. Then, Eggertz wrote a book about his Olympic experiences, listing the abuses they'd suffered and describing the harassment – with a strong hint of Mr Wandering Hands's identity.

The book was drawn to Samaranch's attention at an IOC board meeting in April 1988, in the same Stockholm hotel where the sex-for-votes hold-up had occurred three years earlier. He was furious. We must complain to the Swedish Olympic Committee, he said. It was the book, not the blackmail, that bothered him. The confidential minutes of that meeting reveal Detective Dick's advice. 'Mr Pound was of the opinion that it would be wise to take no action. Decision: The IOC to take no action in respect of the book published by Mr Eggertz.' As well as Pound and Marc Hodler, three other senior members sitting around the table that day later took crucial roles in the IOC's reform process: Kevan Gosper and Chiharu Igaya were appointed to the new 'ethics committee', chaired by Judge Mbaye.

The then secretary of the Swedish Olympic Committee, Wolf Lyberg, raised the case of Mr Wandering Hands directly with Samaranch and later confirmed to Swedish reporters that he had named the man. The revelations in the book came as no surprise to Dick Pound. Lyberg had written to him eighteen months earlier, in October 1986. Pound responded swiftly: 'I appreciate that you have enough confidence in our personal relationship to feel able to write a letter along the lines that you did and I hope that you can accept my observations as given in the same spirit of confidence.'

There wasn't a lot Dick could do. 'It is always with regret that I hear that some IOC members may have made improper personal requests from candidate cities. I expect that if specific examples of this (with names) were reported to the

IOC, the IOC could then be in a position to take appropriate steps. Without formal requests, however, it is very difficult to do anything. That is a judgmental matter which I leave to you.'

Now Samaranch had turned to Dick Pound to look into complaints of systematic and extensive wrongdoing by fellow members. His brief could be as wide as he wanted it to be. There were allegations over the years from many bidding cities. Where would it all end?

Dick Pound is an impressive man in every way. He has the tall, broad-shouldered physique of the athlete who forty years ago swam to the 100 metres free-style final at the Rome Olympics. He enjoys his golf, tennis and squash. Dick is clever, garlanded with a string of degrees in the arts, commerce and law, and he's a chartered accountant. He made his way determinedly up the Olympic tree, leading Canada's Olympic Committee and its team to the Munich games. He joined the IOC a long time back, in 1978, and since 1983 he's been on the executive board, twice being made a vice-president. His base is a prominent Montreal law firm.

Dick's quick and funny; his one-liners can turn a hostile press corps round, and off record the comments on his fellow members crackle. When the going gets rough the IOC waltz him out for press conferences, confident that he will project a lawyerly air of aloofness towards whichever dubious colleagues he's reporting on, people who've been his friends or close associates for decades. Dick remembers every reporter's name. Dick smiles, Dick makes jokes. Dick's an easy-going fellow, warm, handsome and open, he's one of us, signed up to decent values and Olympic Idealism. Of an evening in Lausanne he's likely to drop by the bar, enjoy a cigar, and chat with anybody.

But never relax too far; Dick's lethal on the attack, scything down critics with killer lines.

Detective work is just a sideline for Dick. He's the main Olympic money man, the Super Salesman, negotiating television rights, hunkering down with the sponsors to extract more cash. He's done almost every job that matters at the committee and his anger was heard loudly in the corridors of the Budapest session in 1995 when Samaranch and the freeloaders forced up the retirement age to eighty, jeopardising Dick's obvious long-time ambition to be the next president.

'We're quite capable of investigating our own members,' Pound said after his appointment. 'The last thing we need is another Kenneth Starr out there.' Indeed. Pound was responding to immediate calls for the IOC to hand over the files to independent investigators. A private probe, behind closed doors, with secret files never to be released, conducted solely by IOC members, would have no credibility, critics said.

Dick's screaming conflict of interest passed unnoticed. His most important task, since the 1980s, has been wringing money out of the suits at multinational sponsors and television networks. Every new scandal, every disclosure of chicanery drops IOC stock another point. A wide-ranging investigation – with the results made public – could sink Olympic earnings all round. A clever man like Pound would know this, as he pulled on his detective's boots and got to work.

His squad of truth-seekers, appointed by Samaranch, included his old friend from Germany Thomas Bach. The former Olympic fencer had been a protégé of Adidas boss Horst Dassler, working for his 'international relations team' in the mid-1980s before Samaranch levered him an opening at the committee in 1991. Pound had his own relationship with

Dassler, his law firm picking up the company's Canadian business. There was no conflict of interest here, he said at the time; he took no personal share of his law firm's profits from the account.

Pound and Bach were joined by three other board members: Hungary's Pál Schmitt, another fencer, who supervises protocol at the committee (that's looking after the flag and making sure that during banquets everyone sits in strict order of honour), Belgium's Jacques Rogge and, as ever, the trusty Judge Mbaye.

Straight away, Dick let it be known that success was on the near horizon. The inquiry would wipe out any corruption once and for all. They had been given an 'opportunity' to clean house and he'd set himself a target. 'I'd like to have it out of the way so it doesn't impinge on our doping congress in February.'

Real, full-time investigators, working under orders to dig remorselessly for evidence whatever the cost, weren't offering early deadlines. Two days after Pound's squad was named, the US Justice Department sent FBI agents into Utah. Fifteen months later, as this book goes to the printer, they're still sifting evidence and taking witnesses before a grand jury.

It wasn't lost on Utah's aggrieved citizens that the IOC didn't play by the rules. In Salt Lake City Tom 'n' Dave and Frank and the rest of them were being turned over by the Feds, George Mitchell's grope squad, the SLOC's independent ethics committee and Dick Pound's amateur sleuths. Over in Lausanne, the IOC were being ruthlessly probed by . . . err . . . umm . . . the IOC. And then there were mutterings from Lausanne that the Utahns were the guilty ones, for tempting their vulnerable guests. Anger turned to delight when some helpful soul made it public that even Dick had one of his desires satisfied while visiting their state years before.

The Mormon Church have turned genealogy into an industry, scouring Europe for parish registers of births and deaths to find their own roots. In 1996, on official business in town, Dick had handed over a computer disk with information about his own family origins in Britain. Church researchers went digging and the following year presented him with an elaborate family tree. Estimates of the cost ranged from a few thousand up to $50,000, but the Church explained that the work was done mainly by volunteers and by department staff during times of low workload. So it was not possible to put a meaningful monetary value on the Pound family history. And, they stressed, the gift came *after* Salt Lake won the games.

'I would like to drop a water bomb on the lot of you,' Pound's secretary told nosy reporters, and when they caught up with the man himself, he wasn't much happier: 'After being known for thirty years as someone who's trying to do some good in this, then you become pond scum, it's frustrating,' he said.

Out of the woodwork popped Dennis Loeb, a former cop who'd helped co-ordinate security at the 1984 Los Angeles games. 'Pound was treated like an absolute prince,' said Loeb. 'The only thing missing was people blowing four-foot-long trumpets every time he came into the room. He had the drivers. He had the high-speed Mercedes.' It sounded like Salt Lake in the early 1990s.

Dick Pound pulled off his detective's boots and stepped into his soft-tasselled slip-ons. Salesman Pound had some schmoozing to do at the annual Sports Summit of the American leisure industry in New York. All the big-league American Olympic specialist reporters were there, and I stood at the back of the conference hall listening to Pound lay out the New Olympic Mythology. All the buzz phrases and sound bites the spin doctors could summon up were delivered with Dick's usual fluency.

First, the apologies: 'to the Olympic athletes who have inspired us through the years and whose lives so poignantly embody the Olympic ideals . . . to the millions of volunteers who contribute hundreds of millions of hours of service to promote the Olympic values in their communities . . . and the deepest regrets to the people and community of Salt Lake City.'

Then the diversions: 'the Sydney games will be one of the greatest ever . . . When this is all over, the IOC will emerge as a much stronger and more effective organisation.'

Pound moved on smoothly to The Message. 'The IOC is relentlessly pursuing allegations . . . The Olympic Movement is founded on ideals such as Hope, Unity, Friendship and Fair Play . . . the IOC is here to help the dreams of athletes come true . . . most members are unpaid volunteers . . . If you look at the record of the Olympic Movement the IOC has clearly done an excellent job . . . The investigation has been an unflinching exercise in pursuing the truth and will be unflinching in its recommendations . . . We have tried for years to get something "hard" so that we could act on all the rumours, innuendo and unsupported allegations . . . We have never been able to do so . . . None of the bid cities have ever come forward with any evidence.'

It would be very bad for their image as a cohesive, capable organisation if the boss had to be dumped. 'Some people are even calling for the resignation of President Samaranch . . . I can tell you that he has been a great leader . . . extraordinary vision . . . No-one is more determined to correct this situation than he is.'

The applause rang out. This was what the industry needed to hear.

The first three didn't wait for Pound's judgment and resigned in the space of five days. Finland's Pirjo Haggman went on 19 January. The first woman on the committee, she'd only followed the old men's example: 'My conscience is completely clear.' Bashir Mohamed Attarabulsi went next, telling the Libyan media, 'It never crossed my mind that granting my son a scholarship four years ago by the organising city means a violation forbidden by the Olympic law. I refuse to describe the scholarship as bribery.'

Having procured free education for several of his children, and as much loot as he could stow in the hold and overhead locker in fifteen years of Olympic junketing, David Sibandze sounded happy to call it a day. 'I resigned in the interest of the nation,' he told the *Swazi Observer*.

Three days after Salesman Dick's brilliant New York performance Detective Dick appeared before a packed press conference in Lausanne. Allegations against fourteen members had been substantiated, he said. Six were suspended, Arroyo, Ganga, Gadir, Keita, Mukora and Sergio Santander from Chile. The IOC membership would be asked to expel them at an emergency session in Lausanne in mid-March.

Dick was obviously one of those detectives with a sentimental streak. These members, were 'not accused of any crime or offence', he said. 'They are men and women who certainly have made mistakes, but should not be stigmatized or treated like unworthy human beings.' Investigations were continuing into three more, Vitaly Smirnov from Russia, Korea's Kim Un-Yong and Louis Guirandou-N'Diaye from the Ivory Coast. Holland's Anton Geesink got a letter warning him to be a good boy in future. There was a slap on the wrist for Marc Hodler too. Pound said it came as 'a considerable surprise' that Hodler 'stated that everything he knew was entirely hearsay evidence, the truth of which he was unable to verify personally'.

The same day that Pound named the shamed in public, Samaranch wrote to all cities that had bid for the Olympics since 1996, asking them to divulge what his members had been up to. The first responses were near-unanimous. 'We didn't see any rules being broken,' said Germany. Similar short-sightedness afflicted Athens. One of their two members, Lambis Nikolaou, said there was 'no problem with any member . . . We have no evidence of wrongdoing.' St Petersburg was clean, according to Russia's Aleksandr Ratner. 'We have sent no letter,' he said, 'since there was nothing to report.'

Italian member Mario Pescante told a different story, revealing that he had written a two-page letter to Samaranch the previous April, confessing a 'crisis of my vocation as an IOC member'. The Leader, Pescante said, didn't reply to his 'precise accusations' of wrongdoing. The Italian claimed Rome was asked for scholarships during its unsuccessful bid for the 2004 summer games; he and others were aware that Salt Lake City offered free places to relatives of members. And why hadn't anybody pointed the finger at the winning Athens bid?

An official from Anchorage, Alaska, which failed to land the winter games of 1992 and 1994, said he was solicited for bribes by agents of the IOC, but he wouldn't name names. I did in a previous book. Anchorage was hit by Olympic fixer and agent for votes Anwar Chowdhry, also president of Olympic boxing and an old companion of Samaranch. In Melbourne the former premier of the state of Victoria, Joan Kirner, said: 'I was just amazed, I have never seen a process more open to corruption in my life.' She had approached Samaranch with her concerns. 'We said we thought the process should be made more accountable, he nodded and nothing happened.' She paused and added, 'I think Kevan Gosper ought to quickly examine where he stands. I don't think anything will change until Samaranch is gone.'

The Swedes had been hit again. After Falun gave up in disgust, Östersund had taken up the torch and officials there recalled how one IOC delegate was loaned a new Saab sports car to tour downhill-skiing sites sixty miles away, then balked at returning the keys. He thought it was clearly understood he would be allowed to keep the car. Another member wrote a string of letters asking for a new Volvo, and David Sibandze was in automatic brigand mode again, asking the bid team for his airfare – already paid via the IOC.

To lighten the Olympic gloom came the delightful Prince Frederik von Sachsen-Lauenberg. He carries a torch for the founder of the modern games, sits on the Pierre de Coubertin Committee, and entertained reporters for some weeks with tales of members who visited Amsterdam during its bid for the 1992 games. They were bribed with everything from diamonds to prostitutes, he said, naming two honest members who, he claimed, had reported bribe attempts to Samaranch: 'He didn't take any action.'

Poor Dick, with his two taxing jobs, had fresh trouble to contend with. For all their efforts to tread gently in their detectives' boots, Dick and his team were crushing some people's toes. The dirty messages started snaking out of reporters' fax machines. They reeled off uncouth allegations of illicit sexual relationships which made sleepy Lausanne seem a shaggers' paradise. The messages probably came from a corrupt faction whose best hope was to show Samaranch obsequious loyalty and blame Dick Pound for inventing the Salt Lake scandal to topple the old man and seize power. When they weren't doing it with each other, alleged the dirty faxes, they were doing it with prostitutes in bidding cities. I was quite shocked at the allegations about one member. I didn't think he had it in him. Three in one night in Athens! Good read; shame about the facts.

Salesman Dick didn't have time to worry about all that. He was busy wearing out his larynx trying to reassure the sponsors that the scandal was under control, when so much of what they read and heard said it most certainly wasn't.

Across North America, the sponsor's biggest consumer market, cartoonists were crucifying the IOC. Canada's Cam Cardow invented some new winter games demonstration events for old bald fat men in suits: the 'Pass the money under the table downhill slalom', the 'Highest figure (or best offer) skating pairs', and, for old codgers and their lady partners in high heels and fishnets, the 'Sexual favours freestyle high jump'. Chip Bok in the *Akron Beacon-Journal* drew a torch-bearing codger hot-footing it away from a burning house whose owners bicker: 'Forgot to pay him off, didn't you?' In Cincinnati Jeff Stahler's old fatty, a blonde floozie on his arm, was jumping a restaurant queue and waving a big dollar bill at the maître d', who rebuked him, 'Sir! This is not the Olympics.' New Jersey's Steve Breen put his IOC man in a blazer on a podium with a swag bag marked 'BRIBES' round his neck and the boast 'I went for Gold!'

California's Michael Ramires produced a searing reminder of Mexico City, 1968, when black American sprinters Tommie Smith and John Carlos mounted the podium barefoot and, head down, each raised a black-gloved fist in silent protest at

American racism. The authorities suspended both men, denounced them and packed them off home. Ramires's fat, old white, tracksuited slob, stands on the podium, gold medal round his neck, head down, black-gloved fist raised and clutching a fat wad of dollar bills.

Rat-a-tat-tat through the spring of 1999 came the demands for Samaranch's head. 'There are sackings under way,' said the Sydney *Daily Telegraph*, 'and Mr Samaranch should add the most culpable official to the list, himself.' He wasn't looking welcome at the upcoming games. 'The IOC as presently constituted, with its present leadership and a great number of its members, is incapable of redeeming itself,' added former Australian sports minister Andrew Thomson. 'It's an intensely political organisation. It's inherently flawed . . . Its time has come, it is no longer of relevance to sport.' Belgium's *Le Soir* said the IOC 'has served its time', and in Austria the daily *Kurier* joked that IOC stood for Incredible Organised Corruption.

'The IOC has been exposed as a pig-sty,' said Germany's largest-selling daily, *Bild*. 'Members sold their votes for hard dollars and hot nights of passion. The six who were condemned are only a few fellow travellers in the Olympic mafia.' The French daily *Le Monde* looked ahead: 'A new Olympic ideal must be invented for the twenty-first century and Juan Antonio Samaranch is not the one who can do that.' George Vecsey in the *New York Times* called Samaranch a 'lame duck doomed to waddle through his final two years as the president of this damaged organisation.'

Some of the harshest criticism came from *The Times* of London. 'Señor Samaranch now claims with breathtaking disingenuity that he knew nothing of corruption and is a victim of his underlings. If so, he should be dismissed for incompetence. If he knew but turned a blind eye, he should be sacked for dishonesty,' said a columnist, putting the other boot in and calling the president a 'monstrously self-aggrandising leader'.

The former international relations director for Salt Lake's bid committee, Kim Warren, shared her experience of the Leader with a reporter. 'He had to fly in on a private jet. He had to stay in the presidential suite. It had to be the finest room in the city,' she said. 'We had to have limousines for him – Lincoln Town Cars weren't good enough. That was the example he set.'

Desperately orchestrating the thin small voice of the loyalists was Anita DeFrantz: 'I would say he shouldn't step down. He's been a good president . . . We've got to get back to the athletes,' she appealed, 'we cannot let the athletes down.' Kevan Gosper agreed. 'If ever we need a good president, it is now,' he said. 'President Samaranch has the full confidence of the executive board and the session which put him in place in 1980. Let there be no question of that.' Marketing director Michael Payne put us all in our places: 'It would not be helpful to have a presidential election. It would destabilise the situation. I think that's understood by all of those who closely follow the Olympic movement.'

Europe's national Olympic committees weren't reading their own newspapers, didn't care what the fans or the athletes thought. They knew where their money and perks came from and announced they were unanimous in their support for Samaranch. He was 'taking swift enough action to tackle the problems'.

One member who couldn't contain his devotion was Russia's Vitaly Smirnov. He gave interview after interview. 'I think that Samaranch is a great man, an honest man,' he said.

'I trust him one hundred per cent. I'll do my utmost to protect him, to support him.' The scandal was part of a plot to replace him. 'I'm absolutely certain that someone wanted to get rid of Samaranch, force him to resign under the wave of criticism.'

Vitaly was not alone, he said. 'The Olympic family of Russia, which numbers tens of millions of admirers and supporters of the Olympic ideal, protests against the wholesale slandering of the IOC's achievements, standard of work and leading role.' And they weren't sitting back. 'We are receiving dozens of letters signed by champions from all countries, supporting Samaranch, supporting what we're doing and supporting me.' Smirnov's outpourings came from the heart; he himself was under investigation.

Samaranch was in harmony with Anita and Vitaly. 'In this moment, I have to be at the head of the IOC more than ever,' he told the wire services. Then he counter-attacked. The scandal had been 'exaggerated' by reporters and 'I can't accept that we are depicted as a gang of criminals or that the Salt Lake organisers were victims. They are as guilty as those who were corrupted. They were the corrupters.'

Oh no they weren't, said Senator Mitchell, who'd been doing real detective work down in Salt Lake for months and produced his damning report at the beginning of March 1999. 'The activity in which the Salt Lake committees engaged was part of a broader culture of improper gift giving in which candidate cities provided things of value to IOC members in an effort to buy their votes . . . Salt Lake City . . . did not invent this culture; they joined one that was already flourishing.' The IOC he said, had tolerated it.

From far away Melbourne could be heard the sound of Kevan Gosper gurgling. 'It's quite unacceptable to say that the

IOC has created an environment which has enabled gift giving and rewards to run out of control,' he said. 'I take strong objection to that.'

As the Lords of the Rings packed their Louis Vuittons and set off for their most sombre gathering in decades, they pondered a letter from their Leader. He'd got his chin up. 'We must defend our organisation, and the Olympic Games,' Samaranch said. 'We must also defend the honour and integrity of our members.' Kevan, in tune with his boss, was getting more muscular by the hour. 'We're not out to compete with the media's expectations or the public's expectations,' he snarled.

There was more snarling at the best show in town that week – and not one reporter got to hear it. But we did hear that a discussion of allegations against Kim Un-Yong and his family turned nasty, and the Korean, who is president of world taekwondo, squared up to François Carrard in the combat position.

Eighty-nine members turned up and hundreds of reporters and television crews lined the steps of the Lausanne convention centre, the ugly concrete Palais de Beaulieu, to watch the old chaps and their aides clamber down gingerly from their executive coaches. Britain's Princess Anne had better things to do, and Indonesia's Bob Hasan was detained at home, for 'health reasons', we were told.

I felt mischief coming on. At the first press conference I nudged the BBC reporter next to me and whispered, 'Ask them about their expenses.' I wish now I'd done it myself. Financial controller Thierry Sprunger got in a tizzy and press officers rushed around with varying figures until they pulled themselves together and told us about the good life of an IOC member. They fly business class up to 2,500 km and beyond that are upgraded to the big leather seats – and even more free champagne. When they arrive they are coddled in the finest hotels and every day pocket $150. What do they need this for? 'Meals, laundry, mini-bars, videos (*videos?*) whatever,' explained a press officer. With receptions round the clock, it's hard to see when they have time to buy a meal.

The executive board do even better. They always travel first class and pick up $1,000 for every meeting. The money used to be less but they upped it on 1 January 1999, in the middle of the scandal.

Mr Sprunger told us that the IOC had around $236 million in the bank. A financial reporter did some sums and estimated that the committee would walk away from Sydney with its biggest pay-off ever: around $180 million, tax-free.

We'd all read Dick Pound's second report on the Olympic raiders, to be presented to the meeting. He'd found 'a few cases where IOC members sought or did not resist economic benefits' from Salt Lake, and they were recommended for expulsion, but he blamed the Salt Lake people too, for trying persistently to 'entice and to confer advantages, hospitality and benefits on IOC members, often even after the member had indicated a degree of discomfort with the situation'.

'It is not a whitewash at all. It is a very serious rebuke to the members who were publicly blamed,' Pound told the press. 'We were probably as thorough on IOC members as any outside body would be.'

Why hadn't they cottoned on earlier? Dick dithered. The IOC had been focused on other issues of 'vital importance to the Olympic Movement'. Then came the excuses. 'One cannot overlook the fact that gifts viewed as "improper" in some parts of the world are looked upon with a totally different perception in many other areas . . . IOC membership is unique in the world in its diversity of background, origin, religion, culture, tradition, education, politics, occupation, financial situation, language and opinion.'

That's bunkum. The point about people with a highly developed sense of hospitality is that it cuts both ways; gracious hosts welcome gracious guests. Dick has yet to produce evidence that members arrived in Salt Lake bearing gifts for their hosts. Turning up with empty suitcases, sons and daughters to educate and offshore bank accounts to fill is not good manners in any culture.

The whole crew disappeared into their private conclave to discuss the expulsions and the mildest reform proposals, setting up two more committees to add to the dozens the IOC already had; one would discuss ethics and the other, reform. What only a few executive board members understood at the time was that their deliberations would be guided by a hidden hand, the hand of Hill and Knowlton, mind-controllers extraordinaires.

Chapter 6

Embarrassing Odour?
Call Hill and Knowlton

Tom Hoog helped put Bill Clinton in the White House. He's a world-class master of spin who enjoys the multimillionaire lifestyle that goes with his title, president of Hill and Knowlton USA. Tom has a friendly warning he likes to give clients: 'With the potential for absolutely everything to enter the public domain – from internal company memos to casual washroom banter – the inside must match the outside, the image must conform to the reality. The ability to say one thing and do another has evaporated.'

Believe that, and you have to wonder what's left for people like Tom to spin, but he is right on one thing: absolutely everything from secret battle plans and confidential e-mails to minutes of IOC board meetings have found their way from the files of the spin doctors and their client into this and later chapters, to tell the true story of how Hill and Knowlton tried to spin the IOC out of trouble. It's all here . . . everything but the casual washroom banter.

Another thing Hill and Knowlton people tell clients is that crisis can happen and you should be ready for it. 'Train key individuals who would comprise a crisis response team,' they advise. Conduct 'role-playing scenarios/simulations as the military does'. The IOC didn't have a crisis response team. Why bother? They didn't need one. For decades they'd enjoyed a special double immunity from criticism.

They had the Five Rings and all the noble values of the Olympics to hide behind and, until Salt Lake, they enjoyed the tamest of press. The pack of sports reporters who trailed round the world after the Olympic family behaved, with few exceptions, like poodles, trotting to heel at Samaranch's instruction. Most were delighted to enjoy the lifestyle, the foreign travel, the sport, and easy access to the president, in exchange for retyping IOC press releases and putting their own names at the top. On the rare occasions when the IOC was criticised, the poodles could be relied upon to snap at the critic. (Samaranch's chosen biographer, David Miller, used his privileged position as the London *Times*'s chief sports reporter to rubbish my work – until I disclosed some unevenness in his Olympic reporting. He went on to work as a freelance and not, in Britain at any rate, to write again about his hero.)

Then, one lazy December day in 1998, out of nowhere, it seemed to stunned IOC members, word of their greed and crookery flashed round the world. As the planet revolved, news reporters woke up in different time zones to the prospect of a run of cracking front-page stories. This one was too big for the sports hacks to handle on their own. Across the world, real reporters turned to their telephones and called the IOC, armed with questions about bribery, doping and greed, only to reach the engaged tone.

Sitting in the IOC press office was a thirty-three-year-old electrical engineer, Franklin Servan-Schreiber, who had joined the IOC's 'Cyber Office' two months earlier to explain how the internet worked. He didn't know much about the Olympics, but they'd left CyberMan in sole charge of the phones. At his side quivered a trainee with five days' experience, about enough time to find the fax machine, the kettle and the toilets. In the first terrifying forty-eight hours of the crisis, three hundred callers managed to get through. Help! cried CyberMan. We need help!

Samaranch knew just how to respond in a crisis. Send out orders to the Olympic Family. Instruct them: Stay Loyal! Don't Panic! His confidential letter, dispatched just before Christmas, reads like a tortured howl from the bunker, Samaranch insisting he has done his best to investigate improprieties in the past, making a plea for unity. 'As in all crises, something good and positive will come out, and we must together view this as an opportunity to confront a problem and demonstrate that we are committed to the Olympic movement . . . The personal dedication and commitment of each and every one of you will be decisive.' Then he wished them all the best for the festive season.

Outside the bunker, in the real world, anxious heads of multinational companies opened their newspapers and switched on their televisions to be assailed by hostile stories about their precious Olympic asset. Reporters ambushed them with questions about when they might pull their support. They summoned their sponsorship directors, demanding to be told how come their huge investment in a brand which was supposed to be all about youth, vitality and fair play had decayed into an unseemly connection with a bunch of freeloading old men, some of whom had a penchant for goosing hostesses.

New Year came and CyberMan did his best to respond to a fresh storm of hostile calls. He must have felt like the little Dutch boy poking his finger in the dyke to hold back the flood. The real reporters were unimaginably horrible. A lynch mob, some Olympians called them. 'The crisis brought the attention of the world's general media, who had never before covered the

IOC or the Olympic Games,' Franklin complained when the phones stopped ringing long enough for him to compose a report to the board. 'These media were scandal-driven and attempts to educate them on the role of the IOC amidst the crisis were very difficult and often rebuffed.' Fortunately, some of the poodles carried on retyping press releases. 'Coverage by the regular core of the Olympic journalists was much more fair and balanced,' Franklin gratefully sighed.

Reading their private, for-our-eyes-only report, you can see how close to the edge of catastrophe the IOC tottered in those days. Privately, top sponsors – the IOC likes to call them 'partners' – were telling Olympic marketing chiefs to take control of the scandal or risk losing their business. Their lead attorney in the United States, Peter Knight, advised them to seek urgent help; Hill and Knowlton was one of two firms in the United States who could assist, he said. Someone told them that the firm had only recently succeeded in salvaging Swissair's reputation from the wreckage of a fatal crash. Surely they could do something for the old men at the Olympics.

Marketing director Michael Payne was dispatched to New York to seek Hill and Knowlton's advice. Later, behind closed doors, he told the board that they'd been 'under pressure from all their business partners and, had they not taken the decision to hire an external firm, they would have run the risk of losing several of them on the spot'. That very week he was due to meet sponsors Coca-Cola, Xerox and Visa. The IOC agreed to pay Hill and Knowlton $100,000 for the first month's work; it didn't seem like a lot of money when the IOC's reputation was coursing down the sewer. The firm flew six emergency spin doctors into the disaster zone at Lausanne.

Co-ordinating the operation was Dick Hyde, a former naval commander who had spent more than thirty years taking control of corporate crises for Hill and Knowlton. He secured superhero status in the industry for massaging public concern after Three Mile Island, the worst commercial nuclear accident in United States history. And when people started getting uppity about farmers using the chemical daminozide on apples, to retard growth, enhance colour and lengthen storage life, Dick was on hand to reassure.

With Dick's team in Lausanne and the prospect of lucrative contracts to negotiate, this was no time for reassurance. 'Hill and Knowlton senior management noted immediately that the intensity of the media attention was equivalent to some of the most important media events of the last twenty years,' Franklin wrote to the board. Piling on the pressure, the damage controllers compared the IOC's plight to international catastrophes. This is your Bhopal, they said, recalling the world's worst industrial accident, when toxic gas leaked and killed more than three thousand people in central India – Dick was there too, helping with crisis relief, doing his best to protect Union Carbide corporation profits. This is your *Exxon Valdez*, they said, bringing to mind grisly images of oil-slicked Alaskan beaches and dead sea-birds, otters and porpoises piled high in black, slimy heaps.

Franklin may not have known it at the time, but life was about to get better for him. He was given his very own Hill and Knowlton minder who would hold his hand, calm his fears and introduce him to the sorcerer's arts.

Hill and Knowlton makes the fat end of $200 million in annual revenues providing communications services to top companies around the world including Boeing, Motorola and Barnes & Noble. Feared and admired within the industry, it regards itself as a mould-breaker.

One bold innovation is a trade-marked Reputation Protection System designed aggressively to safeguard a company's profits should it inadvertently kill, maim, poison or in any way upset the public. Clients in trouble can call on the combined services of Hill and Knowlton and its business partners from the world of insurance, law and finance. Kroll Associates, hard-nosed commercial investigators, are on the team too, should clients wish to acquire intelligence on the enemy. The whole idea, the marketing guff explains, is that 'reputation is a state of mind, a set of memories'. Reputation doesn't have to be bound by the boring old facts. The trick is to control people's state of mind, something Hill and Knowlton have been doing for decades and with awesome success.

Over the years, they have sweetened the public's state of mind towards corporate killings, environmental catastrophes and the tobacco industry. When in the early 1990s an independent watchdog looked into how human-rights-abusing nations were represented in Washington, Hill and Knowlton emerged as the repressive regimes' favourite lobbyist, taking $14 million in fees one year from human-rights-abusers. The Center for Public Integrity published its research in a report called *The Torturers' Lobby*. 'I would say they are in the "bottom-feeders" category in Washington,' commented the Center's director, Charles Lewis. 'And that's a remarkable distinction for such a corrupt capital city. In the past, they have fed off the muck in Washington's mercenary culture.'

States of mind were altered, sympathies won and tears shed when in October 1990 a Kuwaiti teenager testified before Congress that she had seen Kuwaiti babies torn from incubators and left to 'die on the cold floor' by invading Iraqi troops. The incubator story was used repeatedly by George

Bush and helped galvanise United States support for sending troops to the Persian Gulf. The girl's testimony was arranged by Hill and Knowlton in the service of a group funded by the Kuwaiti government in exile, and it turned out that the tearful teenager, far from being an independent witness, was the daughter of the Kuwaiti ambassador to the United States.

Hill and Knowlton tend to be secretive about clients and exactly what they do for them. Their private documents rarely leak into the public domain. But their work for Big Tobacco did. Reading their secret battle plans, you can see how tobacco's image problems served as a test bed for the Hill and Knowlton techniques that came in handy, years later, when they set about rehabilitating the IOC.

The firm's own reports, dating back to the 1950s, and collated by Congressman Henry Waxman in 1994 in a dossier called *The Hill and Knowlton Documents: How the Tobacco Industry Launched its Disinformation Campaign*, show how they worked to protect tobacco industry profits from rising evidence that smoking caused lung cancer. Hill and Knowlton devised a brilliant campaign to reassure the public that 'the industry's first and foremost interest is the public health', and 'There is no proof of the claims which link smoking to lung cancer'. They advised the industry to form a group called the Tobacco Industry Research Committee whose purpose, contrary to its public claims, was to 'Sponsor a public relations campaign which is . . . entirely "pro-cigarettes".'

Staff used personal connections with well-respected, authoritative and purportedly independent news organisations to plant positive stories about cigarettes, secure advance warning of negative stories and get them rebalanced, or suppressed. Sometimes they paid freelance reporters to tell the glad tidings about cigarettes and health in articles that readers might assume were independently produced.

'Millions of people are informed and their attitudes influenced by radio and television,' senior Hill and Knowlton executives wrote in one secret report to the tobacco companies. 'The Committee should be on the alert for public discussion programs where spokesmen for the facts as the Committee sees them might be welcome.'

Cancer charities and other anti-smoking groups posed a particular threat, so Hill and Knowlton nurtured personal contacts to obtain 'advance information' of their activities. They canvassed 'long lived, distinguished public leaders' who smoked, to show the public that people they respected weren't moved by the scaremongers.

In the corridors of power Hill and Knowlton's Washington staff cultivated useful politicians and put 'accurate and up-to-date information' into their hands. After the first year's intensive public relations activities the team was delighted to report: 'Even adverse stories now tend to carry modifying statements. Positive stories are in the ascendancy.'

Lausanne, February 1999. Big suits, square jaws, button-down collars. The men from Hill and Knowlton were in town, armed to brief the IOC on how badly they needed the firm's operatives. They came packing an overhead projector and a philosophy that sounded impressive. It was, take a deep breath, 'Active Stewardship for the Future, Rooted in History Faster, Higher, Stronger.'

If the IOC wanted to save their skins they'd have to get the membership on message, said the damage controllers during a confidential briefing. They'd be subjected to 'Blast Fax delivery' with 'key messages' to ensure they would not forget it.

There'd be so many 'action updates' such 'constant com-munication', they would have no time to think for themselves. They'd be Faxblasted.

Only selected spokespeople would be allowed near a reporter: Dick Pound, Kevan Gosper, Anita DeFrantz, François Carrard, Michael Payne and Jacques Rogge. If he checked the list, Samaranch would find his own name at the top of it but that didn't mean anything. Hill and Knowlton has a saying: 'Chief executive officers can be crisis generators or enhancers.' They also have a fancy schmancy system for analysing news, 'a new semiotic technology, which from a quantitative as well as a qualitative viewpoint automatically processes all the articles'. And they didn't need that to tell them that every time Samaranch opened his mouth the press turned more hostile. He'd have to be kept out of the way for a while.

Another painful truth the client had to take on board was the need to involve Hill and Knowlton 'in PR aspects of IOC deliberations'. The damage controllers were not mere message boys, they would help mould the reform process for maximum public relations impact. And they'd conduct opinion polls to check that the public's state of mind was turning positive quickly enough.

In all its contact with the outside world, the IOC must not forget its most valuable asset was there to be milked. 'Tap into respect of the Olympics,' said the firm. It was no use whining about lynch mobs; go out and 'build rapport with reporters', they instructed. 'Raise profile of IOC/Olympic "good works".' When something good happens, like the reopening of Sarajevo's ice rink, apply 'leverage', make it look even better! Boost small events into big, positive stories! Exploit the *Olympic Glory* movie – an inspiring celebration of the Nagano games, which projected core Olympic values on to giant movie screens six storeys high.

Don't let the media decide what it wants to say. 'Co-ordinate media relations. Seize news initiative.'

Naturally, Hill and Knowlton had a long-term strategy too. 'Conduct consumer research to determine any shifts in perceptions of core Olympic entities. Develop, adjust programming accordingly. Use to fine-tune integrated marketing program elements.' And just in case that didn't sound 'action-oriented' enough: 'Accelerate implementation.' And 'Work synergistically with ongoing sponsor programming and utilize the full range of communications options: advertising, web, direct marketing, public relations.' The IOC must 'Secure highly visible, credible platforms, such as speaking engagements, forums, roundtables to communicate leadership role.'

In the public's mind, the client was to be transformed from a 'secretive club,' into a 'modern, transparent and effective trustee'. That might sound like a tall order, but these people could make torturers smell sweet and tobacco taste healthy.

Controlling the media was the centrepiece of Hill and Knowlton's plan. They would 'strategically place op-ed pieces by IOC ambassadors', and 'organize editorial board meetings with key global media outlets'. They threw around some hugely impressive names who might be mustered to come to the client's aid. They'd have Henry Kissinger pontificate in the *New York Times* on the 'geopolitical importance of the Olympics'. They'd even wheel out Margaret Thatcher, revered by many, considered bonkers by the rest, to pen a piece in the *International Herald Tribune*: 'Olympics Good for Global Competition.'

No trace could be found of the articles by Kissinger and Thatcher. But there were other remarkable endorsements.

The very next month, Andrew Young – former aide to Martin Luther King, US ambassador to the United Nations and mayor of Atlanta – put his own fine credentials at the IOC's service. 'It should be no mystery that the International Olympic Committee is maintaining its support for Juan Antonio Samaranch as its president,' he wrote in the *International Herald Tribune*. 'Just as US presidents from the old South became strong advocates of integration and racial equality, so this one-time fascist has been responsible for the democratization and successful globalization of the Olympic movement.'

Meanwhile in Washington, as Senator McCain got suspicious that these Olympic fellows were taking the American people for a ride, Hill and Knowlton put their big hitters on the case. Vice-president Frank Mankiewicz, who'd been press secretary to Senator Robert Kennedy, made a good living out of trading the connections he'd built up in public life for the influence-peddler's dollar. Senior managing director Jeffrey Trammell and Gary Hymel joined the Olympic cause too. Chief lobbyist and vice-chairman, Hymel had been an aide to House Speaker 'Tip' O'Neill and we'll catch up with him later, when we find out how he fixed it for Samaranch to magic his appearance before a Congressional committee from a potential catastrophe into some kind of triumph.

The damage controllers secured a contract that would bring them $1.5 million in the first six months and the prospect of earnings for many more months to come. But they'd made instant enemies within the IOC. Inside the secretive club, the strains of trying to pretend to be a 'modern transparent and effective trustee' showed immediately. Too many members enjoyed the lifestyle, the secrecy, the power, and knew of no reason to change. The more they saw of the damage controllers, the more they detested them.

Coming up to the IOC's big meeting in March, it was feared that the old guard would prevail, refuse to expel their old mates and defeat even the lukewarm reform proposals on the table. A rift was opening up between those, mostly younger, more commercially aware IOC members who could appreciate Hill and Knowlton's work, and the angry old men.

On the eve of the meeting Hill and Knowlton prepared a confidential briefing paper for the executive board only, designed to defeat the sceptics, to demonstrate the depth of the trouble they were in and play up the firm's efforts to pull them out of it. Our objectives, they said, are, 'to protect and enhance the image and integrity of the Olympic committee, its leadership, its members, member organizations' (and, far down the list, 'the Olympic Games'). They aimed to 'minimize the negative financial, legal and public relations impact of the situation on these and future Olympic Games'.

There were 'challenges' to face. There was the danger of a 'public and legal backlash' from members accused of impropriety. This played on IOC paranoia about the prospect of defamation suits. 'Special interest groups may fuel the fire,' said Hill and Knowlton – everyone on the IOC knew there was more dirt out there and feared bid city losers might at any moment throw some. 'Media and sports industry insiders have suspected and been privy to accusations of IOC impropriety over the years (e.g. through such books as *The Lords of the Rings*).' That's Hill 'n' Knowlton-Speak for 'You've known about these problems for years and done nothing, you bozos; that doesn't look good.' Finally, as if the IOC needed any more 'challenges', doping had raised its embarrassing head at precisely the wrong time.

'To overcome these challenges and achieve our objectives we developed the following strategies,' Hill and Knowlton reported. The subtext was 'You need us more than we need you. Listen up and keep paying our bills.'

If the IOC was to survive, the world had to be led by the nose into believing that it was 'proactive, aggressive and uncompromising in dealing with the situation'. Whatever the reality, Hill and Knowlton was busy 'positioning the IOC' to make it look that way. Among other strategies was 'media-training IOC spokespersons'. And here's another one that's survived intact from the tobacco files: 'Identify and media train a team of credible third-party supporters.'

When speaking publicly about Dick Pound's investigation, 'stress the positive dimensions of the IOC policy changes coming from this investigation, that will prevent any improprieties from occurring in the future'. There were to be no more unhelpful off-the-cuff comments from members, no more leaks: 'Establish a system of message consistency and ensure strict confidentiality for all internal communications.'

Hill and Knowlton had all sorts of ideas: 'Play up the IOC's history, accomplishments and successes in judiciously addressing alleged improprieties . . . over the years.' That was a tough one; the IOC had done nothing of the sort. Keep talking to the sponsors, 'ensuring [sic] them that any scandals will not diminish their investments'. Then it got sinister: 'Identify the most vocal potential critics and strategize accordingly.' What could that mean? Would critics know when they'd been strategized? Did it hurt?

Hill and Knowlton painted an impressive picture of the frenetic media manipulation efforts they'd expended on the IOC's behalf. 'More than 15 professional staff representing six cities on three continents speaking four languages' were keeping 'two thousand reporters' in check. 'We've identified third party supporters and are identifying opportunities for them to show wide-ranging support of the IOC and its leadership.' In print, on TV and radio, they'd seem like independent expressions of unprompted opinion. 'The supporters include athletes, non-athletes, politicians and business people who are respected and seen as ambassadors,' said the firm.

'We've created a list of media opportunities including interviews, editorials and by-lined articles for placement in areas with the greatest reach to target audiences.' It was all about reassuring the public. 'Hearing from respected third party officials provides a more balanced position to promote the Ideals of the Olympics,' said the firm, although, just as in the old days with tobacco it wasn't a 'balanced position' Hill and Knowlton wanted at all, but a controlled one, a fix.

They were writing keynote speeches for Samaranch showing 'the President's commitment to reform', plotting with Anita DeFrantz to arrange 'opportunities for athletes' to demonstrate their support, and doing everything possible to control the likely damage of the Senate hearings in April.

Dick Pound had spent the past three months burning up patience and aviation fuel, flying between sponsors, trying to persuade them to keep faith with the IOC. As members gathered in Lausanne for the big session, he understood better than anyone how perilous their position had become. For those executive board members who still hadn't got it, Dick put on his stoniest face and, in private, delivered his own crushing report. The crisis, he told them, had had 'an extremely serious impact on virtually all aspects of Olympic Marketing. The decisions taken by the IOC executive board and the IOC session over the next few days will be critical to establish whether the IOC will be able to restore the damage done.'

As blood drained from some members' faces, they could only try to console themselves that, thanks to their own secretive rules, Dick's damning words would not see the light of day before some of them were dead. 'Any failure or hesitation will have the most grave consequences for the financing of the Olympic Movement from the business sector,' he warned them.

Amid the wreckage of the IOC's reputation, Dick and his marketing team had held meetings with sponsors and broadcasters exhorting them to keep the faith. Sponsors received daily updates too, but all this was not enough. 'Privately,' he said, '[sponsors] have made it very clear to the IOC that if the crisis is allowed to drag on beyond March and the IOC is seen not to have addressed the issues at hand, the consequences could be fatal to their Olympic partnership.'

The crisis was knocking confidence 'at the exact moment that they are developing and "selling in" their Olympic marketing plans to individual countries', said Pound. 'A number of renewal agreements (Kodak, Xerox, Visa, Matsushita)' for Athens and beyond 'have been put on hold', as had 'other negotiations, future technology partnerships, etc.,' he said.

Sponsors Johnson & Johnson and BMW had withdrawn from Salt Lake; the BMW deal alone was worth $45 million. Swatch and General Motors were reconsidering their support for Sydney, whose organisers claimed to be £200 million short of their target, blamed the crisis, and demanded the IOC share the financial damage. (Relations with Sydney were so tetchy that when the Australians suggested IOC members travel by bus to save money, the Olympians retorted that they'd import their own fleet of Mercedes if they had to.)

Several sponsors wanted 'morals' clauses inserted in all future contracts. Such clauses, more usual in sponsorship deals involving young, reckless football players and rock stars, would guarantee them money back if scandal struck again.

'To date broadcasters have not been affected,' said Pound, which sounded like his first piece of good news until he added that they 'are anxiously awaiting the outcome of the March IOC Session, as many prospective advertisers have put their Olympic airtime buy on hold.'

Even if the session does accept the need for reform, he said, 'the IOC will need to begin a major restoration programme for the Olympic brand and consider what structural changes will now be required for future programmes.' They'd need to spend up to $5 million on a 'major, worldwide advertising campaign'.

And if reform is rejected? 'Not only will sponsors fail to renew beyond Sydney, but there will be an extremely high risk that many sponsors and broadcasters will endeavour to renegotiate the terms of their current agreements. Various media reports have already indicated that sponsors are exploring this legal option.'

Dick had no good news at all. Even the *Olympic Glory* movie had turned sour: 'The producers are declaring that the current crisis has had a serious negative impact on their distribution arrangements and are asking the IOC to consider refunding part of the production costs,' he reported. 'The IOC has refused.'

Dick sat down. Anita DeFrantz spoke up. According to the minutes, she said she was, 'glad to see the word "image" being used instead of "brand"'. Did Dick choke? Did he splutter? He had just delivered the IOC's worst news in its history and all Anita could do was babble about a distinction that any first-year student of elementary marketing understood.

Judge Mbaye cut in. He 'thought what he was about to say could be taken as sacrilegious, but he had to clear his conscience. He found this quasi-bribery by the sponsors extremely incorrect.' The minutes don't tell us, but surely Dick Pound was eyeing the windows and wondering if the boardroom was high enough for him to jump into oblivion.

Mbaye wittered on: 'He would not claim to be anything other than ignorant of this sort of world,' but that wasn't going to hold him back for a moment. 'This kind of behaviour troubled him greatly. The IOC and the Olympic Movement needed moral reinforcement after recent events.' Pound reassured the ignorant judge that the sponsors were not, 'telling the IOC what to do, but encouraging them to get it done'.

Michael Payne chipped in: 'Coca-Cola and some other major sponsors had said they were ready to make a strong, positive statement the following week,' that is, once reforms had been passed. That's no use, snapped Thomas Bach. Someone should make positive statements *this* week: 'They had to show the world that the Olympic values and money were not contradictory; in fact money was the way to realize the values.'

President Samaranch 'agreed with Ms DeFrantz that "brand" was the wrong word. They should use "image" instead.'

They still didn't get it! Pound explained as patiently as he could that they 'had to use the vocabulary and concepts that the partners were familiar with'.

Pound left some of the worst news until last. America, biggest Olympic market, home of Olympic broadcasters, most of the sponsors and 70 per cent of the cash, was a disaster area. There was serious trouble with the United States Olympic Committee: 'It was impossible to work with them and the

USOC was deliberately exploiting the current situation. They had to be very careful.'

Just as Dick reached rock bottom, Anita piped up again. She said she was eager to help: 'She attended meetings of both the USOC and the SLOC and would be pleased to help resolve the situation. She felt it was essential that she be involved in resolving issues with the government, as she had a great deal of experience.' Anita taking charge of government relations. That was all Dick needed.

Facing the full session, Samaranch soothed his members that everything would be all right. Why did they have a problem? Because of, 'a virtual firestorm that has consumed the world media which, in turn, has influenced the perceptions of the world at large'. Ah, the media had created the scandal. He concluded with a gigantic nod and wink: 'The legacy of our founder, Pierre de Coubertin, must be preserved for ever.' Most reporters thought it was some sports legacy. The baron's legacy, to his members, was that in perpetuity, they would remain a self-selecting club, admitting only those people they wanted with no silly democracy or accountability. That was the line the members cheered.

Dick Pound laid out the evidence against the suspended few and they put their defence. Members voted reluctantly for the expulsions, the warnings and the reforms. They chucked out five of the already suspended (Charles Mukora resigned ahead of the chop) and with them went the Samoan Paul Wallwork. There were three grades of warnings: Kim Un-Yong and Phil Coles got a 'severe', Vitaly Smirnov and four others were dealt with 'seriously' and two more drew a 'less severe'. Strictly for consumption back home, Smirnov tried his own spinning. 'I want the truth, I am not guilty,' he told *Tass*. 'Many colleagues fully agree with me and I will work to restore justice.'

Members voted to demonstrate their confidence in Samaranch and only the most naive observers were impressed that Samaranch won by eighty-six votes to two. Hadn't he appointed most of them?

At the Palace Hotel Olympians sip tea in the lobby, sink into lush red velvet upholstery, undisturbed but for the occasional tinkle of silver on bone china, gaze about, admiring the door-men in their morning suits, the marbled pillars, sparkling chandeliers and golden balustrades. It's a place to relax and reflect on your own importance.

Not the day of the expulsions. Jean-Claude Ganga turned up with scores of reporters and two dozen film crews in sweaty pursuit. Penguin-suited flunkies looked on aghast as big blokes bearing heavy cameras clambered on dainty chairs, dragged their hiking boots across velvet settees, and elbowed for space. Ganga picked out an ornate high-backed gilt chair upholstered in golden satin – it looked like a Bokassa throne on the evening news – and disappeared under the mob. Press reporters bellied their way through to catch his denials.

Another Olympic reject, Ecuador's dandyish Agustín Arroyo, made his entrance. He sank into a settee, re-arranged his grey bespoke suit and waistcoat, adjusted his red spotted silk tie, twitched his thin moustache and began to explain why everybody had got him wrong. 'I don't think it was a right decision. My conscience is clear,' and, he smiled wisely, 'my soul is happy.' Arroyo ignored questions about the allegations, his colleagues had been rushed, 'forced by circumstances', to let him go. I thought it was time to cut to the chase. 'How can you say your name is clean?' I asked. 'Your colleagues expelled you, seventy-two votes to sixteen at the end of a corruption investigation.' 'Not corruption!' he shouted, 'it was just a lack of judgment.' I asked the question again. He didn't answer this time, and at the seventh asking he sprang from the settee and marched off, turning one last time to ask, 'Are you British?' as if that explained everything. He was shepherded away by his companions, a trio of elegantly dressed, slightly faded middle-aged women with blonde hair set like granite who could have been founder members of the General Pinochet fan club.

The next day Samaranch called a press conference: 'We promised to clean house and we did it.' A reform commission would be created, the IOC 2000 Committee, to examine proposals for democratic elections and accountability. 'In view of the last few months' events, why should you be the Chairman?' asked a reporter. 'Because I am the president of the IOC and it must be presided by the president,' he explained. Samaranch was back in the game. As Hill and Knowlton gleefully reported, 'The immediate impact of the March session can be measured by the return of a positive press unseen since the beginning of January 99.'

Chapter 7

A Handmaid of the Sacred Heart Battles the Olympians

'Mushi, mushi,' Monica answers the phone in Japanese. If she switches to Spanish she may be speaking to a Filipino construction worker fearing deportation – or a Filipina bar girl fleeing her yakuza gangster boss. If Monica slips into English it's probably an American reporter looking for the Nagano nun we've all heard about, the sister who insists that there's a huge gulf between Olympic reality and idealism.

This chilly morning up in the Japanese Alps, a week before the IOC launches its winter games of 1998 in the presence of the emperor, politicians and businessmen, Monica has different concerns. She's busy working the phone, charming her bishop into attending a conference protesting against the cruel occupation of East Timor.

I'd tried being formal, as you would greeting a holy sister for the first time, when I arrived at her cramped office at the Pachichisa refuge in the Nagano back streets – and was swept away with eruptions of delight that I'd found my way from the bullet-train station. 'You want green tea, we have English tea,' says Sister Monica, and Sister Celeste from Manila darts off to the cramped kitchen. 'Thanks, you're very kind,' I say, looking around what will be my home for the next few days. The Pachichisa refuge is a two-storey con-crete block house, not dissimilar from the rest of the

101

neighbourhood, where few Olympic officials will ever venture.

There's no central heating so we share blankets and gather round one of the electric heaters. It is going to be a long cold stumble tomorrow from my bed on the bamboo floor upstairs, down to the steamy bathroom. 'This is one of the places we hide the wives and children,' explains Monica, 'when the immigration police are looking for them.' Hiding from the police! Who is this woman?

Dressed in her not-so-new check jacket, dark skirt and thick, warm woollen stockings Monica could be a modest-ranking, middle-aged civil servant, if it weren't for the chunky silver cross round her neck. Some days she rushes from her convent without it and only when she pauses to give me her card – another Japanese formality she treats casually – do I learn exactly who she is; on one side she's introduced as Sister Monica Nakamura, a Handmaid of the Sacred Heart of Jesus. On the reverse, she's a member of the Anti-Olympics People's Network.

One year to the day after Monica and I first sipped green tea in Pachichisa, President Samaranch had his underlings write to every city that had bid for the games in recent years, asking for evidence of 'inappropriate behaviour by its members'. I called Monica. 'They should ask me,' she laughed. 'They are asking the wrong people the wrong questions.'

From the moment the Salt Lake scandal erupted out of the Great Basin, over the peaks of the Rockies and bounced off transponders into most homes on the planet, the Japanese businessmen who made the Nagano games so much their own closed ranks with their Olympic friends. 'I have never heard of such a thing,' said an indignant Mayor Tasuku

Tsukada. IOC executive board member Pál Schmitt said, 'I fully trust my Japanese friends. I have the sincere feeling there was no bribery.'

How could they be so certain? Might not investigators dig out another cache of documents like the ones that sank Tom 'n' Dave? 'All the records relating to visits by IOC members have been incinerated,' said a Nagano official. 'There was no space for storage.' They contained information that was 'not for the public,' such as 'who had wined and dined with IOC officials and where'.

After a month of holding the line Mayor Tsukada changed his tune and admitted that 'there may have been excesses'. Japanese Olympic officials caved in and set up an inquiry; like the IOC they didn't want outsiders poking their noses in, so it was staffed by their own people and uncovered little. Predictably Ecuador's Arroyo had made the most of local hospitality along with Samoa's Wallwork, but that was all we learned. 'It could spark an international row if we name names,' said an official. 'It's up to the IOC to release names and mete out punishments.'

The Japanese media were less inhibited and kicked in with a scandal story from nearly forty years past, revealing that Japanese boosters had paid a few thousand dollars to a few IOC members in an unsuccessful bid for the winter games of 1968. Coming up to date the *Sports Nippon* paper alleged that not all the Nagano bid team's budget could be accounted for. How much was missing? Only $17 million.

A clutch of prominent Japanese officials swore they had been in the room when Samaranch was presented with an ornate Samurai sword, worth $13,000. 'We have a big painting, two small paintings and lots of knives,' said spokesman Franklin Servan-Schreiber, 'but no swords.'

I think I may have found it. Close by the Palace Hotel in Lausanne where Samaranch lives most of the year, on the precipitous rue du Petit Chêne, is a 'Blades 'R' Us' store, and throughout 1999 among the Swiss army knives, bayonets and Bowie knives displayed in the window was a magnificent Japanese short sword, just as described by the Nagano officials.

'The real story of Nagano,' says Monica Nakamura, 'is the story of Mr Tsutsumi.' Back in the mid-1980s Nagano and three other Japanese cities sought the winter games. The best candidate was Morioka in the north, but railway owner and property developer Yoshiaki Tsutsumi, who had conveniently become a leading figure at the Japanese Olympic Committee, plumped for Nagano. Located in that region of the Japanese Alps was a chain of his Prince ski resort hotels. He had the ski runs and the chairlifts but the business lacked good road and rail connections with Tokyo.

Tsutsumi, then ranked as the world's richest man, operated in that shadowy world where sport, politics and corporatism collide. He delivered $27 million worth of donations from Japanese industry to take care of the overspend on Samaranch's Olympic Museum in Lausanne and was given the highest-ranked Olympic Order. He fixed it for the old Franquista to be received by the Prime Minister. Construction companies raised 1 billion yen to promote Nagano's bid, the IOC members enjoyed whatever was lost for ever in the incinerated files and bingo! the games were Nagano's. And Tom 'n' Dave learned how the Olympics were won.

Japan's taxpayers coughed up $15 billion for a new bullet-train and expressways and the Prince ski resorts were now within reach of Tokyo weekenders. It's easy to know when you've reached Tsutsumi country on the bullet-train to

Nagano. The jagged mountains suddenly turn soft and rounded, artificially moulded to cram in dozens of ski runs. Skeins of chairlifts criss-cross the snowy landscape like zips on a punk jacket.

'My family was Buddhist,' says Monica, 'but in the first year of high school I converted to Catholicism. I became a nun because I cared about human rights. My parents were good people and we were very happy and, somehow, I wanted to share my happiness with people who were not so happy.' Monica peals with laughter.

'I started solidarity work with the homeless and after a time I stopped wearing my habit because . . . how can homeless people feel friendly with me if I wear such formal clothes? It was a barrier. My experience taught me that when I was wearing a habit, people just respected me, bowing so many times. So when I am wearing ordinary clothes I am just another middle-aged woman they can take help from.'

Monica's solidarity work reaches beyond Japan and over the years she's battled her way through South-East Asia, campaigning to free East Timor from Indonesian military occupation. 'It was a terrible experience when they deported me from Malaysia. They took me away in a military truck with iron bars on the windows. It was like a prison. Then they put a stamp on my passport to keep me out,' and her face cracks up, she's laughing again; it was frightening then and funny now, because that wasn't her only passport.

Monica's mission in this week before the games is to serve the invisible tribe of undocumented migrant labourers who trek across Asia building the great signature towers of the East's vibrant capitalism. Japan has tight immigration laws but, with its young men showing little interest in unskilled labouring, the wanderers are allowed to stay, though only until the buildings are topped out.

The Nagano games triggered a construction boom with tight deadlines. An estimated $1.3 billion was spent on vast ice halls, broadcast centres, ski runs and jumps, quite apart from construction work on highways and the bullet-train tunnels and viaducts. 'Foreign workers have done the dirty work,' Monica explains, 'the so-called "three K" jobs shunned by the more affluent Japanese – *kitanai*, *kitsui* and *kiken* – which mean dirty, hard and dangerous. In fact, the majority of the workers on the new Olympic venues were foreigners.'

How nice. Samaranch always says that his sports event brings the young people of the world together. 'These people are hypocrites,' says Monica. 'They say the games are an international festival of peace. When the work is completed, they throw the workers out. And their wives and families. We try and hide them, get them medical help, homes. Some bosses are humane but they worry they may be prosecuted. One kept a Peruvian worker, his wife and their baby hidden in a storage room for two years. I helped translate at the birth.'

A Filipino illegal told a local reporter, 'I worked for 12,000 yen a day, while Japanese workers were paid 15,000 to 18,000. And we were always paid three days to one week late.' Monica counts Filipinos, Thais, Sri Lankans, Bangladeshis and Brazilians working on the Minami sports park which will stage the opening ceremony. 'As the work ended they were coming to me in panic,' she says. The Nagano police had cranked up 'Operation White Snow'. Three months before the games began they swept the city looking for ten thousand foreign workers coming to the end of their contracts.

The girls are the easiest to catch. They can't hide. They have to work. It was late, Monica shut down her computer and as she prepared to return to the convent for the night I said, 'That's all right for you nuns. I'd love a beer.'

'Ohhhh.' Monica lit up. 'You'd better come and meet Sandra.' We walked a couple of blocks and at the entrance to the Gondo shopping arcade ducked into a doorway, went up two flights of stairs and into a secluded, darkened bar. 'They say the man who runs this is a yakuza,' whispered Monica. It was getting unreal. What kind of Catholic nun was this, escorting me into a hostess bar run by a mobster who was probably missing a couple of fingertips, the price paid for offending his under-boss.

Before we could make the twenty feet to the bar we were gently mobbed. Half a dozen lissom young Filipina women, divine in sleek, slit dresses, were all over us. I put my shoulders back, beamed – and was ignored. 'Monica!' they chirruped, 'Monica,' and besieged her in torrential Spanish. It looked as if they hadn't been happy all day until the squat, bespectacled woman with the staid woollen clothes entered this citadel of velvet walls and mirrors.

This was social work in action. While half a dozen salary-men, abandoned, subsided on couches, Monica dispensed advice on everything: sending money home to Manila, getting childcare, divorce papers, dealing with the bosses' unwelcome advances. Sandra, an older Filipina who ran the joint, gave the girls a couple of minutes and then a hard look and they went back to work.

My bill a few beers later had enough yen zeroes to reflect a good year on the Sony balance sheet. Sandra leaned over, 'Half-price, Monica's friend.'

The Tokyo press joked there were fifty thousand hostesses working the shady bars of Nagano during the games. Sister

Celeste told me the figure was more like one thousand. 'Thank God the biggest problem Sandra's girls ever face is harassment,' she said. 'In other bars they are often sexually exploited, forced to do naked dancing.'

The usual sex buzz had run when the IOC came to town to inspect Nagano's facilities. As they weren't designed yet, never mind built, only pleasure could fill the hours before the trip back to Narita and home.

When the cops weren't arresting undocumented workers, they were watching Masao Ezawa, a wiry man in his late forties, with the dark, sun-burned face of someone who spent much of his time in the mountains. It was on these journeys, gathering plants to make natural dyes for his one-man weaving business, that Ezawa discovered that rare specimens were disappearing before the onslaught of the heavy earth-movers moulding the slopes for Olympic competitions.

At first it was just Ezawa against the big money interests. They commanded the media's attention, their insistence that the environment was safe from Olympic development became the conventional wisdom. 'There will be no destruction of nature, because when we cut down one tree we plant two,' said the organisers.

'The answer we came up with,' says Ezawa, over a bowl of noodles, 'was for my wife, Norika, to run for election as mayor of Nagano on a No Olympics platform.' Norika got 15,000 votes against Mayor Tsukada's 107,000, and the earth-movers went on trampling the plants.

'And we set up a site on the internet,' intervenes Monica who is interpreting for Ezawa, 'to send our message around the world.' They scanned in pictures of the damage to the Japanese Alps: the freestyle ski runs in the Iizuna Highlands which looked like dried-up river beds full of crushed stone, the lattice of runs from top to bottom of Mount Yakebitai and the new road, paid for by taxpayers, leading to one of Mr Tsutsumi's Prince hotels. Their claim, 'Nagano's fragile mountain environment is being drastically affected by preparations for an event that lasts only two weeks', got up the collective nose of the authorities and by the time I set up my base camp in the Pachichisa refuge, Ezawa felt sure the cops were tailing him.

'Two rental cars driven by plain-clothed police officers followed me when I drove my car to the station the other day,' he told me. 'And they were there later when I went to pick my children up from nursery school. But I don't care, it's only annoying.'

The environment campaign didn't interest the foreign reporters. By the time they arrived, Samaranch could safely point to hills blanketed in snow and claim, 'This is a green Olympics.' A year later, after the Salt Lake scandals broke, Ezawa was the toast of the Foreign Correspondents' Club in Tokyo. 'The lesson I've learned in the last ten years,' he told them, 'is that Japanese democracy is shallow. Citizens have rights but don't use them.'

Monica Nakamura and Masao Ezawa weren't alone. At Nagano's historic Zenkoji Buddhist temple, was Takakazu Fukushima, who had turned to the priesthood after gaining his chemistry doctorate in America. Fukushima readily gave media interviews in which he accused the Olympic organisers of lying when they assured residents there would be benefits for them after the games. He was concerned about environmental damage and how the Nagano skyline would be disfigured by the under-used, vast Olympic buildings. He told an Australian television programme, 'The best thing to do with the Olympic venues would be to burn them down after the games.'

President Samaranch took up residence in Nagano's Kokusai Hotel and, knowing the reporters needed good stories, initiated a rapid fire of press releases headed 'Agenda of the IOC President'. They were full of scoops like 'The President of the International Olympic Committee, Juan Antonio Samaranch, met with Their Majesties the King and Queen of Spain.' Others included 'The President of the International Olympic Committee met with the Prince of Orange, heir to the throne of the Netherlands', and 'he had a meeting with the Under-Secretary of State in charge of Sports in Greece'. By the time the games ended, forty-nine of these 'hold the front page' stories had been issued.

Samaranch had brought snowboarding into the Nagano games because the sponsors and snow industry needed the business. Skiing was stagnant but the youthful boarders might attract a new television audience with money to spend. Nobody had told him these young anarchists with their screeching music and green 'n' purple hair preferred to sail through the air with a Bob Marley Special gripped between their teeth. Marijuana made it all a lot more fun.

Samaranch's dope police failed for a generation to catch the bigtime dopers of the winter sports circuit. Many of their names were well known in the press room but apparently not to the IOC Medical Commission. One day into the Nagano games, Canadian snowboarder Ross Rebagliati made headlines when he took gold in the giant slalom. Three days on Ross got even bigger attention when Samaranch's executive board took the medal back after a trace of marijuana showed up in his dope test.

Many wondered why. Samaranch hadn't minded when positive tests on big track stars had been suppressed, so why was he declaring war on his new profit prospect – and millions of dope-smoking youngsters? The IOC leadership had got themselves into a tizzy of noisy moral outrage when the phone rang. Er, they'd got it wrong. They didn't have a rule banning ganga and an arbitration panel had just given Ross his gold back. By this time a generation was in stitches as Ross, looking puzzled, speculated that he might have picked up the traces while breathing deeply at a smoke-filled farewell party back home in Whistler, Canada. Determined to make themselves look even more out of touch they set up a 'working group' of Anita DeFrantz, Pál Schmitt, Dick Pound, Judge Mbaye and the Prince de Mérode, head of the medical commission, to figure out how to ban a drug that is otherwise non-existent in the games – unless you count the press room.

Every night during the games the medals were presented at a ceremony in Nagano's Central Square. Visiting reporters sensed something wrong; crowds of citizens applauded, but without vigour. The English-language edition of the *Yomiuri Shimbun* explained what was going on. Olympic organisers, nervous that an over-taxed population would boycott the ceremonies, had imposed quotas to be filled by each of the town's twenty-six wards. A minimum of seven hundred bodies was required for each medal ceremony; each ward must produce between three and fifty flag-waving celebrants. The *Yomiuri* commented, 'Local citizens appear less than enthusiastic about attending ceremonies in the night-time cold.'

Sister Monica elaborated. 'This is "Tonarigumi", the old-fashioned style of community mobilisation. Ours is a society which puts great store in consensus and harmony. Most people are frightened of being seen not to conform.' Older people were especially vulnerable. 'When the IOC session opened,' said Monica, 'hundreds of them were mobilised alongside local council employees. They were sent to wave flags, and each was given a Yen 500 – that's £2.50 – phone card as a reward.'

At the session Samaranch co-opted nine new IOC members, two of them European princes, from Holland and Luxembourg, another a billionaire from Asia, and then he went back to working for the increasingly elusive Nobel Peace Prize he thought should be his. He organised a march through the town, celebrating the fiftieth anniversary of the Universal Declaration of Human Rights, prompting much crude comment among reporters who had seen the pictures of Samaranch wearing his fascist uniform.

Some had trouble keeping a straight face when Samaranch tried to get reporters to write about his call for an Olympic Truce during the games. Others, like Bob Verdi of the *Chicago Tribune*, couldn't stomach any more posturing. Samaranch, Verdi told his readers, was a 'doddering little dictator . . . a hypocrite . . . a cretin . . . a liar . . . a dictator'. That was the warm-up; when Verdi hit his stride he still had room in his 646-word column for 'babbled . . . arrogance . . . stupidity'. He dismissed the rank and file as Samaranch's 'fellow windbags'.

It got worse. Surely, if there was one arm of the media Samaranch could trust to be uncritical, it had to be the CBS network, which had paid $375 million for the rights to screen the games in America. CBS has a popular current-affairs programme, *60 Minutes*, transmitted at peak time every Sunday night. They asked for an interview and Samaranch was delighted to accommodate what he assumed was another emissary from Brown Nose TV. Reporter Bob Simon was charming, even as he raised the question of Samaranch's fascist record. His report was intercut with grainy black-and-white archive shots of the Olympic Leader in his favourite Nazi-style uniform. More and more the American media were thinking the Olympic unthinkable – and then publishing it.

Father Otaro Hamada is the priest of St Joseph's Catholic Church in Nagano. Chatting in his austere office, he told me: 'I received a phone call from a young woman involved in the Nagano Olympic organisation a month before the games. Could I attend President Samaranch in his hotel room at nine o'clock on the following Sunday morning?'

'I told them, no, I cannot go,' Father Hamada went on. 'Here in Nagano prefecture we are one priest short and on Sundays I have to travel to three churches in the region. How can I have time to go to Samaranch's hotel?

'If a parishioner is sick, I will try and go to him. If he is dying I will certainly go and hear his confession and give him final Communion. They told me that in Tokyo a priest had been to his room. I guess they were saying that, if it was possible in Tokyo, it should also be in Nagano.'

Father Hamada, slim, in his mid-thirties and wearing cords and a sweater, explained that a decade ago the Japanese Catholic Church resolved to be 'on the side of the minorities, the oppressed and the poor. Many of the foreigners who came here to work as cheap labour in construction and factories are Catholics.' One of his favourite books is George Orwell's *Homage to Catalonia* but the priest was unaware of the IOC president's political background. 'I cannot ignore my parishioners and the Filipinos for Samaranch but I invited him to come to our church,' he said.

It's barely a mile from Samaranch's hotel to St Joseph's

Church but the Leader was in no mood to step into one of his many limousines and take the five-minute drive to share his devotions with the common people who'd built the Olympic venues for him. Rebuffed by Father Hamada, he summoned a priest to make the 400km bullet-train round trip from Tokyo and this time, God went to Mammon. Again and again and again on successive Sundays until the games had ended.

Father Isidro Ribas, an old school friend of Samaranch's who was teaching at a Jesuit university in Tokyo, made the journey. I caught up with him on the phone in Nagano and asked, 'Why doesn't President Samaranch want to share mass with the migrant workers who made all this possible?'

'He's very busy' said Father Ribas tautly.

Chapter 8

How Atlanta got the Games . . .

'There was nothing untoward, nothing unethical' about the way the Olympics came to Atlanta, insisted Billy Payne as the Salt Lake scandals unfolded. Billy, a bulky, bespectacled former college football star, had sired the bid back in the spring of 1987 and swiftly enlisted the backing of the local big money. An airline, a bank, Coca-Cola, the local media monopoly, AT&T, the construction industry, all invested in the exciting possibilities that would come from bringing the world's most cherished sports event to their town.

'We are proud of the way we won the games,' said Billy. 'There were no payments, direct or indirect, no scholarships.' We could take his word for it; indeed we'd have to, because Billy and his friends in Atlanta's white business elite had no wish to release the files accumulated when IOC members came visiting and he'd been chasing what was later spun as his 'incredible dream'. But they kept the files, thousands and thousands of pages of receipts, memos, lawyers' letters marked 'client privilege', notes of candid conversations, private and confidential, all under lock and key.

One of Billy Payne's closest aides was Horace Sibley, an attorney with Atlanta's blue-chip law firm King & Spalding, whose senior partner is Griffin Bell, once attorney-general in local boy President Jimmy Carter's administration. They handled the Coca-Cola account and they've earned millions representing Billy's team since 1987.

From the bid's early days, Horace filed memos as he learned what you had to do to win IOC votes. One reported a lunch Horace and Billy had with John Martin, who negotiated TV rights when American network ABC screened the Olympics from Moscow and Los Angeles. 'Martin asked me to come out half an hour early,' wrote Horace. 'When I arrived, he told me that he had wanted a minute with me because he had some things he wanted to talk very bluntly about, and did not want to run the risk of offending Billy Payne whom he had heard was a very optimistic and positive person. I told him . . . he ran no risk in saying whatever was on his mind because Billy was also very much a realist.

'He said that what he really wanted to say, bottom line, was that the IOC members were a bunch of "sleaze bags" who could not be trusted and were not the kind of people that we wanted to deal with. I told him we were fully aware of this and named a few whose reputation had already preceded them.'

The other King & Spalding attorney who joined the optimistically named Atlanta Olympic Committee was Charlie Battle. One of Charlie's earlier memos covered a dinner he shared in a Los Angeles Chinese restaurant with IOC member Anita DeFrantz and her brother James. 'One of the main things that we discussed [was] that somehow she be kept in touch with our bid process so that she knows what's going on in Atlanta on an ongoing basis like a weekly communication.'

Charlie went off to Colorado Springs to talk to the US Olympic Committee's Alfredo La Mont. Alfredo ran international relations and knew better than most who was dirty and amoral in the Olympic family. You need Anwar Chowdhry, said Alfredo. Charlie reported back to Atlanta, 'He apparently can deliver from 15–20 votes if handled properly . . . it would be expensive as Chowdhry likes to do everything first class and you in effect had to give him a blank check.'

Chowdhry was president of Olympic amateur boxing and worked for the international relations team assembled by Adidas, when it was family-owned, to rig elections throughout the Olympic world. He couldn't stop boasting about the bribes bidding cities offered him to get them votes, and before long his two daughters were installed in an apartment in Atlanta and signed up to study at local colleges.

Calgary, who were about to host the 1988 winter games, generously shared the dossiers they had compiled on the IOC members. The Atlanta team turned Olympic intelligence-gathering into an art form, creating a four-page questionnaire which asked for intimate details on every member. Blank spaces were left for points like 'Is member highly ethical?' and 'What is member's long range business objective?'

The man who led Barcelona's bid informed them that 'the Royals on the IOC operate as a group' and another file recorded the shoe size of most members, their wives and children. Billy's boys and girls had opened a corporate charge account with the local branch of Tiffanys. As a losing rival commented later, 'Atlanta were talented gift givers.'

Atlanta's challenge was to win over forty-four members. Sure, the IOC told the public that they didn't accept gifts valued at more than $200. Why they *should* have gifts of that value – or at all – was never explained. Everybody in the game knew the rules were a joke, never applied, offenders – members or bidders – never punished. Looking back later, the affable Charlie Battle pleaded their naivety: 'We were true believers in trying to build a relationship, a real true friendship.' Billy's boys were tough operators and they knew an opportunity when they saw one. They built themselves into a well-oiled machine. Into one end they channelled public money, land, effort and goodwill. Out the other end came enrichment for the few. What a beautiful machine!

They had an uphill job; many members seemed not to know much about Atlanta, home of Coca-Cola, CNN and the self-proclaimed Southern 'city too busy to hate'. Members confused it with the New Jersey resort of Atlantic City. 'Several of the people we spoke to said they were looking forward to gambling in our casinos,' recalled Billy, 'and watching the Miss America pageant.'

Another IOC rule was that members shouldn't need to holiday in the applicant cities more than once. This didn't stop members who thought Atlanta's commitment to hospitality should be tested rigorously. Ecuador's Arroyo (shoe size 9.5) and his wife Raquel (shoe size 7.5) were more than conscientious, jetting in twice first-class in 1989 and coming back to check again the following year. David Sibandze (shoe size 7) was on autopilot, visiting twice and inquiring about college places. He brought with him a pal described as 'a prince in the royal family of the kingdom of Swaziland', who had to be bought a $470 jacket to go out to dinner.

A friend of the Atlanta bid warned them that Sibandze was 'Greedy and self-serving. Will sell his vote and will do so openly. Will try to have Atlanta set him up in business. Do not waste your time on him. To cave in to his wishes will get Atlanta into trouble.' Another memo noted that his two wives 'run his two fish and chip shops in Swaziland'.

Others, too, made multiple trips and some even came back after 1990, when Atlanta won their vote, just to check the mint juleps were still being served full-strength. Still more, on their way to and from Atlanta, were compelled to visit other favourite haunts around the world, all on Billy's dollar. The purpose of these trips was to check out Atlanta's competence to host the Olympics and many chose to vacation at Disney World in Florida.

All the established rackets were worked, free dental and medical treatment, discussions of business deals and attempts to share in the billion-plus of Olympic contracts on offer in town. The shopping was truly wonderful. Members and their wives, sometimes together, sometimes not, were escorted to Atlanta's finest stores by hostesses with credit cards that became dull and worn by the end of the couple of years of pillage. The hostesses, often wives of the men who built the Machine, were told to be 'gracious, accommodating, and hospitable'. In the evening they took their guests home to dine in the city's finest mansions.

Hostesses who escorted members in Atlanta had to fill in another questionnaire. There were five sections.

1. Personal likes and dislikes of the Member's spouse.
2. Any comments about Atlanta's candidacy and other bid cities.
3. Advice regarding our candidacy.
4. Other pertinent information.
5. Rate on a scale of 1–10 your observation of the sincerity of the member's comments about Atlanta's bid.

One hostess, Mary Drye, coped magnificently with the Arroyos. 'Dr and Mrs Arroyo took the lead and set the pace,' she reported. 'They were happy with the original agenda, and very happy that their other desired activities could all be incorporated . . . the afternoon at World of Coke was a real favorite though the experience of *Cats* at the Fox [Theatre] was greatly enjoyed – almost overwhelming, it seemed.'

Mary worked as an efficient double act with driver Susan Smith. 'It has been a definite plus working with Susan these last two times . . . we both enjoy going the extra mile to work everything out for the Arroyos because they're so much fun to be with – and so appreciative . . . working out of the Marriott Marquis was a pleasure (good cooperation from doormen, bell-check – as well as conveniently located ladies room for quick changes.)'

Arroyo became a fervent advocate of Atlanta's bid and shared family secrets with his new friends. 'Arroyo says that Samaranch does not like controversy on the floor of the Session,' reported one Atlanta scout. 'If there is an issue of debate Samaranch will personally call the opposition and diplomatically make compromises or promises to keep the debate from happening. He says that Samaranch can be extremely convincing in these one on one conversations.'

Horace Sibley, asking Arroyo how to win one member's vote, was told, 'Get him a girl who speaks Arabic. Treat him with a silk glove as a sheikh and give him a bottle of wine named for him.' Princess Nora of Liechtenstein, he said, 'will do whatever the royalty do – most likely [vote for] Athens.' Billy's boys and girls warmed to Prince Albert of Monaco. 'Honest, open and fun,' read his file note. 'Likes the good life, wine, women (some say men as well) and song. Visit to Atlanta should be low key with press but an all out orgy for Al and his friend.' Orgies were sought by a member (shoe size 9.5) who 'accepted two ladies from Barcelona' and another great Olympian (shoe size 44 – European) of whom they were told, 'Gifts are OK. Gift of female OK.' These secret lists of IOC names often carried the reminder 'Will not accept gifts' but as

often 'Will accept gifts' and 'Can be bought'. These people
have survived Pound's purge and remain IOC members.

An encounter with an African member was alarming. 'He
talked again about the eye clinic so prepare yourself, he is
asking for open heart surgery and eye surgery for his wife.
Probably he does not have any insurance. I hope he has
insurance. We are well aware of the prohibitive hospital costs
in our country for surgery in Atlanta.'

America, to some members, was a gougers' paradise, with
some of the finest medical facilities in the world. Free medical
treatment was a routine request. After meeting one elderly
Asian member (shoe size 8, narrow) the scout reported: 'He
indicated he is coming back to LA for a visit to his doctor
around February. It did not dawn on me that what he was
probably asking for was for us to pay for his ticket until I heard
him tell the same thing to Paul Henderson', who led Toronto's
rival bid: 'We need to send him two open round-trip first-class
tickets.'

Britain's Mary Glen-Haig (shoe size 8) told Billy privately
that she was 'totally against this entire bidding process, as
cities spend too much money and bring out the worst in some
of her dishonest colleagues'. Another file note, from yet
another adviser recorded, 'Mary Glen-Haig is ineffective.'

You couldn't blame Billy for stretching the rules. Look what he
was hearing about the rivals. Carol, wife of Willi Kaltschmitt
from Guatemala, told him, 'On the boat in Barcelona Mr XX
from Athens asked her to come into the room and to take off
her necklace and he presented her with the new Greek gift –
the gold necklace. He told her the gift in Tokyo [will be] a pair
of earrings to match the original necklace given to the IOC
wives in Seoul.'

The story was seemingly confirmed by another of Atlanta's best friends, Flor Isava. The Venezuelan dowager (shoe size 7) told Horace Sibley 'about the gold necklace that one of the Athens Bid Committee gave all the women members of the IOC and the wives. She said Raymond Gafner from Switzerland 'had protested this but had been told by the donor that this was not a gift on behalf of the Bid Committee, but was a personal gift; so she decided to keep hers.' Flor didn't have to be grateful, though. 'She commented several times about the "disagreeable" personalities of the two Greek members of the IOC.'

Billy persevered with the capricious lady. 'Flor Isava continues to be most impressed by the city she last visits. She takes great joy in telling us how wonderful the competition is. However it is very true that we have a special and sincere relationship with her.' Flor's assigned hostess noted, 'loves to be the center of attention – particularly with men. Hates early morning events.'

Vitaly Smirnov got up early for a free medical consultation with Billy's personal physician. Then he was taken to Chuck's Gun Shop. Mrs Smirnov shopped at Saks and met Vitaly for lunch at the Cherokee Town Club. They squeezed in more shopping before a Tchaikovsky concert – Vitaly is a talented pianist – then dined late at The Country Place. As a bonus and to remember his days in Atlanta, Vitaly took home a 'glow-in-the-dark' dog collar for one of his Irish setters.

More dog collars went to Sweden's elderly Gunnar Ericsson, coincidentally, another Irish setter man. He could be hard work, as Billy lamented. 'Gunnar continues to ramble a lot and is not a good listener and will be difficult to ask very direct questions. Nevertheless, we will try.' Maybe some easy money would concentrate his thoughts. 'Perhaps we should pursue putting Gunnar on an American affiliate Board of Directors in Sweden,' mused Billy.

There was much talk of helping members' offspring attend college in America but Billy's boys seemed to have stopped short of paying fees. They did fix to get one child a discount rate at a local college and Billy helped the son of Vitaly Smirnov enrol at the University of Georgia in 1991 but Daddy is said to have paid the bills. This was commendable on Smirnov's part. By the following year he had the additional burden of building and equipping what looked to me on my visit there like a palatial home in the pine forests outside Moscow.

Hungary's Pál Schmitt was hoping to place his talented tennis-playing daughter in an American university and a scholarship was offered at the University of Georgia. Calls were made on her behalf by Olympic family member Anita DeFrantz and she ended up in California. The highly moral Nigerian member, Henry Adefope, was troubled when a scholarship at Georgia Tech was offered to his daughter Toyin (shoe size 6.5) in late 1989, in the run-up to the vote. 'The spontaneous offer can be misinterpreted,' Henry wrote to Charlie Battle, 'so she has my blessing to pursue the pro-gramme after 1990.' Billy's boys now say she never did.

While chasing votes Billy's team had to look ahead to see how they would fund the event if they got it. Television cover-age was crucial and so Billy went to talk to Alex Gilady, an Israeli-American entrepreneur and producer who schmoozed the IOC on behalf of NBC. 'Gilady certainly confirmed his reputation for being abrupt and even rude,' wrote Billy. A year later an Atlanta lawyer working for Billy filed a memo about his own approach to Gilady for advice. 'It was interesting to note

THE GREAT OLYMPIC SWINDLE

that Alex did not mention anyone other than those at NBC or affiliated with NBC,' wrote Joe Bankoff. 'He did not have a kind word to say about ABC and never mentioned CBS at all. His list included only Peter Diamond, the head of NBC Sports, and Manola Romero, NBC's adviser for Barcelona.' Gilady has since been elevated to full membership of the IOC.

When Billy insisted that 'there were no payments, direct or indirect,' he couldn't have been thinking of the favourite sport of many IOC members, the airline ticket contest. They competed to see who could squeeze the maximum number of first-class return tickets from their homes to bidding cities. The front runners cajoled applicants into handing over tickets for wives, pals, kids and probably the chap loitering on the corner over there. Then they cashed them in, and bought cheap bucket-shop tickets or didn't visit at all.

The rival Toronto bidding team were milked by an estimated eighteen members. A similar number are thought to have repeated the exercise in Atlanta. Ten of them, feeling Atlanta's enthusiasm and the warmth of Southern hospitality, demanded and received thousands of dollars in cash without receipts for flights they claimed to have made. One scored more than $11,000 in a single hit.

It was all being paid for by donations from the business sector, claimed Billy. These were the private-enterprise games he said, overlooking the $900,000 donated by the city, the state and neighbouring Fulton County. One of the more enterprising endeavours was taxpayer-funded visits by American ambassadors around the world to members' homes and inviting them back to the embassies for fine luncheons. Billy asked Vice-President Dan Quayle to drop in on members during his foreign tours – but that doesn't seem to have lost any votes. President Bush sent personal letters to every member; he might have been less effusive if he'd known of the stroke pulled by Jamaican member Tony Bridge.

Charlie Battle and a colleague and their wives spent a weekend visiting ageing Tony, a member since 1973. Part of the discussion was about Olympic gold, more precisely about how to suitcase some of Tony's gold into a Florida bank account. Charlie reported that Bridge owned a publishing business somewhere in south Florida. 'Tony had $15,500 in cash which he wanted paid to them and suggested that we facilitate this payment for him as he sometimes has difficulty transferring such funds from Jamaica in a timely fashion. Since you are permitted to bring into the United States cash in an amount which does not exceed $10,000 I brought in $8,000 and Bobby Reardon brought in $7,500. I truly believe no laws were broken and certainly no illicit payment was made.'

The bidding team opened a Very Special Dossier on a most important guest. 'Mrs Samaranch,' one of her friends told them, 'absolutely loves to shop.' Billy filed his thoughts: 'Mrs Samaranch does not like to get up early and likes late nights . . . Mrs Samaranch does not like adhering to his very tight schedule and prefers to shop (line up a Saks and Lord & Taylor visit with the store managers and when she selects something, make them insist it's on the house because she is such an important person, etc. Make it convincing by prior arrangement with the respective stores).'

Her visit was fixed for late spring 1990. Billy sent another memo passing on advice from the head of world volleyball, Rubén Acosta and his wife. They emphasised that 'she loves the high society and artsy stuff and despises any of the venue plans. We ought to go over her entire program and find out if she will at least attend the race.' The city was staging a road-race, to demonstrate a belated interest in amateur sport.

Would Atlanta be stimulating enough for Bibis Samaranch? Just in case, they arranged a trip to neighbouring South Carolina. Three days before the Great Lady arrived from Barcelona, hostess Linda Stephenson hurriedly faxed her fixer: 'Dear Kathleen, I have just talked with Mrs Samaranch in Barcelona. She is very excited about her trip to Charleston. In conversation she told me that she will be bringing two guests: Mrs Malvehy and Mrs Comazran. Both live in Barcelona. I am sorry to change the number but I did not know.'

The excursion couldn't be tied remotely to the question of whether Atlanta was capable of staging the games. So the IOC sent Billy a bill, from Lausanne, for first-class return tickets: $11,620. Once she had her hands around the plump Atlanta teats, Bibis milked madly. A year later Linda Stephenson winged a memo to Billy. 'Subject: Mrs Samaranch's Request to Attend Academy Awards. This is to remind you that we must secure at least three tickets to the Academy Awards in Los Angeles for next Spring. Mrs Samaranch, Isabelle and Cecilia would like to go to the Academy Awards. The last time Mrs Samaranch went to the awards was right before the Games in 1984. She was introduced and was very pleased.'

Her husband also loved to meet the stars. Billy Payne remembered, 'I met with Samaranch in his room to invite him to meet with President Bush . . . he was immediately affected and impressed . . . then for the first time ever made an attempt to make small talk to me.'

As Samaranch's first visit loomed, Linda's memos piled up 'Samaranch is a Catholic. It is important for us to invite the Archbishop to either the breakfast or reception and introduce him to Samaranch. He was in contact with the Bishop in Calgary and asked for special spiritual guidance.'

Samaranch certainly was well looked after. His personal secretary, Annie Inchauspé, they wrote, 'will travel with him. Bill says that she acts as his "mother" – lays out his clothes, etc and must have an <u>adjoining suite</u>. She is a valuable source of information and needs attention. We should spend time getting to know her and <u>must</u> pronounce her name correctly.'

Linda did get to know her and reported further: 'Re Samaranch visit. He does like to be addressed as His Excellency or President. He is very aware of his position. Samaranch likes in his room the following: weights, a chinning bar to be hung at the very top of the door to his bath with just enough room to get his fingers around the bar, a stationary bicycle, sparkling water, postcards, small gifts from Atlanta, flowers, printed schedule, extra non-slip treads in the bathtub, pulsating shower head. He brings his own skipping rope.' There must be gifts for Annie and, 'The Governor and Mayor must present a gift to Samaranch.'

The old jackbooter knew how to squeeze the teats. Billy wrote to the manager of the Omni Hotel in Atlanta's downtown. 'The president of the IOC has sent us a personal request to assist his personal doctor, B. Ruis from Barcelona.' Apparently space was limited at a cardiology conference and 'anything you can do to assist will be greatly appreciated'. But not by Samaranch.

In April of 1990, election year for the games of 1996, Billy wrote confidentially to Anita DeFrantz. 'Dick Pound says . . . Samaranch is making an all-out effort in support of Athens. He says Samaranch has been asked by the King of Spain (brother-in-law of King Constantine) to work for Athens in the hope that their victory would somehow permit King Constantine to come back into Greece on some official basis.' Constantine, an IOC member, has lived in exile since he fled Greece in 1967 after a military coup.

By July, two months before the vote, Billy might have been despondent. He'd been tipped off that Samaranch was up to his old tricks. The IOC sent an Evaluation Commission to every bidding city to examine its ability to put on the Olympics. Two of its leading characters were IOC members Pál Schmitt of Hungary and Finland's Peter Tallberg. Billy's memo to his team said, 'Pál Schmitt mentioned to me that the Evaluation Committee had listed Atlanta number one and Athens last. The president refused to accept that report in those terms and made the commission rank the cities either excellent or good. Atlanta, Toronto and Melbourne were excellent – Belgrade, Manchester and Athens were good. I get the feeling that Schmitt and Tallberg are a little bit resentful that all of their work was glossed over.'

Early in Atlanta's bid Horace Sibley had visited Marc Hodler, the man who later gave the Salt Lake scandal wings and wheels, at his law office in Bern. The shrewd old Volvo-driver, who'd seen presidents and members come and go, was frank. 'First class hotel space and first class air travel are of major importance,' he told Horace. 'A number of the voters are interested in their accommodations above all else.' But Atlanta could provide something no rival could match. 'There are about 15 avid golfers on the IOC. They would die to play on the Augusta national course.'

And play they did. In May 1989 Gunnar Ericsson and his son, Denmark's Niels Holst-Sørensen and his wife, Mr and Mrs Tallberg, Japan's Chick Igaya and spouse, and Ireland's Kevin O'Flanagan, spent a night at the Buckhead Ritz-Carlton ('recently selected as one of the world's 15 best hotels'), then took off in a fleet of corporate jets for the brief flight from Atlanta to Augusta.

O'Flanagan had started eating his way into Atlanta's budget a few weeks earlier, spending a vacation at The Cloisters hotel-to-die-for on Sea Island, off the Georgia coast. He was accompanied by Patrick Hickey, the Irish Olympic official who succeeded him in 1995; Hickey's return airfare from Dublin was a snip at $5,344. Holland's Anton Geesink (shoe size 15) and his wife kept them company. They relaxed in the sun by the seaside while O'Flanagan played golf for two days. Their greeter noted, 'Gee, they all eat a lot.'

The Olympic golfing party had dinner in the Clubhouse, spent a night in one of the course's 'world famous cottages', played a day's golf followed by a second night amid the finest fairways and foliage in the world. Then they transited through Atlanta back to their distant homes. This vacation of a golfer's lifetime was declined by sleaze-buster Dick Pound, who had also declined a private jet ride from his home in Montreal to Atlanta. 'I did not want to waste my time or their money,' he told me.

Dick made up for this a year later when he, too, spent a couple of days golfing at Augusta. His bill, for himself and his wife, was $2,589.79. 'I only agreed the next year at Billy's insistence,' explained Dick. 'I told him that with Toronto in the race I was not going to support Atlanta, but he said I was a vice-president and it was important that I come. I do not know the cost of the trip.' A couple of days later Judge Kéba Mbaye, the member from Senegal, made his one-day golfing pilgrimage. It nearly didn't happen. Billy had filed a worrying memo, reporting a conversation in a hotel; Mbaye had said he hadn't received an invitation to Augusta – he assumed black people were not permitted to play the National course.

'Immediately after the lunch Dick Pound came up to me and told me about the conversation and asked me if it was true.

I denied it was true and indicated that the racial barrier had been broken at Augusta many years ago. He advised that I hurry up and extend an invitation to Mbaye before any damage was done.'

Billy's boys trooped off to Tokyo in September 1990 to arm-wrestle with their rivals, Athens, Belgrade, Manchester, Melbourne and Toronto, and, after a final splurge of gifts, took the gift of the Olympics home with them. At the end of the campaign one of Billy's aides told him that a local archive had offered to store the bidding committee's files and weed out any 'sensitive' documents. He replied, 'No way – you must be crazy or drunk. Total files must be reviewed by us first.'

Chapter 9

. . . And how it Hurt the Poor

Anita Beaty was busy chasing her own dream in parts of Atlanta that Billy and the boys and their friends in the IOC didn't often get to visit. 'People like me in our community didn't really notice the bid for the Olympics. We were too engrossed fighting for social justice,' says Anita. Her community? 'The folks who help the poor and homeless people get access to shelter, food and health services. We thought, "Who in the world would want to come here when we have poverty and racism to the degree that we do? It's all a big joke."'

Short, round and red-haired, Anita was born into one of South Carolina's finer families and made her social debut dancing across high-society ballrooms in a long white ballgown four decades ago. Growing up privileged, she saw injustice, didn't like it, and has been fighting it most of her adult life. She and her husband moved to Atlanta in 1984. 'We came here to do our mid-life artsy thing. Jim's got his doctorate in British lit, and a master's degree in theology. We were doing some volunteer work, and one day a homeless, mentally ill woman turned up with a year-old baby boy. This woman was living on the street with this infant. Outside at night in Georgia that winter it was nine degrees Fahrenheit below zero and the baby was going to die of hypothermia.'

After months of Anita trying to get mother and baby a permanent home, a city hall official said, 'Why don't you put

131

your money where your mouth is?' Anita and Jim already had six children. 'We took him for the weekend and never let him go. We wound up adopting him, and Donnie is sixteen now.'

Soon after, Anita was asked to work full-time on the city's Task Force for the homeless. 'We said, "Hey, we can't live on that money," and prayed a little bit and laughed a little bit and said, "What else can we do? Clearly it's meant to be", so we did it.'

'The Olympic movement in Atlanta was an incredibly wonderful experience,' says irrepressible Billy Payne, who's made his way in life as a lawyer specialising in putting together speculative land deals. Billy prides himself on being ahead of the game; he can see a million-dollar profit where others see only scrubby woods and fields.

Just a year before Billy announced he was going after the games, he spent an afternoon trudging some fields in Rockdale county, twenty-five miles out of Atlanta. They were part of a 56-acre parcel of land at a junction on Interstate 20 which runs eastwards all the way through Augusta and on into South Carolina. Billy saw a potential missed by other speculators and moved smartly to persuade one of his backers to take care of the price, $1.5 million, and become his partner.

In the months that followed Billy backed his judgment and added another 123 acres. This time the $2.1 million needed came from Gus Barkworth who, the local paper had it, owned half the county and ran the rest. Billy was promised 35 per cent of the profits when the time was right to sell. An adjacent 116 acres of scrub and pine forest soon became available for $1 million. A group of investors put up the money and this time Billy got 20 per cent. The deals done, Billy moved on. He launched the Georgia Amateur Athletic Foundation to bid for the Olympics and at its first meeting in June 1987 he said, 'I've already been asked several times, "What is my angle?" . . . My angle in this deal is the incalculable emotional high that will flow from the tears of joy that we all share [when we] hear the announcement that Atlanta and Georgia have been selected as a site for the summer Olympic Games.'

Billy's dream to bring the Olympics to Atlanta, so we learn from dozens of press profiles recycling the same heroic clichés, was the challenge he set himself after a fund-raising drive to build a sanctuary at St Luke's Presbyterian Church, his place of worship in the leafy suburb of Dunwoody. The games, he promised, would leave 'a legacy of facilities and housing which will benefit this community, its young athletes and citizens for decades to come'. But which community was he talking about?

'Between 'eighty-five and 'eighty-seven all we tried to do in our community was open church basements for the homeless to take shelter in,' says Anita. 'And we were trying to get folk to understand that it wasn't a problem of the ageing white alcoholic, the vagrant image you have. This was about a younger population of African Americans, people who couldn't get work because the jobs had moved to the suburbs, people being displaced from housing.'

They were on the street. In the years before the bid the city lost two thousand beds in cheap rooming houses. Anita recalls her hero Andrew Young, later a three-term congressman, ambassador to the UN, mayor of Atlanta and, later still, co-leader of the bid with Billy Payne, telling 'anecdotes of how when he first came to Atlanta as a young man to work with Dr [Martin Luther] King, he could stay for two or three dollars a night in a rooming house.'

In 1985 Anita's Task Force reckoned there was a solid core of up to five thousand homeless people sleeping on the streets of Atlanta, a city damned with America's second highest poverty rate. Five years later, when Billy's boys secured the games, there were fifteen thousand of them and they were no longer being left to rest in the parks or draped round heating ducts. The city had found new, temporary accommodation: the old city jail. 'We were naive,' says Anita. 'We didn't connect what was going on with the Olympic bid committee, the legislation that began to appear and the actions of the police. There was a guy who was getting regularly busted. He would be stopped and put against a fence and oppressed, roughed up, not with a billy-stick necessarily but kinda pushed around a little bit.

'This became a common experience for men who were homeless and on the streets. And for the chronically homeless, who are in the minority but very visible, the harassment often resulted in jail. They were being generally harassed – "Don't be here when I come round again or you're going to jail." Usually they stayed in jail for a few days before any charges were brought. Frequently, the charges would then be kicked out of court.'

And there were other new laws. 'By 1987 Billy Payne's crowd were nothing if not ready to pass state laws and local ordinances that gave them the power to condemn property if they needed to. They had a vision of a great and beautiful city which didn't include poor people and the Olympics gave them that excuse. Their idea of downtown looks more like Disney World or Dallas.

'Atlanta is a debutante with dirty tennis shoes and she leans over and exposes them at every turn,' says Anita. 'It is so adolescent, the way Atlanta has tried to hide its poverty; we should include it, acknowledge it, and celebrate the real solutions to it.' What happened to the chronic homeless when the posh folks from the IOC came a-visiting? 'They were swept out of sight,' she says.

Victory swept $1.7 billion worth of business into the hands of Billy and the boys. The Atlanta corporations that had stumped up the money for the bid were vindicated. The city network of public and private interests, which often appear to zigzag into each other's arms, was mobilised and Billy's Beautiful Money Machine hummed into action.

He discarded his bid-leader hat and took the leadership of the new Atlanta Committee for the Olympic Games (ACOG) at a salary of $519,000. It was one of the highest in America for a chief executive of a non-profit organisation – and it went up by $249,000 over the next few years. The ACOG, a private foundation which would dramatically alter the city's towering skyline and lowly neighbourhoods, hand out millions of dollars on Olympic-related construction and pay several of its leaders enormous salaries, met in private. The major players came from the pre-eminent law firm King & Spalding, alumni of the Georgia Institute of Technology, Georgia Tech, which absorbed $170 million in new construction, and, sensibly, the local construction industry. They all knew each other well, had done business together for decades and could think of no-one better qualified to share Olympia's gold.

At first ACOG thought it was business as usual and began granting contracts to friends at City Hall. They were taken aback, surprised, a little discomfited, when the public started paying attention to how the Olympic windfall was being cut up. An outcry stopped the first share-out, so the politicians had to settle for their kin being employed by the committee. Coca-Cola appeared to sit back, raising its head occasionally when the exploitation of the majority African-American community became embarrassing enough to figure in the foreign press. Ethics committees were set up by the public oversight board and the ACOG but they didn't seem overworked.

The Atlanta boys had studied the Olympic blueprint. First, choose a neighbourhood with no sports venues. Set up a committee of politicians and businessmen and announce your Olympic campaign, motivated by love of country and municipality. Make it private so nosy reporters can't find dirt. Talk a lot about Olympic Idealism. Behave amorally to obtain the contract to organise the event; if caught, claim it was done for the community's benefit. Pass dream laws giving yourself power to seize property for commercial redevelopment – in the public interest. Mix public and private money, divide up the contracts between your friends. Get rich.

Oh, and clear the streets of the poor and anybody who fails to share your glee. The Russians cleansed Moscow of dissidents in 1980. Los Angeles made sure that demonstrations weren't held near the press headquarters and cleared homeless people off the streets. The Korean police, trained to club and teargas, sanitised Seoul. Barcelona's gypsies were banished from Olympic areas.

'When Atlanta won, we couldn't believe it, we were absolutely stunned,' says Anita. 'The minute it happened we said, "Oh My God, this is going to increase the pressure on the homeless in the downtown. This is going to give them an excuse to crack down."'

Ten months later the new laws came. The Quality of Life Ordinances outlawed homeless people sleeping in derelict buildings, being in a car park without owning a car and begging any way the police didn't like. 'And then,' says Anita, 'they opened the first new Olympic facility, the municipal jail. It over-crowded the day it opened.' Anita's Task Force took the city to court, but had to go to Boston in New England, far from the South, to find a law firm prepared to take on the work.

The churches and volunteer groups came together and formed the Olympic Conscience Coalition. 'Our declared aim,' says Anita, 'was to hold the line on funding emergency services. We lost. Programmes were bled of money. Money was spent on cosmetic work, on the streets that led to venues – on street scapes, not on proper renovation or new homes for people without any. They were like set paintings in the movies.' Soup kitchens came under pressure to feed fewer people, because the authorities didn't want visibly homeless men to be given any encouragement.

Atlanta mayor Bill Campbell took reporters to the home of eighty-year-old Alberta Mitchell in the decrepit Summerhill neighbourhood, in the shadow of the new stadium. Her grubby white house had been painted pink. It would make good pictures. The reporter from Associated Press went inside and found the electrical wiring was so dangerous that the upstairs supply had been disconnected. But look what the Olympics had done for Alberta. She didn't need her own lighting: the stadium floodlights had plenty to spare, illuminating her bedroom at night!

With all that Olympic idealism pumping out of the ACOG offices downtown, you might think there'd be a meeting of minds between Billy and Anita's Olympic Conscience Coalition. Their first bodily meeting was in the boardroom with Big Billy and Quite A Lot Smaller Anita faced off across the table. 'He was saying social services were none of his business, but he and his people weren't going to negatively impact on what we did. And we said, "There's already been some diversionary impact on resources and we've had this criminalisation of people on the streets."'

Anita eyeballed the Olympian. 'You can, in your position, declare publicly that this is not to happen, give us something to hang our hats on,' she recalls. 'And he kinda rose up, pushed himself up from the table and leaned forward to me and said, "Anita, you and I have never agreed on anything" – and I looked round to see who he was talking to because we'd never met before.'

Then Anita leaned towards him and replied, 'We have no power, we have no money, we have only our experiences and what we know. And we are going to tell the truth and if there are continued arrests, and we see a worsening of the condition, we will tell the world.'

The oldest public housing project in America, Techwood Homes, built slap up against Coke's world headquarters and Georgia Tech, would celebrate its sixtieth birthday in Olympic year. But it stood in the way of a 'sanitised corridor' running through to CNN headquarters and the city centre, a dream long cherished in the business community. Anita noticed from the late 1980s that as units fell vacant they were boarded up, not re-let. 'We were sure it was part of a closing down of the area for redevelopment. They removed any management interest, repairs, maintenance and police protection for the few residents that were left in what eventually resembled a bombed-out war zone.'

And then popped up The Plan. Half the eight hundred houses would be knocked down. Of the remainder, after refurbishment, only a fifth would be reserved for poor families, and strict new credit and criminal-record checks would exclude many of the families who most needed the units. Anita reckons only five of the original families remain in what have become middle-to-upper-income apartments. Georgia Tech got new student dorms, built with public funds. That was a good piece of business. The excuse? For a few weeks they would be the Olympic village.

Former president Jimmy Carter came into town with his answer to the city's ills. His Atlanta Project, taking care of poverty with volunteers and his own political weight was, says Anita, 'a colossal failure. There was the kind of noblesse oblige that permeated that whole effort. It was the do-good white community coming into the poor community to say, "Don't worry, don't organise, don't push for your rights. Let us provide leverage for you." It let the steam out of the kettle in terms of organised protests around the Olympics.'

President Samaranch, on a visit to Atlanta, caught a glimpse of a neighbourhood protest against the new Olympic stadium and showed instantly that he sensed the community's mood. 'Always, you have problems after getting the games. But I believe this community must be very happy to have these games.' He paid ritual tribute at Martin Luther King's tomb. When the great man was murdered in 1968, Samaranch himself was a high functionary of the Franco regime, whose cops treated demands for the ballot box and free speech just like the goons with clubs had treated King and his cohorts in the South.

During the bid Billy Payne and Andrew Young pitched Atlanta as 'the modern capital of civil rights'. This opinion wasn't shared by New York-based Human Rights Watch who shortly before the games accused the state of Georgia of police abuses, racial discrimination, intolerance and undermining freedom of expression. In a detailed report it highlighted the fact that young people in custody were subjected to 'cruel restraints and punishment forbidden by international standards'. This kind of thing wouldn't happen to the other 'young people of the world', the privileged ones with the good fortune to practise athletics.

As ever on his travels, Samaranch demanded from the local Catholic community special treatment usually reserved for the very sick and dying. The Church obliged, supplying a Spanish-speaking priest, Father Luis Zarama from the Sacred Heart Church, to attend his hotel suite and say a private Mass. Then Samaranch's vanity got him into trouble. On the eve of the games, when the old man's ego had inflated to bursting-point, he gave an interview to HBO's star reporter Frank Deford, who was curious about why Samaranch awarded Olympic Orders to Nicolae Ceauşescu, the Butcher of Bucharest, and other dictators.

'I'm proud of him,' Samaranch said, then he glibly proclaimed, 'We are more important than the Catholic Church.'

Samaranch tried the usual damage limitation, denying he'd said anything of the sort, although millions of Americans had heard him on TV; he made himself a laughing-stock. Atlanta's archbishop, Monsignor John Donahue, failed to see the funny side, and withdrew Samaranch's private Mass privileges.

Under the headline 'Sin and Penitence in Atlanta', Pedro Ramírez, editor of the leading Spanish daily *El Mundo*, wrote of accompanying a nervous Samaranch to the Archbishop's palace. Ramírez stayed in the official car with Samaranch's secretary, Annie Inchauspé, speculating how many Hail Marys were being imposed. Eventually Samaranch emerged from the palace and instructed Annie: 'Three tickets for the closing ceremony and another three for the track and field!'

At a gala night to welcome Samaranch's retinue to town Billy erupted, 'I feel the same love and devotion for this family that I feel for my own.' Now was the time, with the world's media on hand, to pump up a mythology of peace and love, distracting attention from Atlanta's dirty tennis shoes.

It didn't work. It wasn't only the foreign reporters who'd been filming and photographing poverty and exclusion in the neighbourhoods. The organisers became increasingly embattled as all but the local media poked holes in Billy's preposterous claims about a universal, inclusive idealism that could only be practised behind chain-link fences and security guards. The broken promises went on. The city had been persuaded to lend its name to these private Olympics in return for a profit – Billy called it a legacy – of nearly $160 million to bring sports facilities to inner-city kids. Sorry, said Billy, keeping the ACOG books close to his chest, we ain't got no money after all. His private committee was paying him $670,000 a year at the time.

They broke faith with the athletes too. IOC members were wafted through Hartsfield airport into air-conditioned VIP limousines, cheered by the good news from Michael Payne, the IOC's marketing director, that revenues for 1993 to 1996 'are likely to exceed three billion US dollars'. The athletes had to queue at undermanned desks for credentials. The team from Papua New Guinea took thirty-seven hours to fly from Port Moresby to Cairns, Australia, on to Brisbane, then Sydney, then Fiji, Honolulu, Los Angeles and, finally, Atlanta. Then they waited six more hours for credentials before they could travel to the Olympic village. Norwegian tennis player

Christian Ruud reported, 'The bus driver who picked us up at the airport did not know where the Olympic village was. We drove past it three times and, after two hours, we ended up back at the airport.'

Then the Flame arrived, the exclusive property of Coca-Cola, who swamped the media with poignant press releases like 'Coca-Cola salutes all the fathers who will carry the Olympic flame on Father's Day . . . Fathers serve many roles: giving advice, driving the children to soccer practice, fixing a leaky faucet. For those carrying the Olympic flame, the experience will serve as the ultimate way to honor them for all that they do.'

General Motors, who'd snapped up the sponsorship for domestic trucks, rammed thirty of their chrome-painted beasts into the opening ceremony rehearsal with the brand name picked out in huge blue letters. 'Those who view the ceremonies will recognize that we elevated GM and the Chevrolet brand way above the field,' said GM's John Middlebrook. This had been cleared, they claimed, with Billy's boys. Maybe, said the IOC, but it's NBC who do the advertising around here.

'We are disappointed with the Olympic Committee's decision to cover the Chevrolet badge on our trucks in the Opening Ceremonies,' snivelled a GM manager. GM were left to gnash their teeth on a Japanese press release that said: 'The Nissan Pathfinder will serve as the Official Import Sport Utility Vehicle, the Nissan Truck as the Official Import Light Truck and the Nissan Quest as the Official Import Minivan.' With all that to learn by heart, no wonder Billy's folks had neglected the sport.

They'd also neglected the most important detail of the whole event: getting the athletes to the venues. Athletes who'd trained for years to qualify for the games were delivered too late for their events. Rickety, often unsafe buses had been begged and borrowed from towns all over America. Some drivers wouldn't touch them, pointing to bald and splitting tyres, expired fire extinguishers, and complaining about the lack of two-way radios, air-conditioning and fuel gauges. Volunteer, inexperienced drivers refused to take buses on busy interstates. Other drivers quit when their pay failed to arrive.

British multi-medallist rowers Steve Redgrave and Matthew Pinsent stormed out of the athletes' village and checked into a hotel near the Lake Lanier venue. 'On race days we've given up with ACOG transportation. It's just too risky,' said Pinsent. 'There'll be a teenager with a walkie-talkie telling you, "the bus will be here in ten minutes. Have a nice day."' Later, at the Paralympics, shuttle buses dropped off athletes, many of them in wheelchairs, at the bottom of a steep hill when their rooms were at the top.

IBM's computer system, essential to the media, enraged reporters when it failed to deliver accurate results on time. Sports, names, statistics were garbled.

Then the bomb went off, killing one woman and injuring 111 people. That horror couldn't be blamed on the IOC or the ACOG and was likely planted by a right-wing terrorist.

Towards the end of the two weeks Billy and his boys, the local media and the rest of the world that took any passing interest in arcane Olympic matters waited eagerly to see what Samaranch would say in his closing remarks. Traditionally, he congratulated the hosts on 'the best games ever'.

The stadium darkened, the spotlights picked out the small figure. Get on with it man! Then it came; the 1996 Atlanta Olympics were . . . only 'Most exceptional'.

143

Arrrrrrh! The mean-spirited little fascist had screwed them to the last. They'd accommodated every shrill shakedown from his vain and greedy wife, not called the cops when the buggers stole money on the ticket swindle, pulled every lever to get them on to the sacred Augusta fairways, buried them in 'gifts', sent them home newly shod – and now the whores wouldn't do the one last trick they'd been well paid to perform. 'The best ever': that was all he had to say. And he didn't. Billy's 'love and devotion for this family' had to be strained.

Awarding Olympic gold didn't end when the athletes flew home. Billy still had some unfinished business with that parcel of land out in Rockdale County, the acreage he and his partners had acquired before he ever announced his decision to bid for the games. It had become inextricably mixed up in the Olympic business.

The ACOG needed a venue for the equestrian events and one of the bids came from Rockdale's county seat, Conyers. An international, equestrian park could put the sleepy little town on the map! Create jobs! Anything local folk wanted to be told! Around a dozen locations applied and the ACOG whittled them down to a final four, including Conyers. Billy disclosed his land holding near the Conyers site and stepped back from the decision. His fellow members of the ACOG board and its ethics committee ruminated; and then they gave Conyers the prize.

Billy's land was plumb on the Interstate 20 exit for the new Horse Park. Prior to the games he and his partners sold some of the plot for retail development, taking an estimated $500,000 profit. The road to the Horse Park had to be widened for the Olympic traffic and the value on his remaining land crept up. When he washed his hands of the last plot in the late 1990s it brought him a further profit of nearly $700,000.

The Money Machine hummed for lawyers King & Spalding, who picked up nearly $2 million in fees in the two years after the games. More money swirled round the two private organisations created and led by Billy in his pursuit of Olympic gold and glory. ACOG had been the love-child of the Georgia Amateur Athletics Foundation (GAAF), the non-profit organisation created by him in 1987 to bid for the games. Ten years later, the GAAF was almost penniless. Then the ACOG gave it a few million dollars and – whoosh! – a sizeable chunk rushed through and straight into Billy's pocket. There was a good reason, according to his friends. He had amassed a wonderful collection of memorabilia during his Olympic years and everybody agreed it was his personal property so he was free to sell it to GAAF for a trifling $975,000. The price was arrived at by an independent assessor but GAAF declined to reveal the individual valuations.

The local paper was baffled. Curious to know what kind of money Olympic memorabilia could raise, they called some collectors. One of the great prizes of the Olympic world, a letter from Baron Pierre de Coubertin, was valued at only $100,000. One of Jesse Owens's four gold medals carried the same price. What had Billy got that could possibly add up to $975,000?

Billy wasn't happy about these queries. 'I made a private and confidential transaction,' he said. 'There was no attempt to hide anything on this issue. The people who brought the Games to Atlanta are not dishonourable people.'

The ACOG's staff were told at the end of the games, sorry, guys, thanks for your loyalty but money is so tight we can't pay you bonuses. They weren't told about the confidential 'extended resource availability program' that made $1 million available to Billy's friends, even though most had found new jobs. Billy got one of the lowest pay-outs, only $69,000, but others went as high as $400,000. The needs of amateur sport weren't forgotten: the GAAF made two donations of $10,000 each for youth golf, not a sport much played by inner-city kids.

'I wish Atlanta had never had the games,' says Anita Beaty. 'All our predictions have come true. Homelessness is worse and the impact on the meagre supply of affordable housing has been dramatic. Devastating. We're now tens of thousands of homes short of what we need.

'One of the things that made me saddest of all was the businessmen who run the downtown saying after the games, "Now we've taken the city back from the homeless and the vagrants, we need to keep it." That's what the Olympics did for our town. They didn't bring us together – they worsened the divisions in our community.'

'I wish they'd just investigate us, because I don't think they'd find anything,' said Charlie Battle when news of the Salt Lake scandal went global. 'They'd give us a clean bill of health and we could get on with things.'

As the rumours from Mormon country grew wilder, Andrew Young produced a formidable argument that Atlanta's credit cards hadn't been used for salacious purposes. 'I can't imagine anybody on the IOC that's able to engage [in sex]. They are too old and broken down. You would have had more heart transplants.'

Atlanta's denials continued and they began drafting their 'nothing to report' memo for the IOC. Then a reporter acquired a memo that Billy had written a month before victory in Tokyo way back in 1990, suggesting what they could do to win. Here were listed all the things that Billy said had never happened, offers of college scholarships, free medical treatment, complimentary airline tickets to IOC members.

'It was nothing,' said Billy, 'I was just thinking aloud. I was brain dumping, under great pressure.' His plans were dismissed by his subordinates, he explained, and 'This is testimony to the high standards, under enormous pressures, used by our team in pursuit of the games.'

All went quiet in Atlanta. The 'nothing to report' report that should have been so easy to deliver was delayed. Charlie Battle didn't want folks getting the wrong idea. OK, their gifts exceeded the IOC rules, 'but we had not tried to buy votes'.

Billy decided to hold the line. All the memos, receipts, invitations, itineraries, shoe sizes, invoices, ticket receipts were safely locked in the GAAF archives. They were private documents and nobody would get near them.

Billy got back on track and wrote to Samaranch that there was 'no evidence in Atlanta's bid of improper inducements, scholarship programs or an excessive number of visits to Atlanta by IOC members or their families. We believe there was no wrongdoing on the part of the IOC members or the Atlanta bid committee during the bid process for the 1996 games.' No further comment.

The local paper, the *Atlanta Journal-Constitution*, went to court to prise the archives open. Public funds had been distributed by Billy's friends, public officials had sat on the ACOG; the public had a right to know what had been done in their name and with their taxes. Billy resisted and then the state governor and attorney-general joined in. OK, said Billy, we'll select some records for you to see. But not everything.

This was the way the good ol' boys had always done business in Atlanta: give a bit, take a bit; everything in this economically and racially divided town had to be a deal.

Watching in increasing disbelief in faraway Washington was Congressman Fred Upton. He chairs an investigation sub-committee of the Congress Commerce Committee. 'When I read in the *Atlanta Constitution*', Fred told me, 'that they had applied for the documents and been turned down I thought, I wonder if there's something there, I hope not. As we scratched just a little bit not only did we see Atlanta, but there was Toronto, then there was Athens and we said "Holy Cow, this has got to end."'

Chapter 10

Samaranch's Beautiful Launderette

Samaranch had been in the IOC president's chair for less than five years and already he had taken complete control. He'd recruited a clique of loyalists, new Spanish and Catalan officials imported to form his Lausanne palace guard, he took decisions without consulting the executive board and, worst of all, nobody had the courage to stand up to him.

Vice-President Berthold Beitz had courage – and guile. During the war he'd been sent to Poland to serve Hitler's Reich and he helped more than eight hundred Jews escape the death camps. By the mid 1980s he was in his early seventies, a respected West German businessman, director of the Krupp Foundation and a member of the IOC since the 1972 Munich games. And he was worried, so worried that he would go anywhere for help to rein in the new Olympic dictator.

With a heavy heart he sought out the only people he believed had the power to block Samaranch. It cannot have been easy, confiding in the enemy, but things had got that bad. One chilly day in February 1985, Beitz approached the Berlin wall, the border guards waved him through and he headed for an office in East Berlin, where he confided his anxieties in East German IOC member Gunther Heinz and Wolfgang Gitter, secretary of the national Olympic committee. Please, he begged, you people believe in the Olympic ideals, you have to help. Samaranch is filling the IOC with sycophants; you must support me in opposing him. I'm one of the few inside the IOC who can, and that's only because I'm a wealthy man and don't need him. The communist officials listened politely and agreed to talk again.

Eighteen months later, in August 1986, Beitz slipped back into East Berlin and this time he met Manfred Ewald, East Germany's sports supremo. We know what was said because the communists filed minutes in the archives of the Party's central committee. The tone of the meeting was 'open and relaxed', they tell us, and Beitz spoke his mind. In his opinion, 'the IOC is in the hands of a Spanish–Latin-American group that sees money as a means to power. This group's primary interest is to use the financial means and opportunities offered by sport, to increase their power and influence. Samaranch pays attention only to Brazil's João Havelange, Mexico's Mario Vázquez Raña and Primo Nebiolo.' They controlled, respectively, world soccer, the world's Olympic committees and world track and field. Go on, smiled Ewald, you are 'the most important person in international sport campaigning for the maintenance of the Olympic ideals'. Tell us more.

He did. Samaranch's behaviour was so autocratic that Beitz 'was considering resigning from his IOC membership'. He explained that he was trying to restrain the headlong descent into commercialism and professionalism but he felt isolated. He found no support on the executive board; with the exception of the Chinese member, He Zhenliang, who rarely turned up, they subordinated themselves to Samaranch who, he said, 'behaves like a stockbroker, demanding to be kept abreast of stock market and currency values, then deciding, with the aid of his friends and the Secretariat, how to spend the IOC's funds'.

The problem was that the IOC had too much money. And

there were no rules on how it should be spent. 'Therefore the IOC president can decide about the fate of large amounts without consulting either the Executive or Financial Commission – of which I am a member.' Beitz wound up his tale with an appeal for the Soviet-bloc countries to join him and other Western progressives in an alliance against Samaranch. 'He will retreat when he realises that other forces are against him,' Beitz told them.

It was remarkable that a pillar of Western European capitalism such as Beitz felt that only the Stalinists of the East could help salvage decency in sport. And he was wrong. They betrayed him. The Soviets had made their own accommodation with Lausanne; they rivalled the West in the doping wars, were equal partners in the conspiracy to hide positive tests, and were happy to depart each Olympic Games with a truckload of medals. Samaranch suited them fine.

A quarter of a century earlier, seven years before Samaranch was admitted to the IOC, the bureaucracy in Lausanne heard reports about his freewheeling attitude towards money and the law. In 1959 Otto Mayer, the grandly titled chancellor of the IOC, wrote privately to his president, Avery Brundage, about some unfortunate gossip concerning the ambitious young man from Barcelona who was trying every which way to gain membership.

In Spain the Franco dictatorship had passed strict laws to protect its faltering economy. It was illegal to move money out of the country without a permit. Permits weren't easy to get. Exchange-control laws had been common in Europe after World War II but only the junta in Madrid still needed them. This didn't suit the rich who wanted to swap their weak pesetas for strong dollars and Swiss francs. There had been press reports of a $100 million money-laundering operation, and Mayer told Brundage, 'Following a telephone call [from a Barcelona journalist] I had the other day, I am afraid our friend Samaranch must also be in that scandal . . . of course, I have no official confirmation, but this is what I understand from that call.'

Later, Mayer wrote again, with more news. There had been another press report, this time pitching the amount of money much higher. 'Our friend Samaranch is also in the scandal of finances in Spain. One [report] says that about $400 million have been placed in Switzerland and the USA. Important political personalities are also in it.'

From his late teens Samaranch had been drawn to General Franco and his muscular fascists, who'd risen in 1936 against Spain's elected leftist government and, with Hitler's and Mussolini's support, crushed democracy and imposed a brutal police state. Franco modelled himself on Adolf Hitler. As an ambitious young fascist Samaranch aped Franco's rhetoric about fascism's role in cleansing and renewing Spain. Like many opportunists who flocked to the cause, he enjoyed a double standard, parading the streets of Barcelona with his comrades in their immaculate military-style uniforms, declaring loyalty to Franco while lining their pockets at the expense of their oppressed fellow citizens.

Life for Barcelona's poor was so bleak that even some fascists joined workers who risked a general strike in 1951, but Samaranch was a true hard-liner, a keeper of the faith, a strike-breaker. In the archives of the civilian governor of Catalonia lies a report written by the secret police who commended the young man's loyalty. 'He is one of the few Falangists who were present on the days of the strike.'

152

Three years on, in November 1954, the investigators reported again on thirty-four-year-old Samaranch. There was no doubting his loyalty: 'Politically he identifies with the present regime,' they said.

Such endorsements opened the door for Samaranch's rise. By November 1956 he was signing off his political correspondence with the slogan only someone indifferent to the Holocaust that had ended a mere dozen years previously could employ. It can still be read in the Barcelona archives: 'Siempre a tus órdenes, te saluda brazo en alto [I am always at your command with my arm raised].'

Political acceptance came speedily. In two previous books I published photographs of Samaranch at later stages of his long political career, wearing fascist uniform and swearing allegiance to Franco. I've unearthed two new pictures, one from 20 November 1956, an important date in Spanish fascism's mystical rituals. It's after dark and Samaranch heads a procession of the political elite along the cobbled streets of the old city, through a guard of honour saluting with Olympic-style flaming torches. To his right parades Felipe Acedo Colunga, civilian governor of Barcelona, regional boss of the fascist party, the Movimiento, and the man who'd ordered the secret police to check out Samaranch's loyalty. Both wear the complete rig, smart blue shirts and ties and military-style coats with gleaming buttons and epaulets. Young, handsome, stylish and the centre of attention, Samaranch proudly bears a wreath to lay at the wall of the cathedral in memory of José Antonio Primo de Rivera, founder of their creed. On such occasions, arms were raised in the salute they shared with their Nazi comrades who, to their great disappointment, had lost World War II.

Few Spaniards and even fewer Catalans committed them-

153

selves so devotedly to the Movimiento. There was a heroic resistance, many people fled and most waited sullenly, decade after decade, for the dictatorship to crumble away.

Samaranch had been an active fascist for around fifteen years before he discovered his perfect route to advancement. He became a co-opted member of Barcelona city council – as with the IOC, there were no elections – and he spotted an opportunity. Sport. It was at the energetic centre of fascist ideology and aesthetics. Fit young men, flexing their muscles, were as much a part of propaganda in Spain as in the Third Reich. From the late 1950s through to the early 1970s Samaranch clambered his way up the political ladder on the back of sport until he became the country's sports supremo and a member of Franco's rubber-stamp parliament, the Cortes. In 1973, as Spain became increasingly isolated by the democratic nations of Europe, he told a local paper, 'I'm a man loyal to all that Franco represents . . . why not say it? I'm a man of the Movimiento . . . and of course I'm going to lead my whole life in this same way, with the loyalties that I have already mentioned.'

Sport delivered him the greatest prize in 1973 when Franco appointed him president of the region of Catalonia. Samaranch served his master well, looking the other way during the regime's final crackdown on democrats whose heroism and suffering are exemplified in the story of Salvador Puig Antich, a young dissident who was among the last political prisoners executed by the regime.

After a one-day military trial Salvador was found guilty of killing a policeman during his arrest, and sentenced to death. His lawyers claimed the court had suppressed vital evidence and Puig became the focus of an international appeal for clemency. The Pope pleaded for his life, Catalan artist Joan Miró made his plea in paint, a triptych entitled *The Hope of a Man Condemned to Death*. Puig's supporters believe to this day that he might have been saved if only Samaranch had intervened with Franco, but Samaranch did nothing and Salvador Puig Antich was garrotted on 2 March 1974 at the age of twenty-six. His sisters still campaign to clear his name, and they still grieve.

The future IOC president never wavered in his support for the most repellent rituals of the dictatorship. Eighteen years on from the picture of him carrying a wreath for Primo de Rivera, the cameras recorded again his firm convictions. Aged fifty-four and greying, Samaranch donned his blue shirt and uniform on 26 January 1974 to celebrate the anniversary of Franco's rebel army entering Barcelona. The city's leading Franquistas paraded at the monument to their fallen comrades and Samaranch took his place in the front row.

The picture, taken just over a year before the dictator's death, shows Samaranch flanked by grim-faced military men, the kind who turned the screw in the metal collar that choked life from impertinent young Salvador Puig Antich, whose judicial murder followed five weeks later. That year Samaranch, already a member of the IOC executive board, was promoted to vice-president. The Olympic message of peace, reconciliation and redemption he preached wasn't extended to the condemned man's cell. If anything, Samaranch's exalted position in international sport lent the regime legitimacy, helped blur its atrocities in the eyes of the world.

There was one more opportunity for some enthusiastic arm-waving before the ghastly era ended. Again, this time on 20 November 1975, Samaranch joined with the ageing rump of the city's fascists to celebrate their ideologue, Primo de

Rivera. Right arms were raised and then, that night, the people's hearts nearly burst with joy. Franco was dead!

But not for Samaranch. Over the next two years, as riot squads roamed the streets, he spoke out through local press and radio, praising Franco. He was a co-founder of a neo-fascist party, Concordia Catalonia, the only one of seven fighting the first free elections in four decades which sought to maintain the status quo. Humiliated at the polls, he gladly accepted exile from Spain to the ambassador's residence in far-away Moscow. From there he would run his campaign to capture the IOC presidency. He tossed his blue shirt into the Olympic reputation laundry and it came out sparkling white.

Madame Monique Berlioux, forceful IOC chief executive since 1972, clashed with Samaranch from the moment he chose to reside mostly in Lausanne and become the first hands-on president. Something would have to be done about her; Samaranch started plotting.

Tension simmered until he had his loyalists in position. Three months after Beitz's first visit to the comrades in 1985, the president struck. As it happened, the IOC's annual session was in East Berlin, at the Palast Hotel. The confidential executive board minutes, documents they still won't release to the public, tell a little of the tale.

On 1 June when 'Other Business' came up, Berlioux was shown the door, and in private her Olympic career was terminated. Beitz was one of three senior members, the others being the Prince de Mérode and Judge Mbaye, to work out her severance payment and gagging agreement. Her lawyer was given 25,000 Swiss francs for his work, and four days later she faced the session, read the statement written for her and left, clutching a cheque.

Samaranch remained twitchy about what she might reveal, and three years later the board earnestly discussed a disclosure they thought shocking made by Madame Berlioux in a British television programme. Asked what cities should do if they wanted to win the games she replied: 'Be good friends with the IOC president and the wives of IOC members'. The minutes of that board meeting continue, 'It was believed this statement could be interpreted as a violation of the duty of discretion as per the agreement made in 1985, as facts deemed confidential had been revealed.' A day later they decided it might be wise to take no action.

The new president found it easy to continue the authoritarian traditions of the committee. Numerous German, French and Italian fascists were appointed in the 1930s and the last to go was an unrepentant German, Ritter von Halt, who died in 1964 after thirty-five years practising his straight-arm salute in Vidy. Samaranch continued the tradition of recruiting characters with reputations in need of a good scrubbing at the Olympic laundry. And when he couldn't find a space on the committee, they went into business together.

A special favourite was 1920s French tennis star Jean Borotra, who'd enthusiastically joined the collaborator Marshal Henri Pétain when he set up a 'New Order' pro-German government after the fall of France in 1940. Borotra was put in charge of youth affairs and ordered youngsters to practise sport vigorously, despite food shortages. When the allied armies invaded in 1944 Pétain ordered the French not to aid them; after the defeat of the Nazis he was sentenced to death, commuted to life imprisonment, for his treachery.

Borotra's two great achievements in the 1960s were his prominent role in the Association for the Defence of the Memory of Marshal Pétain and his very own reputation laundry, the International Committee for Fair Play, which awards trophies and certificates of honour at an annual ceremony held in the Paris offices of UNESCO. Samaranch and his phalanx rarely miss these occasions.

Having studied the arts of statesmanship at Franco's feet, Samaranch knew how to build and maintain power, how to turn the institutions under his command into instruments of self-promotion. It was all done under the stirring principle of 'sacred unity' and Franco, from his home in hell, must have laughed to see his little disciple keep the faith so well.

Just like Franco, Samaranch promoted people, not according to their competence, but as pawns in his own political game. He permitted the national Olympic committees to fall into the hands of his loyal supporter Mario Vázquez Raña. He watched as the Adidas international relations team fixed federation elections to put men in power who favoured the commercialisation of sport.

He flattered and rewarded loyal lieutenants, kept them happy and let them have their way. As some members of his retinue neared retirement age, Samaranch changed the rules and raised the age limit, not once but three times. They liked that, and so did he: the new rules meant he could stay president until the age of eighty. He gave an Olympic Order to rightist Swiss politician Jean-Pascal Delamuraz, a man who described calls for Swiss banks to compensate Holocaust victims as 'blackmail'. Later, Samaranch was to show another Franco trait, and start building a grandiose monument to himself, the Olympic Museum.

Astonishingly, Samaranch denies ever having been an active fascist. Like the worst kind of Nazi revisionists, he insists, against all the evidence of photographs, documents and eye-witness accounts, that he held only a minor bureau-cratic position in the regime. And his loyal cronies in the media have helped support the myth. 'He has, by the catholicity of his public and private behaviour, been able to rise above any criticism of his involvement in administration during Franco's time,' wrote his official biographer, David Miller, who found room for thirty-three photographs in his 1992 book on Samaranch, not one of which shows the dashing fascist in his stylish uniform. Miller travelled the world with Samaranch and was granted audiences with friends in high places who certified him fascist-free, a sportsman through and through, a shy, retiring fellow, and surely a worthy candidate for the Nobel Peace Prize.

Reliable reporters have told me of their suspicions that especially sycophantic colleagues have been 'helped' with their expenses. The *Wall Street Journal*'s columnist Frederick C. Klein noted in early 1999, as the Salt Lake scandal took off, 'An acquaintance of mine who's had dealings with IOC agencies says their web of cronysim is so thick it's a miracle the people who work there can keep track of who owes what to whom.' Klein added that such scandals had, 'not been uncovered by any member of the sizeable journalistic corps that covers the organisation'.

Over the years the hacks have regurgitated Samaranch myths ranging from 'We are winning the war against doping' through 'He rescued the Olympics from bankruptcy' to 'I trust my members. They are one hundred per cent clean'. Even in 1999, when Samaranch's credibility zeroed, the wire services re-ran patently unresearched biographies of Samaranch and his merry men.

The old man's fantasies of winning observer status for the IOC at the UN were reported straight-faced, as were the time-wasting sessions in which Samaranch and Prince Albert of Monaco won UN endorsement for their Olympic Truce, drowned out by the small-arms fire from thirty-odd regional wars going on at any time. Samaranch has poured money into unreadable publications – *Olympic Message, Olympic Review* and the piles of obscure pamphlets that load the tables at any Olympic press gathering. My favourite offering, which set a tone for the years that followed, was in the *Review* back in 1968 when an apostle of idealism, by-lined as 'Dr Ferdinand E. Marcos, President of the Republic of the Philippines', wrote that sport teaches 'honesty and the sense of fair play and therefore a deeper comprehension of justice'. I bet that went down well in the jails of Manila.

Some excesses, ignored even by a weary press pack, still soak up funds that should go to sport. Every couple of years the IOC promotes a World Conference on Sport and the Environment. In October 1999, the reform process safely under control, they partied in Rio, producing guff like 'The IOC has made environmental conservation the third pillar of Olympism along with sport and culture.' There's a special commission, of course, placed in the reliable hands of Samaranch confidant Pál Schmitt, the Hungarian diplomat with the talented tennis-playing daughter. He has recruited noted environmental warriors like Samaranch's friend Bernard Nicod, a Lausanne real-estate agent, and Nagano's Sol Yoshida who, if he simultaneously fired up his collection of several dozen Bentleys from the 1940s and 1950s, would block out the sun with fumes. Sol owns a chain of gas stations, too.

Such is the IOC's concern for the environment that whenever there's an Olympic banquet at Vidy they send a flotilla of limousines to Geneva airport to collect members. The gas-guzzlers roar away, leaving the rest of us to take the swift and comfortable electric service from the heart of the airport to the centre of Lausanne.

The regular reporters who've downplayed Samaranch's peculiar political record have taken their lead from sponsors like Kodak, who claimed, bizarrely: 'Many key figures have cast off doubtful backgrounds to make achievements in recent years, even David Duke, an ex-Ku Klux Klan member.' If American anti-drugs czar Barry McCaffrey hadn't enjoyed himself many times in 1999 referring to Samaranch as a 'fascist' the issue might have gone unremarked.

Members' opinions vary on Samaranch's right-arm activities and how they sit with Olympic ideology. Some of them cherish his political experience because it's theirs too. Most may never have heard of Franco or his dictatorship and wouldn't care if they had. Others believe what they're told. 'Everybody knew that he had never been active but had always been concerned to take care of sport in Spain,' says dear Marc Hodler. 'Under any political system, if you want to do a job you have to accept the government rules.'

'We owe so much to him,' Anita DeFrantz told the *New York Times*. 'Women are now members of the IOC. More women compete in the Olympics. He should be allowed to complete his job by cleaning things up.'

Kevan Gosper gulped when I asked him in a television interview about the Leader's past, collected himself, then said how very efficient Samaranch was at chairing meetings. I e-mailed Dick Pound to tell him I had two new pictures of Samaranch in the funny clothes. 'Regarding JAS, I think you should be careful about the allegations unless you are very, very certain,' cautioned Dick. 'A uniform doth not a politician make and one needs context when going back that far in a difficult period.'

And that's another of the apologists' techniques. It was all a long time ago, there was a different scale of values then. To the grieving Puig sisters and countless other survivors of fascist repression, it doesn't seem so long ago.

'Good morning President Samaranch, British television!' We meet at last, early one bitterly cold morning under the Grecian portico of the Lausanne Palace Hotel. My colleagues and I have tried everything, phoning and faxing appeals for an interview over four months through the winter of 1991, always rebuffed. So, in spring 1992 we go looking for him, to show television viewers what he has to say about his fascist past. We've been staking the place out for hours, and now here he is. To help jog his memory I've framed two pictures of him in fascist uniform with Franco.

There's Samaranch in blue shirt and white ceremonial jacket with shiny-buckled belt, kneeling before a crucifix, being sworn in as a national councillor in 1967, watched by General Franco. And another proud moment: a smiling Samaranch in his best fascist outfit complete with medals, shaking hands with an avuncular Franco just a year before the Dictator's death. Juan Carlos, Spain's future king, is in the picture too, sporting his blue shirt.

As Samaranch moves towards his Mercedes I intercept him, holding out the photographs, 'I'd like to present you with these pictures for the Olympic Museum.' Cameraman Graham Smith moves smoothly into place and the president gazes at the pictures, holds out his hands and takes them, and for one moment, captured on film, looks almost nostalgic. Sensing there's something going on that he isn't controlling,

Samaranch hands them swiftly back and heads for the safety of his limousine. When he's settled inside I pass the pictures back to him through the door, before it closes.

'President Samaranch, I'd also like to ask you, how do you reconcile your past with your guardianship of the Olympic Ideal?' I call through the glass. He points to his ear as if he can not hear me, and gestures to his driver to get him out of here. Sitting in the back with him and trying to look casual is Judge Mbaye. The limousine glides away. To this day my gift has not been displayed in the Olympic Museum.

Two years and eighteen months later, I paid the price for being cheeky. Detective Sergeant John Warren of the International and Organised Crime Branch of Scotland Yard, called round for a chat. Samaranch had started libel proceedings against me in Lausanne, where libel is a police matter, a criminal offence. Among my supposed crimes in *The Lords of the Rings* were presenting 'a particularly distasteful portrait of the IOC and of its President, Mr Samaranch' and giving readers the feeling, 'that the members of the IOC are mainly preoccupied by their own personal interest rather than by the interests of the Olympic Movement.' Samaranch was particularly offended by what he saw as a depiction of him as 'a man who, through astute lobbying, has perverted the IOC so as to reconstruct it in his own manner on the lines of the Franquist regime'.

I took no part in the proceedings. In my absence, Judge Jean-Daniel Martin inspected the book and its photographs, observed the eminent Judge Mbaye taking a morning off from his duties at the International Court of Justice to sit and look wounded, heard Samaranch assure him, 'I never exercised any political power. I was a high-ranking civil servant. It is wrong to say I organised the repression,' and gave me a five-day suspended jail sentence.

Judge Martin's fellow lawyer in this small Swiss town, François Carrard, the IOC's director-general, denied knowing of any improprieties by members. This was in 1994, four years after Toronto's damning report on members had been buried by the executive board. Justice done, they all went off to lunch.

Chapter 11

The Rainforest Logger, the TV Executive and Boris Yeltsin's Tennis Coach

Don't dare to sit in Alex Gilady's dark leather and brass-studded corner chair in the bar of Lausanne's Palace Hotel. If there's an Olympic meeting in town Alex, his domed forehead gleaming, will be there, exuberant, glad-handing, a man of substance. Even when the dimly lit bar fills up as members come in from dinner, Alex's throne is left vacant until he arrives.

If he catches your eye his broad face opens, an arm waves you to a seat at his table, a waiter appears, soon your drink follows. When the box with the very biggest cigars comes round, they're offered, too. 'Does NBC pick up your tab?' I asked once, and was blasted, as you are when Alex declaims, with an explosive 'No!' His exclamations are often joined to physical movement, a playful punch on the upper arm, a tight grip on your forearm to squeeze his point home.

Alex, in his mid-fifties, has the aura of a big man. He holds court in every bar on the Olympic circuit, building bridges between critics like me and the IOC members who might otherwise turn away. At his TV station in Tel Aviv, at NBC's offices in London and New York where he takes care of global sports for the American monolith, working the phones from his other homes in London and Spain, you feel that he's reached a height that few can attain. He affects to adore

Samaranch, and genuinely has his ear, a privilege granted to few. It could be because NBC pays the IOC billions of dollars for American rights to the Olympics and that investment needs protecting, especially in this year of scandal.

Alex Gilady joined NBC from Israeli television in 1981 to boost their international business. 'He developed relationships for us in Europe so we weren't perceived as strangers,' says his ultimate boss, Dick Ebersol, chairman of NBC Sports. Strangers? By the mid-1980s Alex was one of the family, eased on to the private but powerful television advisory committees of both the IOC and world track and field. Samaranch co-opted him into full membership in 1994 and gosh, didn't business boom.

The next year, without any open tendering, any competition from hungry rivals like Rupert Murdoch, NBC signed up all the winter and summer Olympics until 2008. Outsiders scratch their heads, and wonder which side of the table Alex occupies during NBC–IOC negotiations. Alex himself says his two positions are 'a wonderful combination'. Dick Ebersol insists that at all the key moments Alex is left out of the loop. He's a global sports executive for the company negotiating a $3.55 billion deal, and they say Alex isn't told a thing about it.

Immaculate in his tailored suits and hand-made blue shirts, Alex wants to share his good luck. 'Look,' he says helpfully, suggesting you follow his example. 'Look at the quality, I get them made in It'aewon – it's the special shopping area for Westerners. As soon as I arrive in Seoul I go and see my tailor and order some more.' From Korea to Switzerland in 1999, I've sat with Alex in the best corner of the best bars. 'In ten years' time I will take you to lunch, a long lunch, and we'll talk and you'll see how you got it all wrong in your books, absolutely wrong,' he'd boom. He's very good at talking for hours without disclosing a thing, but one night he said something worth putting in my notebook.

Alongside Alex and his NBC colleague Peter Diamond on the IOC's television commission sits Bob Hasan, the mogul from Indonesia. Bob was slipped on to the IOC the same year as Alex, America's Jim Easton and Britain's Craig Reedie. In the Palace bar late one night Alex was trying to persuade me that I was jaundiced, their reform process was a success, the IOC was, as Samaranch claimed, cleaning house. 'Not until you get rid of the likes of Bob Hasan,' I said. The banter stopped. Alex's broad shoulders slumped. 'Yes,' said Alex quietly. 'Bob will have to resign.'

I was standing by Dick Pound in the glass-walled atrium of the Seoul Arts Centre. We watched, through the milling crowd of IOC members and solicitous hosts, as Germany's member Thomas Bach, with his natty little moustache, threw his arm round Bob Hasan's shoulders. Bob, who's also a small chap and has a darker, trimmed moustache, hadn't been seen at an IOC function for the first six months of this year of scandal. I turned to Dick and murmured, 'I thought they'd taken Bob's passport away?' Dick shot back in his quick way, 'Maybe he got a one-way ticket out.'

The Seoul IOC session in June 1999 gave Bob Hasan a break from his own personal scandal, twelve months of company liquidations, bailiffs seizing his airplanes, suddenly emboldened government investigators summoning him to answer questions about his forty-year relationship with the deposed dictator Suharto. And again, please, Mr Hasan, how did you amass your $3 billion fortune? they asked him in the attorney-general's office. Outside, unruly teenagers, free at last of the army and riot police on the streets, were shouting 'Thief! Thief!' from their high-school windows.

It shouldn't have turned out that way. When Bob met Suharto all those years back in the 1950s after the Dutch colonialists had been kicked out, the future father of the nation was an army colonel and Bob was a young businessman. His birth name was The Kian Seng. He was from Chinese stock and to avoid the prejudice that still bedevils Indonesia, he converted to Islam and became Mohamed Hasan, for ever after known as 'Bob'.

Together they'd taken an agrarian archipelago of fifteen thousand islands stretched over three thousand miles, home to two hundred million souls and a multitude of races, cultures and faiths, and built it into a country foreigners wanted to invest in. The newcomers set up sweatshop factories churning out clothing and running shoes, mined precious metals and tore lumber from the rainforests. Their taxes, when not diverted from the national Treasury, bought a mountain of military equipment to help keep Indonesia a safe place for business.

It had been bloody at first. Half a million men and women perished, gunned down, assassinated, tortured, starved, or disappeared in Indonesia's gulags in the 1960s, but that was the price of progress. Anybody who opposed Suharto's police state must be a communist and wasn't fit to share in the wealth that was there to be taken. The army didn't just do the shooting. The officers wanted their share of business and they needed pliant partners who'd deliver. Suharto, by now a general and the country's president, imposed his New Order ideology, eerily reminiscent of Franco's Spain, a seamless blending of public and private interests.

Every business deal was an opportunity to set up a monopoly, grant a licence, hijack a stake without risking their own money. The country became Suharto Inc. The general and some of his family established themselves as gatekeepers to the nation's wealth, in time owning half a million acres of the country, shares in insurance, shipping, construction, mining, the oil and gas industry – if it made money they'd take their cut. Eldest daughter Siti took road tolls on the new highways, Tommy got a chunk of the car import business, another son the cigarette monopoly. If the national airline wanted new aircraft, the family brokered the deal. When they had to put up cash, banks were forced to supply loans which were rarely repaid.

Bob Hasan became business manager to the Suharto family. He warehoused their commissions and shares in seven foundations which at their peak were said to be worth $5 billion. He took 10 per cent. The censored press couldn't repeat what people said: that their country had fallen victim to 'KKN', the local shorthand for corruption, collusion and nepotism. The Suharto foundations didn't pay taxes or make financial disclosures and were presented as charitable trusts, created to 'alleviate poverty.' Everybody was encouraged to join this high endeavour and for those who were too busy, or too poor, to put their hands in their pockets the family imposed laws that took deductions from wages and profits. Bob explained, 'In the interest of the people, monopoly is allowed.' He and Suharto played golf several times a week – 'Your course or mine?' – and went deep-sea fishing together.

For Suharto, Bob and their KKN clan, the biggest blots on the landscape were the rainforests of the larger islands. They cut down as much as possible, as fast as they could sell it abroad.

Borneo – as big as Britain and France – was ravaged first. In 1972 the American Georgia-Pacific corporation acquired a concession on the island, but couldn't do business without a local 'partner'. Bob's your man, said Suharto. Hand over a share to him and he'll repay you from his dividends. Two decades later Bob was the world's most prolific lumberjack, exporting pulp and plywood from factories built with taxes raised for re-forestation. The forests levelled, Bob planted orderly rows of palm-oil trees.

Environmentalists mourn the devastation of Borneo. Bob, his bulldozers and his chainsaw gangs have displaced two and a half million Dayak people and destroyed their traditional crops and homesteads. It's their own fault: they don't understand progress, KKN-style. 'The older people that is a little ignorant,' Bob explained to the BBC, 'as soon as we build the roads they say "Oh this is the grave of my ancestor". We want to raise their standard of living. We don't want them to roam around in loincloths.' The army doesn't want that either and they were especially helpful when Bob, with vast logging concessions throughout Indonesia, decided to plunder East Timor, the Portuguese colony annexed at gunpoint by Suharto in 1976. The dictator and the logger enjoyed the protection of armed militias who went on to murder and to lay waste much of the country in the wake of 1999's pro-independence vote.

Even Bob couldn't destroy all the forests single-handed – a staggering 70 per cent has disappeared – but he could pimp off other logging companies. Suharto permitted him to set up what he described as a marketing company. Every timber exporter in the land was forbidden to speak to foreign buyers and had to do business through Bob. He set prices, and compelled them to export only on his ships and to insure their goods with him. He had to be rewarded for all his trouble; not one log or sheet of plywood could be exported without paying Bob a commission of up to $20 a cubic metre. It has all helped build his $3 billion fortune.

In the summer of 1997, three years after Bob joined the IOC and signed up to Samaranch's concern for the environment, his timber companies started lighting fires. That's the lazy way to clear undergrowth. Other companies joined in, but Bob was among the worst. 'When we do deforestation, we do organised burning,' he explained. 'Organised burning means we clean up the shrubs, we clean up the grass because if you do not clean the shrubs, it might become a fire hazard.' The fires got out of hand, encouraged by El Niño-induced dry conditions. An area the size of England and Wales went up in smoke and the toxic haze spread and spread across the countries of South-East Asia, darkening the skies. The rich fled to safety abroad. The rest put on smog masks if they could afford them and did what little they could do to shield their children from the poison. Bob had an answer for his critics: 'They come in and say you're violating environment rules, you're violating human rights, but usually things like this comes from communist individuals.'

Why should Bob be bothered by such whingeing? Earlier in the year he'd acquired – in partnership with a Suharto son – a significant slice of the world's richest gold mine in the remote province of Irian Jaya. It was being developed by the Louisiana-based Freeport-McMoRan company, who hoped to extract at least $50 billion worth of gold, copper and silver. Bob's share was valued at a quarter of a billion dollars.

Later in 1997 Suharto Inc began to crumble. The family and friends had boosted their currency, the rupiah, to dizzy heights with creative accounting and unrepaid bank loans. The cold wind of currency collapse swept through Thailand, the

Philippines, Korea, and eventually reached Indonesia. Inflation rocketed, living standards collapsed and students took to the streets of Jakarta and the regional capitals demanding reform. Troops, under orders to beat and shoot their countrymen, did their worst, and Suharto rigged the elections again, giving himself, in his late seventies, a seventh five-year term. As the protests mounted Suharto appointed a new government. 'We will give our support,' said daughter Siti, 'since this is the people's wish.' The trade and industry minister was . . . Bob Hasan. He didn't have to divest himself of his business interests, explaining they were 'non-profit'. The people bravely returned to the streets and the regime collapsed.

Bob lost a lot – perhaps a billion dollars – but he looked a cheery chap in Seoul a year later in summer 1999, surrounded by his good friends. Bob isn't just an IOC member; he's also made it to the executive committee of world track and field. In a private meeting I asked a member of the IOC executive board, how on earth did Bob Hasan get on the Olympic Committee?

'Samaranch called Suharto and asked him who he wanted to nominate', was the reply. 'Bob was his choice, Samaranch was happy and that was that.'

How could Samaranch cosy up to Boris Yeltsin? Who would open the door and get him inside the Kremlin? Late in 1993 the perfect candidate hove into view. This was going to be better than sex! An international tennis champion, a smooth operator with rare access to Yeltsin, Shamil Tarpischev had captained the Russian Davis Cup squad and was now the president's tennis coach and trusted confidant. He was so close that he'd been given an apartment inside the Kremlin.

There was another lip-smacking temptation for Samaranch. Yeltsin created a National Sports Fund to replace the money the state had given to sports development in the good old days. Tarpischev was the boss and Boris granted him the most staggering tax break in history. The fund had the exclusive right to import liquor and tobacco duty-free into the whole Russian Federation, right across all ten time-zones, and then decide how to use the cash. How much did it rake in? The Moscow press drew breath, counted on all its fingers and toes. Could it be true? Yes it was. The fund was swelling to the tune of one trillion roubles – $200 million – every month. Oh yes, Mr Tarpischev was the ideal candidate to join the IOC. He was appointed in 1994, at the Lillehammer Games.

The tax-gatherers didn't like it, but they couldn't teach tennis. Boris had his way and Tarpishev got the title of sports minister – and the money. From time to time sports administrators complained that they didn't see much of it, but who cared about them? After its first year's operations the fund was reckoned to have pulled in at least $1 billion. And still Russian sports stars were emigrating to Europe, America and Australia to find decent facilities for training.

Where was all the loot going? When Tarpischev was appointed deputy chairman of the Campaign to Re-elect Boris Yeltsin the press caught on and re-named the Sports Fund the All-purpose Kremlin Slush Fund. Tarpischev rose from volleying a ball around the court at his Pyotrovsky Park tennis club to number two in the respected *Interfax* annual list of Russia's most influential businessmen. The commentators reckoned he'd become one of the richest.

The foreign governments bailing out Russia were irked. They told Yeltsin again and again, close down this racket and collect some taxes! He fended them off for months and then decreed in late 1995 that the fund was closed down. Informally it ran on well into the following year.

Inevitably, such huge amounts of money sloshing round the Kremlin attracted sharks. The rumour mill cranked up: Tarpischev, like so many of Yeltsin's entourage, was seen in the company of gangsters. Russia's sports facilities got poorer as the tennis coach got richer. Then an assassin struck, not at Tarpischev but at his disaffected lieutenant, Boris Fyodorov. The hitman shot Fyodorov once in the stomach, then when his 9mm Luger pistol jammed, pulled a knife and stabbed him four times in the chest.

That was in June 1996, as the Russian Olympic squad prepared to leave for Atlanta. Russian media said the attack was aimed at stopping Fyodorov disclosing racketeering at the Fund. He survived and a month later a reliable Moscow paper, *Novaya Gazyeta*, disclosed his insurance policy. Anticipating the shadow of the gunman any time, Fyodorov had taped an interview with a reporter. In the transcript Fyodorov alleged that the former tennis coach was in league with two sacked Yeltsin aides in huge illegal transactions. Tarpischev was linked to mafia figures, he said, and he claimed that a week prior to the taping Tarpischev had relayed a demand from 'Sasha and Misha' for $10 million in cash. There were also connections to a gang boss by the name of 'Taivanchik', to Moscow's Ismailovskaya mafia group and to powerful figures in the Russian aluminium industry.

The newspaper named Mikhail Chernoy, one of three brothers whose activities in the Siberian smelting business had brought them attention from investigators world-wide. Originally from Tashkent, Uzbekistan, they had become fabulously rich, acquiring businesses in Russia, Ukraine and Bulgaria. Brother Lev moved to Israel for a time and made headlines in late 1999 when his estranged wife, who'd taken refuge in a five-storey house in London's Mayfair, denied to the *Independent* that she'd paid £400,000 from a Swiss bank account to have hubby liquidated.

Tarpischev threatened to sue his accusers and claimed somebody was trying to discredit him. Time was running out for him. 'To say that the sleaze season has opened over the past few weeks does not begin to describe the rash of accusations and counter-accusations being flung among Russia's rivals for power,' reported the *Moscow Times*. As soon as he sobered up, three months later, Yeltsin gave his coach the Order of the Kremlin Boot. The state television channel, ORT, asserted that Tarpischev was resigning from the IOC too, because 'scandals recently linked to his name may damage the international reputation of Russian sport'.

That was in October 1996. Early in the new year Samaranch's mouthpiece Karl-Heinz Huba, publisher of the fortnightly newsletter *Sport Intern,* wrote: 'Tarpischev's days at the IOC are numbered. It is assumed he will resign.' He didn't and you have to wonder why Samaranch didn't tell him to go.

Karl-Heinz Huba was back on the case in March 1997 reporting that Tarpischev had travelled to Lausanne to seek an audience with the Leader. He'd been foiled by senior IOC member Vitaly Smirnov and his chum, the wealthy Russian businessman Boris Berezovsky, who were in town lobbying for St Petersburg's Olympic bid.

Tarpischev's dismissal from sport and government in his own country makes a mockery of his continued membership of the IOC. Yet three years after he was dismissed, the IOC's internet site still had him listed as sports adviser to the Russian president, with an office in the Kremlin. His IOC seat looks secure for several years into the new century.

*

Korean magnate Lee Kun-Hee needed the Olympic laundry, and fast. His reputation was about to be muddied. Samaranch's wash 'n' scrub service might shift some of the dirt.

The Olympic one-stop is mostly reserved for the rich, and Lee qualified easily. His personal fortune of $5 billion would make him the richest IOC member – as far as we know. He'd controlled the Samsung conglomerate for a decade, overseeing everything from semiconductors to genetic engineering, fibre optics, petrochemicals, shipbuilding, banking, insurance and an expansion into the entertainment industry. He made warplanes too.

To grow as fast as it did, Samsung, like many other Korean businesses in the 1970s and 1980s, routinely fiddled the books – there were often three sets – and Lee paid kick-backs to the military junta to look away. To offset such seediness, Lee spent hard to link his name with sport. The company's colours were pasted on the backs of soccer players, wrestlers, golfers and athletes in seven other sports. Employees were urged to show loyalty by taking up three sports. 'Playing golf we learn rules and etiquette,' explained Lee. 'Through baseball we can learn about the meaning of the star player and rugby will teach us how to struggle.'

Successive generals who'd traded their uniforms for presidential suits honoured Lee. From the early 1980s he was given the Sport Merit Medal, Order of Sport Merit, Maengho Medal and the Cheongryong Medal. In 1988, after the Seoul Olympics, he won the Korean Sports Award with Presidential Commendation and you'd think grateful governments would be running out of gongs. Not at all. 1990 brought a Presidential Recognition Award, the following year he qualified for the Sixth Annual Sports Seoul Athletic Award and after that came vice-president and finally president of the Korean Olympic Committee.

Lee has a personal Sports Philosophy and he propagates it on Samsung's internet site. His thoughts on sport, he says, 'coincide with the spirit of Olympism'. And what does that mean? Handing over $40 million a time to become an Olympic world-wide sponsor. 'Samsung can achieve global recognition,' he says, 'and as time passes, the group will become known as a progressive global concern, which in turn greatly helps product marketing.' Another Samsung venture coughed up $2 million for Samaranch's Olympic Museum. At the IOC session on the eve of the 1996 Atlanta Games, Lee Kun-Hee was inducted.

A month later Lee, shining bright from his first cycle in the laundromat, donated $60,000 to Jimmy Carter's Atlanta Project for the Homeless (unloved by local activist Anita Beaty). Carter should have flung the money back; the going rate for presidents in Korea was considerably higher. And then, two weeks later, Lee was off to the Seoul courthouse with bowed head.

It was the corruption and murder trial of the century! Television cameras were excluded, officials said because the pictures might damage the country's economy. Lee and eight other company bosses pleaded guilty to carrying sack-loads of cash into the presidential mansion of the then leader Roh Tae-Woo in the 1980s. It must have taken a lot of sacks because when ex-president Roh stopped his ritual sobbing he admitted that the figure of $667 million might be about right.

Lee got a two-year jail sentence for bribery and corruption. As he always says, 'Through sports, complicated diplomatic situations and political differences can be solved,' and they were for him: the sentence was suspended for three years – he could carry on attending IOC meetings. Perhaps the hearing should have been renamed The Two Olympic Orders Trial. Lee had got his Order in 1991, three years after another defendant, ex-president Roh, was declared by Samaranch to be 'the real inspiration behind the Seoul Olympics'.

Roh is probably the first recipient of an Olympic Order to *admit* murder, mutiny and treason, although he isn't the first murderer to achieve one. Everybody in court knew that he and fellow defendant Chun Doo-Hwan had led the army uprising in 1979 and the next year ordered the massacre of hundreds, if not thousands, of pro-democracy demonstrators on the streets of the southern city of Kwangju. Roh was jailed for twenty-two years – let's hope they let him take his Order to jail with him for comfort – and Chun received the death sentence, subsequently commuted to a jail term.

One year on, at the end of 1997, Lee and his fellow business leaders and their corrupt business practices brought the Korean economy close to collapse. Plants were closed, workers sacked and Lee and three other businessmen, after a public dressing-down from the president, admitted: 'We deeply feel responsible for the current crisis and humbly pledge to create a transparent business climate.'

Lee's spokesman said he would give up 'most' of his $6.5 million salary and sell $75 million of personal assets to plough into Samsung. The IMF lent $60 billion to prop up the country and Lee intoned, 'I, as a businessman, repent having not fully performed my duty to head off the economic catastrophe.'

Samsung funds prizes worth up to $10,000 for the best of Olympic reporting after every games.

There's a conceit at the IOC that members are terribly important people without whom world sport wouldn't function. Any real reform process would bid farewell to most of them and replace them with dedicated sports fans who don't mind travelling economy-class. They could start by expelling the member who makes as many first-class long-haul flights to Lausanne as he can get away with, at IOC expense, to sleep with his girlfriend.

A good gesture would be to invite those members linked to the old Adidas manipulations, including Germany's Thomas Bach and 'Sepp' Blatter, president of FIFA, to pack up their things and move on.

You don't have to be a republican to ponder the usefulness of the clutch of European royals recruited by the Marqués de Samaranch, whose own title came late in life, awarded to him by King Juan Carlos on the eve of the Barcelona games. Samaranch likes royals; they put a little gloss on his personal photo album. Consider Spain's Doña Pilar, Infanta de Borbón. 'In her youth, took part in various local horse shows and in the point-to-point organised by the Equipagem Sto Huberto as the closing event of their hunting season,' says the IOC publication summarising her total sports career. Without being unkind to the Infanta, her youthful exploits happened around the time Samaranch was first photographed marching through Barcelona in his blue shirt. She's since risen to preside over world equestrian sport, an Olympic event in which few can afford to compete, and she has not served on any Olympic commissions since she joined in 1996.

A neighbour in Madrid is Princess Nora of Liechtenstein of all places, who succeeded her papa on the committee. She's been so engrossed in the workaday world of being a princess that she hasn't played any serious role at the IOC since 1991. The Liechtenstein family fortune of more than $5 billion makes them Europe's richest royals. Running a close second, at $4.5 billion, are the Luxembourgs. Grand Duke Jean packed it in recently after fifty-two years' membership, during which he devoted exactly four years to sitting on working parties. It was such fun that he bequeathed his seat to his son Prince Henri, who lists among his achievements honorary doctorates in humanities, law and economics from universities in America and Thailand.

The Windsors of Britain come third in the European royalty wealth league with around $4 billion and Princess Anne, an IOC member since 1988, spent four years in the early 1990s serving on a commission. She often misses Olympic sessions – which may be a tribute to her taste but hardly benefits world sport. Because of her royal status, reporters can't just ring her up. Her thoughts about Samaranch's past, medal-fixing and dope cover-ups remain a state secret. Chambermaids at an Olympic hotel where she stayed confirmed that she abandoned all gifts in her room when checking out.

Fourth wealthiest royal family in Europe are the Orange-Nassaus of the Netherlands, with roughly the same amount of moolah as the Windsors, and their Prince of Orange got the summons in 1998. The young prince has opinions on everything and helpfully offered most of them during the IOC reform debates of 1999.

The Grimaldis of Monaco come sixth in the league with a puny $1 billion. Prince Albert, who followed his father and grandfather on to the committee, seems happy to sit back, reminisce about his Olympic career in team ice-sledging and let Willem Orange do the chattering.

They lost a royal in August 1999, when a lifetime of chronic drug addiction and debauchery finished Saudi Prince Faisal Fahd Abdul Aziz at the age of fifty-four. Few members will have met him. Since Samaranch bowed to the serious money and anointed him in 1983, he'd turned up for only six annual meetings. This broke the IOC rule that if you miss three you'd better have a sick note. The IOC don't talk about him or about a sex scandal on one of his few visits to Lausanne. His critics among the Saudi exile community allege on their internet sites that his quarter-century running sport at home and building venues was 'a particularly lucrative source of graft'. His dad, the king, gave him $20 million a year to spend on youth welfare, and no doubt he did, when he wasn't taking commissions in the arms trade.

Chapter 12

Just Another Family Man

They're more than deferential. Under the low ceiling of this dimly lit, windowless convention room they give their president the status of a god. He's the provider, the great architect, their unquestioned leader, and the delegates, a couple of hundred of them, radiate obedience. The microphones – one each, sixteen abreast at the rows of tables spanning the room – are barely used. This is the Congress of the World Taekwondo Federation, Edmonton, Canada, June 1999.

Four of the five dark-suited men on the low platform are Koreans and in the centre sits the president, guiding them through the agenda. He is the ultimate Master, the highest-graded in the sport, an honorary ninth Dan, the only leader since he founded the Taekwondo Federation in Seoul in 1973. Dr Kim Un-Yong speaks softly, is warm and attentive to every face before him, inviting a question, a contribution, as he eases them through the roll call, the finance, operational and budget reports, selection of the site, in Korea, for the next world championships.

Business doesn't take long when Dr Kim is in charge. There were no questions at all at their last congress, two years previously. It says so in the minutes on my table at the back of the room. There is something missing from today's agenda. I turn to the delegate next to me and whisper, 'Don't you have elections?' 'Oh, we dealt with that last time,' he replies. I check the minutes and sure enough there is an item headed 'Election

182

of officials'. Kim was the only candidate for president. He was re-appointed with 'big applause'. There was 'big applause', too, for the re-appointment of the general secretary and the treasurer. I read on: perhaps they had voted for the five vice-presidents. No, the existing vice-presidents got 'big applause' and kept their positions.

What about the remainder of the executive committee? How had they been selected? The minutes say that a British delegate had 'suggested that Dr Kim decide the list himself'. That was seconded from Finland and Dr Kim presented his choices.

Who needs elections when Dr Kim has painstakingly steered their ambitions to the big breakthrough? In fifteen months' time taekwondo will make its Olympic debut in the Sydney games. The good times are about to roll. The hardest years are behind them. Over three decades they've left their homes in the Korean peninsula and fanned out across continents, setting up schools, scraping by, always working towards this day. As taekwondo is an official Olympic summer sport, the federation will get a share, millions of dollars, of the profits from television and sponsors, and in their adopted home towns instructors can raise banners across the front of their martial arts academies: 'Join me, the only path to the Olympics'; students' fees will multiply.

Near the end of today's meeting a voice from the platform announces that sitting at the back of the hall is an honoured guest. 'Mr Andrew Jennings, will you please stand up so all the delegates can see you.' I stand up warily – and am greeted with big applause. For all I know I've been elected to the committee. This is surreal. For years I've been an irritant to Kim, revealing his spooky past, his dubious present, and how he came by his academic honours. Then one morning, the postman delivered a letter from Kim's federation: 'We think you have taken a wrong view of Taekwondo,' it said, 'and we invite you to attend our world championships in Edmonton, Canada.' They flew me in, expenses paid, business-class, to have my wrong view righted.

The Congress begins the day before the sport, at 10 a.m., and ends well before lunch. Dr Kim, two years short of his seventieth birthday but looking younger, comes down and mingles, moving smoothly in his Gucci loafers, light-blue Aquascutum shirt, his dark-blue tie, and charcoal suit. He's in a good mood, the sensual lips on his flat face smile and his rimless glasses twinkle, drawing you to his eyes, narrowed to almost parallel lids since recent surgery.

We trickle out of the hotel into the June sunshine and promenade the wide pavements of this meandering, green city in the vast Canadian plains, forty-five minutes' flying time north of Calgary. Here, admiration for the leader is unqualified. We are a long, long way from the real world where Dr Kim's name has become known to millions for the first time this year, though not in the way he likes. Kim's family has endured six months' vilification since the Salt Lake scandals broke. At that time he was poised to launch his bid for the Olympic succession. Now his ambition is frustrated. His family has been impugned, his son risks arrest by US immigration officers and trial on a dozen or more charges. The Doctor himself may face the same indignity; for all he knows, the FBI has left his name at US airports, and the Olympic family couldn't risk electing a president who might be detained in custody on his way to Salt Lake City to open the 2002 winter games.

The rise of this talented sports politician, a linguist, a clever plotter, once a leading figure in his country's intelligence service, reflects all that has gone wrong at the IOC. He saw how Samaranch rose, through back-room deals with commercial interests, the same with Primo Nebiolo, and many others who will decorate the VIP seats in Sydney, and followed their example. Samaranch steered Kim on to the executive board two years after appointing him to the committee in 1986. Kim steered Samaranch to receive the especially created Seoul Peace Prize. Samaranch shoe-horned Kim's minority sport of taekwondo into the Olympics. Kim levered himself on to the short list to succeed Samaranch. Then Salt Lake's Howard Berkes called Marc Hodler, the documents poured out, the expulsions and resignations removed some of his most reliable supporters – and Kim was history, a victim of his own flawed political culture.

'If you can read this, the bitch fell off', says the message on the back of one man's ragged T-shirt, the guitar band thumps out R & B and we're slurping sixty-four-ounce jugs of beer and bopping in an Edmonton bikers' bar. It's comforting to be accompanied by half a dozen of the world's finest taekwondo instructors, good company and unimpressed by the beefy hulks with bike chains for belts. My new friends are loving their week of championships, love seeing the dedication of their well-schooled young competitors fighting through the qualifying rounds towards world titles in the University of Alberta Butterdome. But they are worried. For all the gifted fighters with their spectacular spinning back-hook kicks, too many contests don't look world-class.

Too many bouts look like this: 'Joonbi!' spits the referee and the fighters take their positions. 'Shijak!' is the command to begin, they eyeball each other from under their red or blue plastic safety helmets, bounce up and down and let out the occasional intimidating holler.

This can go on for some time as they bounce, waiting for the opening to spin a scoring kick to their opponent's head or chest. 'Keuman!' Stop! calls the referee if neither launches an attack, and they're warned for time-wasting. They bounce some more, yell again and then one sweeps a leg upwards, misses and they stumble into each other's tight embrace, pogoing around the fighting square like two amorous cranes.

They are separated and the bouncing, circling and yelling continue until the end of the three-minute round. They break for a minute and then go on for two more rounds. This, the masters know, produces kamikaze television. Synchronised swimming has more drama. No network outside Korea is going to screen eleven-minute Olympic contests in a minority sport where the winner may deliver only one scoring kick. The coaches tell themselves that world-wide television exposure will grow their sport – but admit they'll be lucky to get more than late-night highlights.

The coaches have their tickets booked for Sydney but the unspoken fear is that they won't be asked to Athens four years on. Dr Kim's power is in decline, his mentor Samaranch retires in 2001 and there's guerrilla warfare on the executive board between Kim and Pound and Carrard. If Pound wins the succession, he's likely to evict taekwondo from the games and Kim from the executive board. There are plenty of other sports eyeing an Olympic berth, who argue that taekwondo is not a universal sport, has not grown far enough beyond its Korean roots and should be shown the door. Life after Dr Kim could be downhill.

It was tough on the way up. The World Taekwondo Federation was created in the early 1970s at the command of

Korean dictator, General Park Chung-Hee. Kim was given the job: take the Korean federation and make it international. Kim, an ex-army man, is widely recognised in Seoul as a former senior member of the Korean Central Intelligence Agency, the state's brutal secret police. He abandoned his army career for a mix of diplomacy and spookery that took him to postings in Washington, New York and London. Congressional documents in Washington suggest he was an assistant director, disclose his nickname, 'Mickey' Kim, and reveal that one of his chores was sidling up to American companies doing business with the Seoul government to squeeze them for 'campaign contributions'.

He stopped off at a small college in St Louis one afternoon and acquired the honorary title of 'Doktakim', respectfully used by his instructors and pupils ever since. Deploying his connections and his personal charisma, Kim set up global outposts of taekwondo in a government-backed drive to grow the sport. In the long trek to the Olympics it wasn't the sport's popularity that mattered. Kim needed recognition by individual national Olympic committees and support from their officials.

In a cramped Georgian building in south London, home of Britain's Olympic establishment, one of Mickey Kim's friends is having a bad day. 'Andrew, I'd rather that I don't appear in your article,' says Dick Palmer down the phone. It's late 1997, Dick has just reached the end of twenty years as general secretary of the British Olympic Association and I'm preparing an article about feuds in taekwondo.

Back in 1977, when Palmer had just become chief executive of Olympic sport in Britain and Mickey's fledgling group had few friends and no international credibility, Dick gave them both, joining the WTF's Advisory Council. Signing up Dick – and implicitly British sport – was a coup. Three years after Palmer became a consultant to Mickey Kim, the World Taekwondo Federation was granted official recognition by the IOC at its 1980 meeting.

Palmer stood down from the WTF in 1982, but was called back seven years later. Kim had mishandled his strategy to gain admission to the Olympics. He'd grabbed the chance at the 1988 games to make taekwondo a demonstration sport. Unwisely, Korean athletes took all but one of the victories. The world saw a local sport, dominated by local athletes and local judges, an unlikely contender for the full Olympic programme.

Demonstration sports never, ever, get a second outing at the games, but Kim, an ultra-loyal Samaranch supporter, got the boss to breach that rule at the 1992 Olympics in Barcelona. Kim had learned the lesson from Seoul: he left most of his best fighters at home and the medals were shared.

Federation consultant and British Olympic chief Dick Palmer helped again. IOC members had been asked to give taekwondo full Olympic status. 'The only time I ever met Dick specifically on WTF business was at the Olympic congress in Paris in 1994,' recalls British instructor Mike McKenzie. 'He introduced us to some of the voting members just to say we were British taekwondo people. We were there to show that it wasn't just an Asian sport.'

Dick Palmer retains fond feelings for Kim. 'I find him a perfectly acceptable character,' he told me.

'I'm an honest, dedicated, sincere, hard working man,' Kim told me in Edmonton. I asked him why he smiled when he said this. 'I'm happy,' he replied.

One thing that makes Doktakim especially happy is seeing

his daughter Hae-Jung at the keyboard of a grand piano on the stages of the world's concert halls. It's a tough life for gifted soloists, hard to survive without a private income or a rich father, but Hae-Jung seemed to be a rising star. There she was in Atlanta, Berlin, Melbourne, Lausanne and Paris, playing the big Olympic concerts, and if she wasn't on the main programme she'd be entertaining the spouses. Tom 'n' Dave were sufficiently impressed to pay her $5,000 for a two-night Utah gig – a little while before Daddy Kim voted in Birmingham. They spent another $3,750 on tickets to give away; it seems not everyone shared their taste in music, or perhaps they had read her reviews.

'Returning from the much-anticipated Paris debut of a famous pianist, Claude Debussy . . . was asked what he thought of the concert. "It was dreadful," he replied. "He didn't miss a note." That pretty much sums things up here,' wrote the critic John Bell Young of one Hae-Jung performance.

'Kim Hae-Jung is a talented, unexceptional pianist who demonstrates the characteristics of a thousand other run-of-the-mill competition warriors: steely-fingered, driven, unimaginative, mechanically precise and emotionally impenetrable,' Bell Young went on. 'Her tone is hard and clangorous, which is entirely commensurate with an aesthetic (or lack of one) which disparages warmth, mystery and tenderness. As she slashes and hammers her way to the top of every phrase she shows no mercy . . . desperate for control, she rules the musical landscape with the iron hand of a prison warden, locking down every musical cell lest even one note escape.'

Bell Young had a few kind words: 'Ms Kim is a hardworking, well-schooled musician who plays all the notes on time, if not in time. What goes on between them is evidently of no consequence to her. Music becomes no more than an enemy to be conquered, a skill to be mastered, a game to be won.' The daughter played piano like Daddy Kim played sports politics.

When Hae-Jung's name first surfaced during the Utah scandal, a spokesman for Melbourne's bid for the 1996 games popped up and said they, too, had dragooned a 'capacity crowd for a relatively little known artist so that her father would appreciate the extent to which Melbourne liked the work of his daughter'. Phil Hersh at the *Chicago Tribune* fished out Bell Young's review and published a few killer sentences. The *Washington Post*'s Marc Fisher picked it up and ran a clump of stories about the lurid musical world of Kim Hae-Jung. Most enjoyable was the allegation that Daddy Kim had used his muscle to bump Ms Lee Kyung-Mi, a rival of his daughter's, from an enviable slot as soloist with the Moscow Symphony Orchestra at a Seoul concert in 1988. Ms Lee's family claimed that, when they protested, Doktakim left a death threat on their voice-mail.

Kim sent out his new friend Bill Schechter to do the denials. Bill's an American public relations adviser who became Kim's persuasive new voice through the scandals. Friendly Bill Schechter said No, it was the other way round: Ms Lee's dad had threatened to throw fire-bombs during Ms Kim's performance. Then, the *Post* produced evidence suggesting that Daddy Kim had tried to rig the 1990 International Tchaikovsky Competition in Moscow. Hae-Jung was a contestant and judges talked of private approaches, envelopes with cash and the offer of a free Steinway piano.

The *Post* and the *Tribune* together solved the mystery of Ekaterina Soukhorado. Her name had threaded through the Salt Lake investigation. Tom 'n' Dave bunged $15,000 to the

University of Utah for a few months' study for young Ekaterina, although she wasn't related to any IOC member. How come the daughter of a wealthy Moscow businessman gatecrashed this party?

The Salt Lake files hold copies of letters that flew between Tom 'n' Dave, Kim and Russia's Vitaly Smirnov. Ekaterina's dad was boss of Melodiya, one of Russia's biggest recording labels. Melodiya had issued a CD of Kim Hae-Jung playing with a leading Moscow orchestra, with Daddy Kim picking up the bill for the recording. Smirnov had helped, putting a little more IOC squeeze on Utah to make them pay for Ekaterina's education. Friendly Bill Schechter said that Kim's assistance was for 'purely humanitarian reasons, to help a friend in time of need'. You can't buy Hae-Jung's CD from Melodiya any more. You have to call up Samsung Classics, part of the empire of Korean IOC member Lee Kun-Hee.

If you'd like to book Hae-Jung, you can call IMG Artists, a subsidiary of the mammoth International Management Group, which seems a pretty fancy agent for a musician of her calibre. But there again, IMG's television arm, Trans World International, worked for Daddy Kim at the time of the Seoul games, has extensive dealings with the IOC, and has worked for the taekwondo federation. Oh, and Doktakim chairs the IOC's television commission.

Then the US Justice Department started sifting through bundles of under-the-table payment orders, fake invoices, sham consulting contracts, dodgy tax returns and false immigration applications that drew together Tom Welch, Dr Kim, his son John and a Utah businessman called David Simmons.

The IOC's television partners in America, NBC, had given

John Kim a job, then downsized him in the summer of 1990. This was bad news: if he couldn't convince immigration officers he had a full-time job, he would be deported. Documents later filed in the Utah district court allege that Tom Welch and the Kims, father and son, came up with a wheeze to get round the law. A job would be created for John in the New York office of David Simmons's Utah-based television company and if he couldn't deliver any business, not to worry, Tom would secretly refund John's salary to the company. Dr Kim was expected to cast his vote for Salt Lake to get the 2002 games.

The hot money, more than $100,000, went round and round, faster and faster, the friction caused heat and the fraud caught fire in August 1999 when Simmons, in the icy grasp of the FBI, admitted the scam. He was indicted, the Kims named as part of the conspiracy. John Kim flew home to Seoul and, beyond the reach of the handcuffs, came up with a disinformation blitz so bizarre that you hoped Friendly Bill Schechter wasn't involved. First he went to the American embassy and, in an act of ritual sacrifice, threw back the green card that gave him American residency. All it gave him now was the right to be locked up.

If you believed his story, the Kim kid was getting a bum deal. Those horrid FBI men were 'intimidating' him – and he was making a bold and moral stand. How bold was revealed a few days later when Kim Jr swaggered into the Seoul district civil court and stuck a $100,000 defamation lawsuit on faraway Utah businessman Simmons for 'hurting my integrity'.

The purpose of this street theatre became apparent a week later when two federal grand juries returned fraud indictments against John Kim. In New York and Utah he was accused of lying to the immigration service and the Feds and he faces up to five years in jail on each of a fistful of counts.

John had signed another secret contract, this time directly with Tom 'n' Dave. For $20,000 he would work to get the votes of selected IOC members. His contract said he would be 'most effective' with members from North Korea, Bulgaria, Pakistan, Russia, Turkey and Togo.

In mid-1999 the *Los Angeles Times* was tipped off about another sweetheart deal involving father and son Kim. John had been granted an exclusive licence by Daddy's taekwondo federation to sell competition uniforms. No authorised uniform – no competition – that was the rule. I don't recall this concession being mentioned at the Edmonton convention. And it was news to the US Olympic Committee, who were unhappy that young Kim's uniforms carried the five rings, exclusive property in America of . . . the US Olympic Committee.

There was only one more Kim sibling to be named, and Hye-Won – a lawyer better known as Helen – surfaced in the Atlanta scandals. Just as brother John was about to lose his right to reside in America, she was in a similar fix. An Atlanta booster approached a local senator to 'expedite' her application to stay in America. It looked like queue-jumping. And it turned out that Billy's boys gave Doktakim a $600 Tiffany jewel box.

Why was the Kim family name coupled all year with scandal, sleaze, corruption, crime and nepotism? Friendly Bill muttered about 'political overtones' and Daddy Kim blamed 'a dirty plot'. Samaranch wouldn't hear of his close ally being expelled, so Dick Pound and his detectives, Mbaye, Bach, Schmitt and Rogge, had to settle for handing out a reprimand over Hae-Jung's Utah concerts, another one for smoothing the way for Ekaterina Soukhorado and a 'serious warning' about John's crooked deal.

No distance is too far for British member Mary Glen-Haigh to travel if there's an IOC meeting that could benefit from her wisdom. Even at the age of eighty and an honorary, non-voting member, she volunteered to occupy a first-class cabin from London to Seoul for the IOC's June 1999 session. At Kimpo airport, she being a very important person, her welcoming party from the Korean Olympic committee were allowed through customs and immigration. Mrs G-H stepped into the arrivals lounge, stopped, and her right arm snapped up, extended to shoulder height and held out her hand luggage. I watched the hosts hesitate, uncertain, then one leaped forward and took it from her. She marched away to her limousine, leaving them to gather the rest of her bags.

Mrs G-H, a former fencer, was little known in Britain in 1982 when Samaranch appointed her and nearly two decades' fencing for Lausanne in Britain hasn't changed that. In private she has been a critic of Samaranch but doesn't want it known. In 1991 she went on the record, on tape, with pungent comments, then instructed her lawyers to insist that her interview couldn't be published because it was her copyright.

The good times are rolling again. The Lords and Ladies of the Rings are on Kim's turf. He's going to give them the time of their lives, distracting them from the charges levelled at him all year and restoring his power base in the family. They arrive at the Shilla Hotel for a week of coddling. This is confusing for the reporters. Most days an IOC member or booster pipes up to say the organisation never demands luxury from its hosts and will be happy in spartan quarters – clashing with the company boosters at Samsung, who own the Shilla, and brag that it's been declared One of The World's Top Ten, Best Hotel in Asia and Best Hotel in Seoul.

Samaranch, speaking at a meeting in the Shilla, insists, 'We are not looking for luxury.' The hotel, which boasts five hundred and eleven rooms with 'marble bathrooms, incredible views, private dining areas and over-sized executive desks', stands in twenty-three acres of wooded parkland, much liked by 'Royalty and heads of State', say the management. The IOC leadership hold their private discussions in the Orchid Room on the twenty-third floor and cross the corridor for lunch and dinner in Japanese, Korean, Chinese, Italian or French restaurants. Keeping as great a distance as possible from athletes, they take breakfast with the prime minister and lunch with the president.

We are surrounded by an infinite variety of cop. They range from the black-uniformed, red-bereted, dark-glassed para-militaries in the Shilla lobby (with tactical nuclear weapons hanging from their hips) to the dark-suited agents with their video cameras tracking a demonstration of workers just made redundant by Samsung. Round-the-clock shifts of officers occupy a chair next to my bedroom door – 'For security,' one told me – so I carry my notebooks wherever I go.

Every morning the *Korea Times* English-language edition arrives at my bedroom door and every day there is a fantastic-ally positive set of stories about the IOC. Our host, Dr Kim Un-Yong, is prominent in the coverage. This is Doktakim's week; every day he is pictured shoulder to shoulder with Samaranch at some contrived ceremony commemorating nothing in par-ticular, but looking restored to the family bosom.

Kim and Samaranch have the most finely calibrated under-standing of the IOC membership and it shows at the end of this week when Kim publishes his manifesto for the presidential election of 2001. Dressed up as a press interview, it lays out his stall, and panders to the fantasies of the oldest of Old Boys. 'Commercialism is strangling the Olympic movement . . . Atlanta was like a business convention, the sports were a sideshow . . . we should not hang about smoking free cigars during the games when everybody is competing.' That was Dick Pound shafted.

Then he whacked the young people of the world, touching on a distressing discovery made in recent times by older IOC members who like their athletes humble. 'These highly paid athletes have created a regime of money, money. Very soon it will be out of control . . . in fact already, many athletes are beyond control.' And there were whacks for his rivals Pál Schmitt and Anita DeFrantz: 'the IOC should focus more on sport than extraneous issues like the environment and other causes . . . why do they have to have a women's working group meeting in Bermuda, Morocco, Hong Kong, Paris?' Ouch!

There was a scatter-gun blast at some of the goings-on in Lausanne that confused the old duffers: 'we should be dedicated to Olympic ideals through sport . . . not through environment, memorabilia, cultural displays and stamp collections.' Then, one last fusillade at the way Kim had been investigated. 'After this Olympic scandal we are very divided . . . there was leaking to the press, private investigators.' That was one more bullet with Pound's name on it.

Life was returning to normal for the members. They'd had their natural rhythms, moving sedately from one banquet to another, disturbed by the baying of the common media. At last they could enjoy a meeting not forced on them by scandal and be treated as the royalty they feel they are.

They descended on the auditorium of the Seoul Arts

Centre for their traditional opening ceremony. Once again, hooray, they were the object of respect! Korea's president arrived to anoint their meeting! Confidence was returning! At any moment I expected a member to clamber on stage, grab a microphone and croak, 'Shoot the reporters! These are our Olympic Games to run any damn way we want. We demand gifts, sex, luxury, envelopes of cash, scholarships for our children, Kim Un-Yong for president!'

Instead, they got a bout of Doktakim at the lectern. Oh, he was so good at telling them what they wanted to hear. 'I know I speak for the entire Olympic family in expressing absolute confidence in our ability to once again earn the trust and confidence of people from every corner of the globe,' he purred. They all shared his sadness that 'we have done far too little in eradicating hunger, disease, environmental pollution, and an end to religious conflict, racism and war'.

But he had an answer, their answer: 'The gathering of the world's greatest athletes every two years from every corner of the world to compete for the gold, silver and bronze exemplifies the best hope of humanity and improved human relations.' The IOC may have special software to churn out these sentiments.

Now came their host's real message. This week they could look forward to, 'some of the world's most satisfying experiences. I hope you will find the time to share the personal pleasures that await you here this week,' he told them. 'You deserve no less for your contributions to our past success.'

The Leader followed. Samaranch had looked drained when he touched down at Kimpo, his face losing definition, like melting wax. Now, his speech was wooden, and he rarely looked up from his text. His members waited; this was his annual keynote speech, his State of the Olympic Union message to his disciples. How would he explain the corruption scandal?

It seemed they'd done nothing wrong. As ever, it was somebody's else fault. They had been the target of 'an unprecedented world-wide media campaign'. What about the ten empty seats here in Seoul? The nearest he got to the Missing Members was a mention of the extraordinary session in March, when 'proposals submitted by the executive board were discussed and adopted'. Then he looked up at his members and told them what they most wanted to hear. 'We say Yes to reforms,' he articulated slowly so they all got his message, 'without destroying the heritage of our founder Pierre de Coubertin.' That was it. He'd given his word. Coubertin's creation of a committee which would for ever select its own members would be maintained. For his slower members, he said it again. 'We say Yes to reforms which protect the independence of our organisation.' Independence in the IOC lexicon means No Elections! The worst year of their Olympic lives was turning the corner.

The entertainment begins. No opening ceremony of an IOC session is complete without the cultural segment. This could be a good one. Korean music is spell-binding. From the elegant dulcimers, zithers and flutes of court music to orgasmic drumming at peasant festivals, our host Dr Kim has a culture to boast about, if he wants. But he doesn't. Instead, we sit through a serenade of imported European easy listening. The Seoul Symphony Orchestra gives us Verdi, a soprano sings arias from Strauss's *Die Fledermaus*, a baritone sings from *Carmen* and we snooze through 'O sole mio'.

At last comes the star of the East, a performer to close the show. She strides across the stage in a glittering electric-green off-the-shoulder dress with a flowing gauze train, pulls the stool away from the piano and adopts her familiar combat position. All around the concert hall members wake up. Here is a celebration of themselves! An artiste who speaks not a word yet whose presence defiantly screams, 'Screw You' to killjoys like Dick Pound and the media assassins. Kim is a genius. There is no better way to say it: They Shall Not Pass! We Are The Masters of the Universe!

The Mendelssohn concerto doesn't last long. At the height of her attack on the keyboard our soloist's chin is almost on her knees: arms outstretched she beats the instrument into submission. When dark falls, it will probably seek asylum in North Korea. The applause is fulsome for the heroine of Nagano, Berlin, Lausanne, Melbourne, Paris and Salt Lake City. Well done, Kim Hae-Jung!

The swearing-in of a new member is a sampling of the rituals of their own secret societies, the Freemasons, Opus Dei and various Falanges. For the first time the session, in the Shilla's Dynasty Room, is being fed to us hacks watching a video screen a few hundred yards away, and for the first time, we see the ceremony.

Master of Protocol Pál Schmitt (who stood to attention next to Samaranch all through his speech yesterday) swings the big Olympic flag through the air, down to waist level, and, one by one, new members clutch a corner of the flag. They recite the rambling oath, with its one particular phrase that has nourished corruption: they will respect 'the decisions of the IOC, which I consider as not subject to appeal on my part'. Only the kind of people Samaranch chooses for IOC membership would consent to swearing away their rights like this.

Samaranch is unsettled. Over breakfast with half a dozen

usually well-behaved reporters he's had to deny rumours of a palace coup led by director-general Carrard, backed by Pound. We all know something is going on and our suspicions are reinforced when Samaranch waves a letter he claims has been given him by his ten board members. 'In these difficult times of crisis wrought with danger, a strong, wise, trusted leadership is essential,' they tell him, 'We unanimously support you . . . and ask you to continue to devote your time to the Olympic movement as president of the IOC, until the end of your present mandate.'

The essential business is left to last: selection of a host city for the winter games of 2006. Six contenders have set up stalls in the lobby of the Shilla. The Swiss candidate, Sion, is the favourite, Turin, backed by the Agnelli family, isn't far behind and the remainder are lost in the mists. The pretty girls from Helsinki, Zakopane, Klagenfurt and Poprad-Tatry hand out brochures and badges and try to appear optimistic. The IOC members who will vote are sulky; the scandals have ended visits and fun. Who can they blame? That bastard Hodler of course. He's Swiss.

Turin wins by a stunning 53–36. During the night, in Europe, the Olympic Museum in Lausanne is visited. Staff arriving for work the next morning see a single letter painted in each of the five rings: 'M-A-F-I-A'.

Chapter 13

Anwar's Boys Fix Fights

'I never tell a lie,' bellows the Professor, bright brown eyes gleaming in deep black sockets either side of his beaky nose, firing phoney rage at me. 'I'm not a hypocrite, everything I do is straight.' The point made, he pauses, drops his head and spoons more yoghurt from a bowl on his lap. It's ten in the morning and Anwar Chowdhry, the president of world amateur boxing, is slumped in a low armchair, grey linen pyjama jacket open to the navel. His brown chest is disfigured by ridges of purple, knotted scars from bypass surgery a few years back. His belly flops out over his thighs.

I got my summons to hear this ranting back in the downtown convention hall where they're staging the world championships. 'Professor Chowdhry would like to talk with you,' said a silky aide, plucking my sleeve. It's the summer of 1999 and here we are in a suite on the twelfth floor of the Holiday Inn with its view over the flat Houston landscape, already shimmering in the scorching August heat.

I'm here because Anwar's boys fix fights. Olympic titles, world championships: year in, year out, amateur boxers are robbed in his rings. He knows it, I've written about it, but he insists on this hectoring pretence that he's taken aback by the betrayal of his own officials.

'Bastards,' he says, waving a scoresheet from yesterday's bouts. 'Look at this bastard, he's scored zero and the other judges saw ten blows land.' We are talking 'man to man', he explains. Professor Chowdhry, aged seventy-six, a retired engineering teacher, a son of the British Empire, speaks colonial-style, ruling-class English. He wants me to believe that from his home in Sunnyside apartments, Karachi, he wrestles manfully with the depressing stories of fix and bribe coming to his desk almost daily.

'These bloody judges,' and he's off again, shouting. 'The bastards are letting us down, I will get these bastards out!' He bellows, as he has done for the last dozen years, his black hair flopping up from his proud forehead and back down with every gesture. I think he's guessed that I've made the trip from England because I've been tipped off that this time the Cubans are going to get the shaft. One of Chowdhry's closest allies rashly boasted to my source a couple of months back, 'We will get the Cubans in Houston.'

The key component of the professor's survival kit is the verbal ramble. His monologue is a rat-a-tat-tat of boxer feints, sending you off in the wrong direction. Follow one utterance and you've lost the plot. He fills the room with his rich voice, leaving no space for questions, showering me with bouncing balls of quicksilver. Ponder one and you've lost ten more, jigging away under the furniture.

'I give in to nobody! Nobody bullies me,' he shrieks, swallowing a mouthful of yoghurt. 'I will not let them harm our beautiful sport.' I try a question: why don't they display the scores during a bout so we can see which judges are incompetent or corrupt?

His answer is the refrain again: 'Cowards. Bastards.'

'Why don't you get rid of them?'

'We will. We will.'

He sits back and smiles. 'I know many things about Samaranch.' You bet he does. Anwar Chowdhry keeps the black book of Olympic sports officials; he has the dirt on them all. Recently, he told another boxing source of mine, 'I have Samaranch in my pocket. He cannot move against me.' The same person told me, 'Chowdhry? He's a perfidious, cunning old crook, greedy for money and hungry for power. The king of schemers. Face to face he calls you a friend. Seconds later, when you've left, he calls you a bastard.'

Anwar asks me a question and whoosh! we're in Atlanta. 'Are they finding anything out?'

It's a pleasure to look him hard in the eye. 'Yes, congressional investigators have all the documents, they're digging.'

Suddenly he's not so confident, even troubled. But he's the eternal optimist, any problem can be shed, like a snake skin. Whoosh! we're in Nagano. 'They did the right thing,' he chuckles. 'They burned the files, all of them.'

Whoosh! More quicksilver. We're in Madrid in 1978, at the conference of the International Amateur Boxing Federation (AIBA). Chowdhry was general secretary, but that didn't pay. He had lost his teaching job, something about a row with the minister back in Pakistan. 'Mr Horst phoned me. Come to Paris.' So Chowdhry worked for Horst Dassler, the charming, ruthless boss of Adidas.

Perhaps Anwar Chowdhry was a decent man once. He was a noted referee in his younger years, at the Tokyo Olympics, before Dassler recognised his enormous potential for duplicity. Chowdhry had been freelancing for Adidas for several years doing deals with athletes, Olympic committees and sports federations to wear the distinctive three-striped sports shoes and kit. Dassler wanted Chowdhry's special talents at work in the next stage of expanding his empire's influence.

They lived in exciting times, perhaps the most volcanic in

the history of sport. Dassler saw, long before sport's leaders, that the world they'd known, of running federations, committees – even the Olympics – part-time, at evenings and weekends, would soon end. Suppliers and sponsors like himself would be joined by the suits of the television networks as they carved up sport between them. Dassler saw his opportunity: he went from buyer to seller in a run of murky deals. By 1978, when Chowdhry joined the fixer's team full-time, Dassler had already become the key player in world soccer. He devised the marketing plans that brought in Coca-Cola and their millions to fund the game's new Brazilian leader, João Havelange. He plucked the unknown Sepp Blatter from obscurity and groomed him in the Adidas way to become chief executive of soccer. Blatter replaced Havelange in 1998, long after Dassler's death.

The manipulative Primo Nebiolo was elevated from Italian track and field in 1981, in one of the more crooked of sport's 'elections', to take control of the international federation, which he held until his death in 1999. And then there was Samaranch's burning ambition. Dassler masterminded the campaign and Samaranch was relaunched, within five years of Franco's death, from fascist functionary into Guardian of All Things Moral at the IOC. Part of Chowdhry's lifetime insurance policy in world sport is knowing the deals that were done to reinvent the old Blueshirt.

There had to be a payback and sport's leaders gladly offloaded their marketing rights to his Swiss-based private company, International Sport and Leisure. The soccer world cup, the track and field worlds and then the Olympic Games all belonged to Dassler.

In 1986 Chowdhry's turn came. The American Don Hull announced he was to quit the presidency of amateur boxing.

In the late summer Dassler gathered his team of fixers to plan for victory at the forthcoming boxing congress in Thailand. Money was made available to pay the fares of delegates who would vote for Chowdhry, and to buy hookers for the undecided.

Everything went to plan. Chowdhry now controlled an Olympic sport and his replacement as general secretary was Karl-Heinz Wehr. He, too, was steeped in boxing and ran the new office in East Berlin with the financial support of the East German government. The first big test for the new leadership would be the Seoul Olympics.

It was a disaster. The world watched, horrified, as the boxing tournament crashed out of control. Low-ability Korean boxers made their way through the qualifying rounds, relentlessly winning on points against superior fighters. It seemed as though the Koreans knew the fix was in; when one of them lost a decision his coaches started a riot, beating up the referee. Boxing's leadership had to be seen to do something. At a private meeting Chowdhry asked Bulgaria's Emil Jetchev, controller of judging for two decades, to name the rioters. The minutes record Jetchev's reply. 'He felt unable to do so. He said he was filling in score sheets at that moment and did not see anything.'

Wehr suspended some of the worst judges but got no support from Chowdhry. In one of the regular reports that Wehr, as an East German travelling abroad, had to make to the Stasi secret police, he recorded, 'For days there were Koreans constantly at my office, in the boxing hall, and at the hotel trying to influence me to reverse my decisions.' When that failed, they resorted to death threats.

Boxing officials say that maybe twenty fights were fixed;

most talked-about was the theft of a gold medal from America's brilliant Roy Jones by a never-to-be-heard-of-again Korean student, Park Si-Hun. Park got four hometown decisions on his way to meeting Jones in the final. Then Jones battered his opponent to the point where some spectators thought the bout should be stopped. The Russian and Hungarian judges agreed, giving Jones victory over Park, 60–56 and 60–55.

The other three judges had been watching a different fight. Hiouad Larbi of Morocco and Alberto Durán of Uruguay scored 59–58 for Park; Bob Kasule of Uganda scored the bout 59–59, advantage to Park. Durán and Kasule, both suspended for incompetence earlier in the tournament, had been brought back for the most important bouts.

'Fix!' screamed American coaches at the ringside and one of their senior officials, Paul Konnor, drafted a protest. 'A bunch of us surrounded judge Larbi at the ringside,' recalled *Sports Illustrated*'s Pat Putnam. 'The reporter from France's *L'Equipe* sports paper was screaming at him, 'How could you do this?' He did the interview in French and translated for the rest of us English-speakers.' The quotes Larbi volunteered were published in Putnam's *Sports Illustrated* article under the headline 'Travesty', and in papers around the world.

Larbi freely admitted that he had forged his scorecard. 'The American won easily; so easily, in fact, that I was positive my four fellow judges would score the fight for the American by a wide margin. So I voted for the Korean to make the score only 4–1 for the American and not embarrass the host country.'

Putnam didn't believe this feeble excuse. There was little doubt among the reporters that money had changed hands. *L'Equipe* summed up the decision as 'Scandalous. Vomit'.

On the way back from Seoul, English boxing's president,

Rod Robertson, talked with a Moroccan team official. 'He told me Larbi was being prescribed pills because he was suicidal. I said, "Don't look to me for sympathy,"' recalls Robertson. 'Then the man said, "It's all right, you Europeans and your principles, but let me tell you the story. Larbi is a teacher in Casablanca. The mayor of Casablanca is Monsieur Bouchentouf [a senior AIBA official], a business associate of the Korean who paid the bribes. All it requires is a phone call to Bouchentouf saying Larbi is not being very co-operative and that is the end of his life as a teacher.'

The rumbles began that amateur boxing had become as crooked as the worst of the professional game and should be thrown out of the Olympics. Chowdhry, confident that Samaranch dare not touch him, ignored all objections. Wehr was worried and sent Chowdhry a private memo warning him, 'Our situation is disastrous.' The attacks didn't stop and so six months later, at a meeting of his executive committee in Nairobi, Chowdhry knew he had to be seen to take some action.

The boxing world was demanding lifetime suspensions for the three judges who'd gifted the gold medal to Park. Wehr told me, many years later, 'We could not reach agreement so Chowdhry suspended the meeting overnight. He called me to his room and said, "Karl-Heinz, I can't push through life bans, it will split the committee." Then he disclosed, "I have been informed that three of our officials, here with us in Nairobi, received money from the Koreans to bribe judges."'

Wehr says Chowdhry told him that one official was paid $10,000, gave three judges $300 each and pocketed the rest. A second leading member of the federation had been paid $5,000 but disbursed only $1,000 to two judges. The third senior man had also had money – they never discovered how much – to pay off another judge. Wehr reluctantly agreed to two-year suspensions for the three offenders from the Jones fight. They weren't taken seriously and later in 1989 the Moroccan Larbi showed up at the boxing World Cup in Moscow managing his national team. Wehr wrote a report about Chowdhry's admissions and filed it in the Stasi archives in East Berlin.

Despite the daylight robbery of Roy Jones, who'd had the bad luck to be drawn against a Korean, America did well in Seoul, taking three golds, three silvers and two bronze medals. And that was the end of American success for a decade. As Chowdhry's federation spiralled into corruption, Americans rarely figured in the medals tables.

Taking on Chowdhry over the Jones case – and losing it – seemed fatal to American boxing. It would have been imprudent to let bent judges stop lightweight Oscar de la Hoya, America's new hope, in Barcelona and he took gold. But light flyweight Eric Griffin, whose scoresheet gave him the fight 81–48 over a Spaniard, was still a loser when the ringside judges had finished with him. The next year, at the world championships in Tampere, Finland, the Americans were left with only two bronze medals and had to watch Cuba take eight out of twelve possible golds.

Wehr despaired at the growing anarchy in the federation. He wrote to Chowdhry, after the world junior championships in Montreal, that a Russian official had 'demanded that if two Muslims are boxing, no Christian should officiate'. Wehr also told him that another official had been warned, 'as it had become known that his people allegedly bribed officials'.

The more dishonest the federation became, the more sport

honoured Chowdhry. Samaranch awarded him an Olympic Order in 1992, praising him for his 'respect for the rules' and for being 'an ardent defender of fair play'. Mario Vázquez Raña, recalling no doubt the support that Chowdhry had given him at his one-man band the Association of National Olympic Committees, came up with an Order of Merit. Somebody nudged UNESCO and Chowdhry was soon boasting, in a letter to Wehr, that he was to be honoured for 'eminent services rendered to the cause of Physical Education and Sports'. The Russian boxing federation pushed the Kremlin and next came their Leonardo Prize, an honour previously bestowed on Samaranch, Ted Turner and Diana, Princess of Wales. Chowdhry was beside himself with vain delight, firing off letters about being huge on the television news in Azerbaijan and getting an honorary doctorate in the Philippines. 'I am being honoured by all type of organisations,' he crowed, 'which no other person in the sports world is achieving or has achieved.'

Samaranch's normally monolithic IOC cracked, briefly, in early 1994 when the newly recruited and independent-minded Philippe Chatrier, former head of world tennis, presented a report suggesting that, as part of the modernisation of the games, boxing should be shown the door. Chatrier made the mistake of disclosing his report to the press without Samaranch's consent. Friendly reporters were briefed that the Frenchman was out of his mind and had no future at the IOC. Inside boxing, the division between Chowdhry and Wehr was deepening and the German suspected that his time in office would soon be over. After their congress in Beijing he wrote to Chowdhry, 'People were elected into positions whose openly declared goal is to take over. These people have rallied to plunder the cash-box of AIBA without having earned a single penny for our federation.' He added, 'These people . . . are being remunerated with the money AIBA earns thanks to the athletes who are fighting in the ring.'

Wehr claims Chowdhry masterminded the campaign to expel him. 'The whole affair escalated following your behaviour at the reception that was given by Uzbekistan,' Wehr wrote to him. 'Your battle cry "The war begins tomorrow" went neither unheard nor unheeded.' They all moved on, to the next world championships in Berlin, in 1995. The crookery went on, too, and at the end the German national federation produced its own report. 'The cardinal problem remains the sincerity, honesty and fairness of boxing's leadership and its referees and judges,' protested German boxing official Kurt Maurath. Then he made an assertion which could be carved on amateur boxing's tombstone: 'Scoring no longer corresponds to the action in the ring.'

Inside Chowdhry's domain, one brave soul raised his head. 'Looking at the score and at some of the individual results we find out that some of us are not honest,' said Australia's Arthur Tunstall at the next executive meeting. 'What is necessary is a complete reshuffle of the referees' and judges' commission from the top right through the organisation.' Arthur's view wasn't shared by Turkey's Caner Doganeli, who said the Berlin championships had been 'one of the best ever'. His only complaint was that there was no security for officials attacked by spectators and journalists. For the Americans there was the meagre reward of one gold, won by Antonio Tarver in the light heavyweight division.

Chowdhry's approach to the contests by rival cities to stage the Olympics was entirely in character: what's in it for Anwar? He boasted that bidders for the games of 1996 offered him up to $100,000 in bribes to help them win. His years fixing for Dassler's team had won him a reputation for delivering – and he cultivated it. When an applicant seemed too dense to get the point, Chowdhry made a straight approach for cash. He tried that on the Alaskan city of Anchorage when they pursued the winter games, telling their team that if they hired him secretly he 'would be more than happy to help them get the Games'.

Two of his daughters, educated at private school in England, went on to college places in Atlanta as the city worked to win the Olympics. Mina took a course in electrical engineering and Fumi studied computer graphics. During the Olympics, and while tipsy, some thought, Chowdhry boasted, 'It was Atlanta's bidding team who made it possible for my daughters to study here in Atlanta.' A third daughter, Sonia, was found a hotel room out of boxing's allocation for the games.

At a boxing reception Chowdhry was seen with a new associate, Mr Gafur Rakhimov, a wealthy businessman from Uzbekistan. The burly men around Rakhimov were assumed to be bodyguards. The press reported on the number of ostentatiously wealthy new officials from the countries of the former Soviet Union, their female companions wearing fur coats in the stifling Georgia humidity.

Were the judges in Atlanta got at? There was one attempt, for sure; a member of the executive committee was spotted at a draw furtively jotting the officials' names on the palm of his hand. It was said that he was passing this information to the Korean team. The draw was repeated – with stricter scrutiny. After the results they'd suffered in Seoul and Barcelona, American boxing officials were getting twitchy. The Reuters boxing writer shared their view that welterweight Fernando Vargas was robbed, reporting that he hit his Romanian opponent 'with every legal punch imaginable . . . he could very well have won by double digits'. Vargas lost. One judge failed to see him strike a single blow in the second round. Others at the ringside found this incredible. Featherweight Floyd Mayfield lost on a questionable decision in the semi-finals. US Boxing's acting director Dave Lubs had his ringside accreditation pulled after he approached the executive committee's table and asked bitterly what was 'the price of winning a bout'. Later he strode to the jury table and called the result 'bullshit'. Another American official was banished by Chowdhry for discussing judges' scores with reporters.

The Atlanta bouts were fought in the shadow of the grievous mugging administered to Roy Jones by Chowdhry and the IOC. Samaranch made periodic, elliptical mutterings about cleaning up boxing, but to have volunteered an investigation into Seoul would have been an admission that his premium-value sports event might be tarnished.

But his hand was forced in the summer of 1996. I had been digging in the Stasi files and discovered Wehr's report of the bribes paid in Seoul. I published it three months before the games in *The New Lords of the Rings: Olympic Corruption and How to Buy Gold Medals*. The IOC dodged the issue for as long as possible, briefing tame reporters that it couldn't be true because hadn't a Swiss judge convicted me a couple of years earlier for telling lies about them?

The US Olympic Committee, who had shown little interest in fighting for Jones, had to be seen to act once my documents were published in the American press. They lobbied hard and, one week into the Atlanta games, the IOC announced an

212

investigation, not into the scandal of the twenty or so rigged fights in Seoul, not into the plight of the four boxers who had clearly beaten Park Si-Hun in the qualifying rounds but lost the verdict. Only the Jones fight would be looked at.

Nobody held their breath; the inquiry was to be chaired by the safest pair of hands on the committee, Judge Mbaye, assisted by two loyal employees, director-general François Carrard and the IOC's sports director, Gilbert Felli. Everything would be done the IOC's way, in private. This was a delicate matter. Chowdhry needed careful handling or he might reveal the secrets about how Samaranch had become their Leader. And they had a vested interest in demonstrating that the games were clean, that cheating never happened – and would the press please go back to sleep.

My disclosures sharpened the tensions between Chowdhry and Wehr, who wrote to his president in August 1996, after the games: 'How can it be that you are blaming me instead of those who, through their misdeeds in Seoul, almost ruined AIBA? And why was there so much reluctance to take action against the real culprits? To such a point that in Nairobi it seemed as if they were going to go scot free?' He reminded Chowdhry that Gilbert Felli had warned them in Atlanta that, if there was one more irregularity, 'boxing is finished'.

Later in 1996 Chowdhry wrote to Wehr: 'If the IOC decides to give a medal to the USA, it will be very insulting for AIBA . . . let this matter finish in the best interest of AIBA.' In early 1997, as they waited for Mbaye to craft his verdict he wrote again to Wehr, 'I am very worried about the Park–Jones decision . . . If we go in the past many cases can be brought out which are even worse . . . this decision will be just opening a Pandora box, any decision against AIBA will be very harmful to our image.'

Hopes for justice were raised, briefly, when Anita DeFrantz, who talks a lot about standing up for athletes, told reporters, 'If someone was wronged and we can make it right, we should do so.' They should have, but they didn't. Mbaye took ten months and found an answer acceptable to his colleagues on the executive board, and the suave Carrard revealed it to reporters in Monaco in May 1997. Olympic historian and record-keeper David Wallechinsky has written, 'Probably no gold medallist in Olympic history has been less deserving of his prize than Park Si-hun, who benefited from five "hometown" decisions.' This view was not acceptable to Mbaye, Carrard and Felli.

Carrard had flown to Rabat where the Moroccan national Olympic committee produced boxing judge Hiouad Larbi for him. Carrard took a statement and the reporters were urged to pay attention because this man Larbi was one of history's great boxing connoisseurs. So what if the world's press had reported that Jones was robbed? OK, NBC's computer had recorded Jones overwhelming Park with 86 scoring blows to the Korean's 32. But Larbi had seen what others hadn't: Roy Jones had a 'flashy, spectacular style'. He hit in an 'irregular' manner, said Carrard, often with the open glove. Smiling at the reporters, Carrard pulled the rabbit from the hat. Larbi had told him, 'I considered – and still consider today – that the Korean should be declared the winner.' Yes, but had Larbi received $300, as Chowdhry had told Wehr? Yes he had, but it was to buy meals.

What about Larbi's admission that he gave Park his verdict to save the hosts' blushes? 'I never made the comments which were attributed to me by the journalist Pat Putnam,' said Larbi in his signed statement to Mbaye's team.

'Oh really!' Putnam laughed in December 1999. 'I stood next to the guy from *L'Equipe* and he was screaming, "How could you do this?" And Larbi came up with that lame excuse. The French reporter translated it all for me. That judge is a

liar. He's a liar and a thief, and you can quote me.' All right Pat,
I said, did Carrard or Mbaye ever put to you Larbi's claim that
you fabricated the quote? 'Never,' said Pat. Judge Mbaye, who
led the inquiry, felt no need to test Larbi's denial against the
evidence of reporters who'd been ringside. Far more con-
venient to allow Larbi's denial to go unchallenged.

Mbaye's view was rubber-stamped by François Carrard and
the four other lawyers at the executive board, Marc Hodler,
Dick Pound, Thomas Bach and Anita DeFrantz.

There was something else that riled Pat Putnam. There'd
been a programme a year or so back on the HBO cable channel
about the Jones robbery and Pat's story from 1988. 'HBO had
this woman, name like a hooker, one of the high-ranking IOC
people who claimed that he never said this,' rumbled Pat.

Would that have been Anita DeFrantz? I asked him. 'Yeah,
that's right, and the broad wasn't even at the fight and she said,
"I know for a fact he never said this." What the hell did she do?
Follow him around all day?

'I got so enraged. She said there's no corruption at the IOC,
there never has been. I wanted to punch her right in the
mouth. I mean, Jesus Christ. She had to say this to keep her
goddam job – what else could she say? She's an IOC mouthpiece.'

When interviewed by HBO, Anita said: 'The IOC investigated and found that the judges hadn't been bribed. There was
one judge who supposedly was quoted as having said that he
voted for the Korean athlete because he felt sorry for him,
because he got beaten so badly. It's not true. He said he never
said that; in fact, he never did the interview.' Anita was in full
flow. 'That's what he said. And that's what the IOC accepted
and he made his report very clear so the appeal was denied.'

*

That was the end of it. Carrard concluded the Monaco press conference in triumph: 'There is no evidence of corruption in the boxing events in Seoul.' There was no mention of the other bent judges, the wholesale corrupt judging everyone had observed back in 1988, or, most important of all, of the fact that Larbi's judging was so crooked in Seoul that even Chowdhry had been forced to suspend him for two years and Larbi had not been permitted to judge in top-level competitions again.

There had to be a deal, somewhere, to placate opinion in America. Despite Larbi's opinion that Jones didn't know how to box, he had become world light-heavyweight champion, hailed by the press as 'pound for pound, the best boxer in the world'. He never got his rightful gold medal. Instead, the IOC, conceding nothing, bestowed on him a Silver Olympic Order. There was no explanation of why, if he didn't deserve a gold medal, he deserved an award. He didn't even get the premier category, the Gold Order given to friends of Samaranch like Romania's Nicolae Ceauşescu or Bulgaria's dictator, Todor Zhivkov, and Professor Anwar Chowdhry.

A month later Chowdhry, speaking in private to his executive committee, told them that the attempt to get Jones his gold medal 'had been foiled by the IOC, which was to be considered a great victory for AIBA'. The minutes of the meeting continue: 'He said that IOC President Samaranch had personally played a great part in resolving this problem.'

The presentation of Jones's Olympic Order was made in New York by Anita DeFrantz, a sometime bronze-winning rower. The *New York Times* headlined its story 'Nice Gesture Substitutes for Justice', and when writer George Vecsey asked her if she felt justice had been served, DeFrantz replied: 'Justice. That's an interesting word.'

Roy Jones wept.

DeFrantz was – and remains – one of the IOC's ambassadors to America. The message she brought that day from Lausanne to New York was that the IOC sided with spivs like Chowdhry against brave athletes like Roy Jones. Just as they'd covered up positive dope tests in the past – to protect their own image – so they would not admit that athletes had been robbed while officials took bribes. Her message was heard loud and clear at the US Boxing Federation. They would have to find an accommodation with Chowdhry, not fight him.

Chapter 14

Here Comes the Mob!

World amateur boxing met in Havana for its Under-19 championships, three months after the 1996 games. Away from the scrutiny of Atlanta, Anwar's boys were busy fixing fights again. Shortly before a Russian was due to compete, English judge Mick Budden was beckoned to the back of the hall by another judge, a Russian. 'He didn't speak any English,' Budden told me later, 'but he made gestures and handed me a white envelope. When I got back to where the officials were sitting I opened it and there was $1,000. I was so angry I grabbed hold of him and told him I wasn't a cheat and thrust the money back at him.'

The English team lodged an official protest. Chowdhry tried to block it. 'Stop and freeze all actions on this incident and no further action should be taken,' he ordered. When the English persisted he let them have an investigation, but insisted it was conducted by his dear friend Emil Jetchev. The Bulgarian did his best to please, dismissing the complaint as an attempt to 'discredit amateur boxing'. The English threatened to take their grievance outside boxing to sport's court of arbitration. Chowdhry backed down. Paul Konnor, the American head of boxing's legal commission, pursued the case and eventually Russian official Anatoli Khokhlov was suspended for a year. The suspension was backdated to the time of his offence and he spent only five months outside the sport. His $500 fine was just half the bribe he'd offered.

He got a better deal than England's Richard Hatton. The nineteen-year-old from Manchester was boxing brilliantly. He beat Cuba's star light welterweight so convincingly that even Havana's newspapers applauded him. He faced Russia's Timur Mergadze in the semi-finals.

Hatton moved around the ring, smoothly popping in shots. Four ringside judges clicked their electronic counters as Hatton connected. There was no doubt who was winning this fight. The fifth judge, a Turk, clicked fastest of all. He clicked so fast he risked repetitive strain injury. He clicked for the Russian and so furiously that he out-clicked all the other judges together. He gave the contest – and a place in the final – to the Russian by a margin so huge that it outweighed the scores of the other four. It was the scandal of the championships; but only until the other semi-final, where there was another astonishing result. A tough Venezuelan was defeated on points by a mediocre German who went on to lose in the final to Hatton's Russian opponent, Mergadze. The Russian took the gold medal and the world title. 'Unbelievable,' said England's team manager, Clive Howe. Richard Hatton knew what to do with his bronze. 'As soon as I got home I chucked it in a drawer and it has not left there since.' Disgusted, Hatton quit the amateur ranks and signed up as a professional.

A year later Gafur Rakhimov turned up again with his phalanx of bodyguards. He's the Uzbek businessman people spotted with Chowdhry at the Atlanta Games. At the world championships in Budapest, 1997, Rakhimov was listed only as a team official but all the squad deferred to him.

Mr Rakhimov's favourite fighter is his own Uzbek heavyweight, Ruslan Chagayev. A raw and ready upstart, Chagayev made it to the final where he faced Cuba's mighty Félix Savón, the stylish and hard-hitting five times world champion. Immediately, the Cuban was in trouble, not from Chagayev but from the Turkish referee. He stopped the fight twice, warning Savón for hitting with the inside of his glove. The Cuban looked baffled, as did the spectators, who saw no trace of a foul.

One more warning and Savón would be out of the fight. He'd taken a blow to the psyche, he was hesitant to do what he does so well, hit opponents hard. Chagayev's confidence surged, he pressed his advantage and started throwing combinations that connected. Chagayev left the ring with a gold medal and a final pop at Savón: 'Looks like he's getting old.' A security escort hustled the referee from the arena. Spectators sloped off, like the Cuban, feeling cheated. The Reuters man at the ringside reported glumly: 'Savón was the victim of some dubious early refereeing.'

Chagayev's success rang bells in Chicago, where weeks previously a boxer of the same name, age and weight had won two professional fights. A keen-eyed reporter tipped off the boxing association's headquarters in Berlin: 'It seems possible these are one and the same man.'

Berlin started asking questions. The Uzbek federation ducked and wove. Yes, they had sent an eighteen-year-old Chagayev to summer boxing camp in Chicago. But professional fights? Certainly not. The fights were on record at the Illinois Boxing Commission, and they couldn't argue with that.

'I participated in two exhibition bouts,' conceded Chagayev, 'but I didn't believe they were professional fights.' Perhaps he didn't notice that he'd fought without the required amateur kit, headguard, vest and gloves with distinctive white patches. And then there was the matter of money, $800 for the boy. That wasn't prize money, that was 'expenses', he said.

It wasn't looking good for Chagayev, so it was time to

change tactics. Early in the new year, in frozen Berlin, Karl-Heinz Wehr took a call from Mr Rakhimov. He wasn't happy about the threat to take away Chagayev's title. 'Please help the young boy,' he asked. Wehr told him, sorry, it wasn't possible, the case had to be heard.

Soon after, Wehr had a visitor. 'Come for lunch' said Vladimir Shin, once a polished amateur boxer, now an official in Uzbek boxing. Shin took Wehr and his interpreter, Heidi Steiger, to lunch in the Haxenhaus restaurant. Over a knuckle of pork with sauerkraut Shin reminded him, 'Karl, we are old friends. Can Ruslan keep his medal?' Wehr was embarrassed. 'Sorry,' he said, 'you know the rules.'

As they bade farewell on the pavement Shin produced two fat envelopes, one each for Wehr and Steiger. Wehr takes up the story: 'We took them into the office and opened them in front of the rest of the staff.' Heidi's held $1,000. Karl got $5,000. 'We were utterly dismayed by the contents of the envelopes,' Wehr told Shin that same day in a faxed letter to Tashkent. 'Please note they will be handed back to you during your next visit to Berlin.'

Oh no, this is a dreadful misunderstanding, said the Uzbeks. Shin had invited the two officials to visit their country and the cash was for travel expenses, that's all, which didn't explain why the general secretary needed five times as much as his interpreter.

The Uzbeks switched tactics and Ruslan Chagayev found himself represented by one of America's most influential law firms. Charles Manatt, of Los Angeles-based Manatt, Phelps & Phillips, is a prominent Democrat who co-chaired the 1992 campaign that put Clinton and Gore in the White House. For Chagayev, a teenage country boy from one of Asia's poorer states, this was one fancy law firm.

221

Manatt, Phelps & Phillips argued that the amateur association's rules don't prohibit boxers from competing as pros; they only say amateur boxers 'should' not do it. The pro contract Chagayev signed with a Chicago promoter wasn't valid, because the boy spoke no English. Besides, everything he did in America was approved back home by the Uzbek Association, so Chagayev must be in the clear. I asked Gafur Rakhimov, known to be exceedingly wealthy, if he had paid for these expensive American lawyers. 'No,' he replied. The bill was met by 'patriots and boxing lovers who believe in Chagayev'.

In February 1998 the AIBA legal commission, chaired by Paul Konnor, stripped Chagayev of his title and suspended him for a year. The Uzbek association were fined $3,500, and the $6,000 they had left in Berlin went to pay the hearing's costs.

Wehr recorded, in a memo to Chowdhry, that 'never were the attempts at corrupting officials as massive as in Budapest'. One official, Chowdhry was told, 'following a decision which was not to the liking of a certain party, had a sub-machine-gun pointed at his chest in his hotel'.

If Budapest had been bad for the Uzbeks, it was a disaster for the Americans. They didn't win anything, gold, silver or bronze. Nothing. A team that couldn't win medals was soon going to run out of sponsors and television money at home. Without money, they would find it hard to train up new contenders, and without successful young boxers, there would be fewer trips around the world for the officials. Maybe that Chowdhry fellow and his friend Rakhimov weren't such bad chaps after all. 'If you can't beat them, join them' became the new motto of the Americans.

What would please them most? Getting rid of the dogged Wehr who fought Chowdhry every inch on fight-fixing was one priority. The other was sacking Paul Konnor, the lawyer from Milwaukee who had been on boxing's executive committee for fourteen years and showed an unhealthy interest in the rules and Chowdhry's expense claims.

USA Boxing got itself a new president, Gary Toney, from South Charleston, West Virginia. Toney wrote a letter to Konnor: there was news of 'changes in strategic direction' followed by a new 'global strategy' which would need a 'redefinition' of roles. Then Toney noted that 'USA Boxing's relationship with the International Amateur Boxing Association has not been favorable in recent years nor have we been influential for some time.'

Toney wasn't at all happy about this, and he had a solution. Konnor must resign, forthwith, from the executive committee of AIBA. 'This will allow the new administration to take USA Boxing in a different global direction from the present.' The abrupt dismissal was followed, as such blood-lettings usually are, by warm recognition of Konnor's tireless efforts and dedication to their sport. Words were cheap, Konnor was out.

Paul Konnor pondered for some months and in the spring of 1998 wrote to the IOC president. It was a long and dignified letter and began by reminding Samaranch that they had met during Konnor's half-dozen years as a member of sport's court of arbitration. Konnor wanted Samaranch to know that professor Chowdhry allowed the 'barter [of] favors and money for gold medals . . . officials rob our athletes of what is rightfully theirs' at the Olympics and other tournaments. How bad was this? 'Worse than the Jones incident in Seoul,' said Konnor – a tactical mistake. He'd forgotten that Judge Mbaye had ruled there'd been no corruption.

Chowdhry was committing a 'contemptible crime' against the athletes, and when he wasn't doing that he was fiddling the books, Konnor alleged. Nearly $400,000 worth of Chowdhry's expenses hadn't been accounted for, and Konnor ended by asking the IOC to investigate. He says he copied the letter to American IOC members Anita DeFrantz and Jim Easton. That was back in April 1998. When I spoke to him two years later he said he was still waiting for a response.

With only three months to AIBA's next four-yearly congress, the Americans hosted boxing's executive committee in New York in August 1998. Chowdhry wasn't happy about the location, writing in a confidential memo, 'originally my choice was Uzbekistan'. His host, Gary Toney, tried to make up for the disappointment: 'It was a privilege and honour', he told the president, 'to welcome amateur boxing's greatest minds to New York.'

Chowdhry's other concern was his own re-election. He wanted the federation to know that he had support from the world's leading sports figures, Samaranch and Jean-Claude Ganga in particular. Chowdhry loyalists from Africa and Latin America were quick to pledge their continents to his cause, as did Mr Doganeli from Turkey who said he spoke for Europe.

As Chowdhry purred, Gary Toney announced the good news: they were pulling Konner off the executive committee and replacing him with Loring Baker from Atlanta. There were some late nominations for the executive board, to be voted on at the congress in three months' time. One was for Mr Rakhimov from Uzbekistan.

The party-pooper was Gemiliano Lopez from the Philippines. 'It is high time to fight dishonesty and corruption in this organisation and to stop the Mafia taking over,' he said.

And by the way, he wouldn't be standing for re-election. He'd had enough.

Late in November 1998, as the Salt Lake scandal lifted off, the amateur boxing community gathered in the Hotel Zeynep, a concrete pyramid overlooking a strip of grey sand on Turkey's Mediterranean Riviera. It was their four-yearly congress. The signs said we were 40km from the old city of Antalya, where the gangsters from the central Asian republics reputedly buy villas for R'n'R – and it's a brief hop over the water if they want to inspect their wealth in Cyprus banks. I joined them, the only foreign reporter.

'Hello boys!' smiles Ms Unbuttoned Big Bouncing Bosoms, and lovely she is, too, with perfect teeth, big eyes, and tumbling black mane. She's the official greeter in the lobby. We can see what she wants us to do. She wears a big badge begging votes for Chowdhry's faction. It moves up and down a lot. Until all the votes have been cast, two days later, she never stops swaying through the delegates, with a smile for every-body, often partnered by Chowdhry's daughter Mina or Michiyo, his Japanese wife.

Her badge reads, in gold lettering on blue, 'Loring Baker for General Secretary'. So Mr Baker is about to become one of boxing's greatest minds. Back in the 1980s he'd stormed out of the sport ranting, 'I want you to know that as of this moment I am a foe of amateur boxing. I plan to do everything I can to see it disbanded . . . I am your enemy.' Times change. Chowdhry, casting around for a reliable man to replace the increasingly obdurate Karl-Heinz Wehr, alighted on Baker, and reinvented him.

'History demonstrates that I am a man who moves FORWARD,' shrieks Baker's humourless election manifesto.

'FORWARD' appears fifteen times. He seems more at ease with capital letters. 'The most important aspect of serving as GENERAL SECRETARY is this: HE MUST BE ABLE TO COOPERATE AND WORK HARMONIOUSLY WITH THE PRESIDENT. These two officers, the highest in AIBA, must be PARTNERS – ALLIES – NOT ENEMIES.'

Baker circulates a full page of biography with everything you didn't need to know about him since the 1930s – except his age, which he later tells me is seventy-one; he is four years older than Wehr, whom he is intended to replace, and four years younger than Chowdhry. Baker is not tall, nearly as wide as he is high, he's bald and wears rimless glasses. His round, featureless face and frame reminds me of a grizzled Teletubby.

His running mate the Professor's manifesto is an attempt at something more sophisticated. One side of the glossy cardboard is given over to a large photograph of our president sitting alongside Muhammad Ali. The Great Man turns his head away, as if he doesn't know this fellow. The other side, headed 'Who is Mr. Anwar Chowdhry?', tells us: 'Professor Chowdhry invented a Computerised Judging System which has stood the test of time.' This will surprise the Russian and German technicians whose pioneering work was reported over the years in AIBA's magazine. The result of his technological genius is this: 'Professor Chowdhry saved the future of Boxing as an Olympic sport for which he will be remembered for years to come.'

There's a rival manifesto from Karl-Heinz Wehr and IOC member and architect Dr C. K. Wu from Taiwan, who runs against Chowdhry for the top job. As IOC members go, Wu is an excellent fellow whose name has never popped up on my corruption radar. Their manifesto confronts the problems that

Baker and Chowdhry ignore: 'We are fighting for honesty and fair play in Olympic-style boxing,' they say, 'and against all forms of manipulation, corruption, bribery and doping.'

It's the first day of the congress and President Chowdhry sits at a small table to the front of the platform in the Zeynep ballroom. At his left is Wehr, still functioning as general secretary. To his right is our host, Caner Doganeli. He's a wealthy man, a mining engineer and construction company boss. Doganeli is a screamer. I've listened to tapes of him performing at executive committee meetings. Disagree with Doganeli and you get the tantrum. Today he is happy, sitting next to Chowdhry, his brother in Islam, as they frequently call each other. The word is that if Chowdhry retains the presidency he'll take his money and run after the Sydney games and Brother Doganeli will replace him without a bothersome election.

Behind them on the platform sit the senior officials. Among Chowdhry's allies – or dependants, depending how you see them – is Uganda's IOC member, Francis Nyangweso, who shows Chowdhry the same deference he showed Idi Amin when he was the dictator's defence minister. Immediately behind Chowdhry, in darkened glasses, is Bulgaria's ageing bureaucrat Emil Jetchev, under attack for corruption in the press back home.

Picking his nose is Scotland's Frank Hendry, who represents little more than his own shrinking constituency. In recent years the Scottish press have competed to libel and defame Frank, and most of his coaches and boxers have set up a rival federation. The Scottish Sports Council removed his funding and tried to act as midwife to a new organisation. If Frank is ejected from the sport in Britain – as many boxing fans hope he will be – he's unlikely to lose his privileged place in international boxing as long as Chowdhry needs sycophants. Frank told me in a BBC interview just before Antalya, 'He's doing a good enough job. The AIBA seems to be thriving.'

Frank shares a Tweedledum–Tweedledee existence with rotund Terry Smith from Wales, friend of fast-food vendors everywhere. Terry, like Frank, has seen his national association shrivel as boxers and coaches have defected to form a new federation. But Terry, like Frank, has been permitted to keep the AIBA franchise and its travel perks. And, again like Frank, he is loyal. 'We support you and your policies one hundred per cent,' he wrote to Chowdhry. Sitting next to Terry in the delegate ranks is Frank's wife, Nessie. She's a delegate too, representing, they say, women's boxing in Scotland. Frank and Nessie arrived early, putting in more days in this rainy beach resort than most, and so they're likely to take home quite a fistful of dollars in allowances.

There's around five hundred delegates, translators, and bodyguards at the rows of tables, with their little national flags, stretched across the hall. Half a dozen rows from the front sits Mr Gafur Rakhimov, stolid and thoughtful. He has the firm build of the light heavyweight boxer he once was, a military-style short haircut; he's quietly well-groomed and has delicate high cheekbones that hint of the steppes and mountains of Central Asia, although he and his associates are listed as Turks at the hotel. His bar and hospitality bill over the long weekend is the highest, at just over one hundred million Turkish lira. Chowdhry comes second with forty-six million lira.

Some of the funny business happened last night, before the congress began. Wehr tells me that when Rakhimov walked into a hospitality room Chowdhry jumped up and chattered 'This is my friend Gafur. If I need $100,000 he will give it to me immediately.' It's also whispered to me that last night a Russian-speaking man approached some African and Latin delegates offering the equivalent of $1,500 each for their votes. Later, Wu and Wehr lodge an official protest that eight African and three South American delegations took bribes.

Chowdhry has his votes bought up and he isn't letting a single one slip away. Early in this first morning's business England's Rod Robertson, a naval commander, takes the mike and asks, 'Is every national association here today up to date with its dues?' If you haven't paid you shouldn't be in the room and can't vote.

Wehr purrs, almost as if it were pre-arranged, that of the one hundred and twenty nations present, thirty-four are in arrears. Defiantly, Chowdhry announces they can pay during the congress. He is applauded. He ventures further: 'They can pay any time they like.' More applause. There's some whispering among his allies on the platform and then Chowdhry shouts, triumphantly, 'Everyone has paid!'

Chowdhry launches his presidential speech. For nearly forty minutes his mind is at its greatest, rambling incoherently without notes or structure. He is probably as surprised as his audience by what he hears. On such a day, seeking four more years' power, he doesn't mention 'bastards' but does acknowledge bad judging. As ever, it is a phenomenon which surprises him, is detached from him, and which he will FIGHT! In a touching piece of theatre Chowdhry says of the man who has presided over the corrupt selecting of judges for so long, 'Emil Jetchev is my friend and I beg you to support him, to give him the strength to take action.' Chowdhry swings round in his chair and looks fondly at Jetchev, who, as much as a grey and grizzled old apparatchik can, simpers and responds, 'I can only thank President Chowdhry. We will definitely overcome this problem.' Big Applause.

The rest of the day evaporates in mumbled reports from committees that deal with rules, youth, women's boxing, matters legal, scientific, business, financial, followed by alcohol abuse at the bar for the rank and file. Some of the delegates, from poorer countries, are making beers last a long time; I redistribute a little of my sports editor's budget. Someone gives me a list of the officials, twenty-nine in all, who will be elected in the secret ballot tomorrow. I have the results in my hand a full twelve hours before the ballot slips are handed out. Rakhimov will come from nowhere to be voted a member of the executive committee. And Dr Wu will be thrown off.

Overnight the Zeynep's atrium lobby is festooned with hand-lettered, painted banners, demanding Chowdhry's re-election. There are more bribes after breakfast. Hoping to counter Chowdhry's bought votes, Wehr and Wu propose that for the first time delegates be paid travel and hotel expenses, plus $50 a day subsistence. Chowdhry's wunderkind, the excitable Doganeli, hits back with a similar offer – plus $100 a day pocket money. It's not his money, it's not their money, it's money earned by the sweat and courage of boxers in the Olympic ring. Boxing has virtually no other income. Delegates take the $100, and in the night $750,000 flown from an Istanbul bank is handed out. From the floor it's proposed that the $10 a day allowance for young boxers when abroad be raised to $20. There is no vote. 'Rejected' comes the cry from the platform, and so it is.

Chowdhry is enraged by the persistence of the Western Europeans – not including Frank and Nessie and Terry.

Whatever they propose, he will oppose. They must be seen by his tribes to be pariahs, trouble-makers, buffoons to be struck down. The English, Danes, Dutch, Swedes, Germans and their allies have got hold of a letter Samaranch sent the Professor a year back, after the Budapest world championships. It's a coded warning that, if specific changes are not made, Olympic boxing is dead. Chowdhry has been too busy travelling the world, building his election coalition, vacuuming up hospitality, to bother with the sporting side of things.

So the Europeans move to have Samaranch's recommendations brought in. The number of rounds should be reduced from four or five to three. This cuts out some boring one-minute breaks that lose television viewers. Up goes Doganeli's red card on the platform and up goes a plantation of red cards on the floor. 'Rejected!' bellows our president. All Samaranch's other proposals, for better judges and more transparent scoring, are 'Rejected!' Chowdhry controls the meeting tightly, except when he makes a fool of himself. More than once, when reading documents aloud, he turns two pages at a time. His aides fidget nervously as they wait for some brave soul to risk telling the great man. It's a long wait.

Election time. Doganeli takes the mike and announces, 'My friends, the payments will be made after the congress.' Wehr states: 'Now we vote for president. Dr Wu Ching-kuo has the endorsement of the IOC,' and Chowdhry, suddenly angry, shouts, 'Don't bring the IOC into this!' Wu is trounced 75–38 and Chowdhry, unable to manage his bulk, stumbles down from the stage and waddles across the room to kiss the Uzbeks and the pliant delegates around them. As they embrace, the lights go out. The hall is in darkness for a few seconds. An electrical fault. It's spooky. Chowdhry kisses Nyangweso, cradling the man's head in his hands, then hugs Jetchev. Doganeli gives

Chowdhry flowers. Rakhimov hugs a Pakistani. My colleague, the photographer Morten Bjørn Jensen, is on motor-drive.

Now it's time for the public execution of General Secretary Wehr. Baker's 78–42 vote kills him but he finds a beautiful way, from the platform, to say goodbye to his old friends: 'We wouldn't be here if we weren't fans of boxing.' And that brings warm applause that was missing for Chowdhry and Doganeli and Baker.

It's all over, so down with the notepad and up with my radio reporter's mike. First to Loring Baker. Why, I ask, does he think he was elected? 'We need to go to another elevation,' says Loring, an anthropological marvel who speaks a language known only to himself. 'And I think people thought that I was better qualified to go to the next elevation than the present administration.'

Brain-numbed by this gibberish, I seek out defeated Dr Wu. Will Chowdhry do anything to clean up boxing? 'I doubt this will happen,' says Wu. 'In the last twelve years he has had many opportunities to make changes.' Wu hates to say it but he knows that today's rigged ballot will likely encourage the fight-fixers, and doom boxing in the Olympics. 'When the IOC review the future Olympic programme I believe boxing will be on the top of the list for what should remain in the Olympics or not, and I doubt how many people within the IOC will speak up for boxing.'

Later I talk to Australia's elderly Arthur Tunstall, long time on the executive committee. 'Rakhimov?' says Arthur. 'He's the one who swung the support behind Chowdhry.' How? 'Nobody actually said, "I saw the money being given." That's been one of the problems. Nobody has ever said it. And they're not likely to. You wouldn't expect anybody to come out and say, "I took a bribe."'

I look again at the list I was given last night in the bar. Should have got to a bookie. All twenty-nine are elected. Mr Rakhimov has come from nowhere to be voted a member of the executive committee. And Dr Wu has been thrown off.

We go to the bar. Over in London this Saturday night reporter Michael Gillard is completing his story about the Moscow Mafia for tomorrow's *Observer*. He mentions that a Mr Gafur Rakhimov is 'The Godfather of Tashkent . . . a major figure in Uzbekistan's booming heroin trade.'

Chapter 15

Masters of the Universe

Gafur Rakhimov returned home from the Atlanta Games to a hero's reception at Tashkent airport. 'He was welcomed back with great ceremony by officials who had come to meet him off the plane in a fleet of black limousines,' reported a source whose account quickly found its way into drugs intelligence files across Western Europe.

Rakhimov had good news for Uzbek sports officials and the government. The Marqués de Samaranch, the president of the International Olympic Committee, would visit in a month's time. This would bring glory to everybody and transform Gafur's own fortunes. Fifteen months earlier his progress up the ranks of the Russian Mob had taken a humiliating knock.

When the Russian Godfathers take time off from drugs, fraud, assassination, prostitution, extortion, gun-running and smuggling plutonium, they like to have fun. Mob bosses' birthdays are occasions for special celebration. And so it was on the night of 31 May 1995 when the crime chiefs of the new Evil Empire flew into Prague for a night of debauchery.

They gathered at the Black & White, one of a chain of strip clubs owned by the Godfather of Russian Godfathers, Ukrainian-born, Israeli-naturalised Semion Mogilevich. A podgy, charmless chain-smoker, 'the most powerful mobster in the world', according to the FBI, Mogilevich controls a fortune estimated at $100 million.

It was a great night to remember, full of surprises. A cheery chap nobody recalled seeing before videoed near-naked girls cavorting around the banqueting tables. To close the night, a bunch of guys in black uniforms and balaclava helmets, packing mock sub-machine-guns, abseiled down ropes slung from the upper floor and jovially clapped the whole bunch in handcuffs. How richly comic. They looked just like a Prague SWAT team. Gafur Rakhimov laughed as much as anyone, though weren't the actors going a bit far, cuffing the girls too?

The joke was turning sour. These hooded characters didn't know when to stop. They hauled the gangsters and lap-dancers out on to the street, lined them against a wall and continued videoing them, one at a time, full face. Then the commander stepped forward and said something along the lines of 'Good evening gentlemen. We are the Prague organised crime squad. We've recorded your faces, but you're not seeing ours. These are real guns. You get a free one-way ride to the airport and don't ever, ever come back.'

The picture they had taken of Rakhimov smiling earlier in the evening was pasted into the file the FBI opened on him ten weeks later. It was headed 'Russian Organised Crime/ Racketeering Enterprises', numbered 033, and held in their office in Miami. The Feds had his date of birth, 22 July 1951, description – black hair and black eyes – and a list of associates that put him in the premier league of the new Eastern Mafia.

Topping the list was Sergei Mikhailov, boss of the Solntsevo crime syndicate. Also named was Vyacheslav Ivankov, head of the Russian Mafia's operations in America until he was jailed in 1996. The Feds said Rakhimov worked with Ivankov's lieutenants the Kandov brothers, Mark and Boris, fronting one of their operations, a Vienna-based company called Agrotek. It was alleged that he had been involved in distributing counterfeit US dollars in Poland and might be connected with 'major cocaine smuggling operations'. Rakhimov had come a long way in the few years since the collapse of the Soviet empire. Now there was nothing to hold back his spirit of enterprise, which would link the Olympic money machine to some of the most fearsome criminal gangs the world has ever seen, with a little help from one of Juan Antonio Samaranch's closest associates.

The tribes of the mountains and deserts of Central Asia were conquered by Alexander the Great and Genghis Khan. Life was so hard that most people didn't notice Italian ultra-runner Marco Polo jogging through in the thirteenth century on the Silk Road to China. Not a lot happened for the next six hundred years and then they disappeared into the Asian underbelly of the USSR.

The plains were irrigated as the Aral Sea was drained to force huge cotton crops but the Soviets never tamed the Kazaks, the Tajiks, the Kyrgyz, the Turkomen and the Uzbeks and in the early 1990s they formed independent states. In Tashkent the local communist boss, Islam Karimov, had himself declared president of the new Uzbek republic and its twenty-two million souls.

There's no free press in Uzbekistan, and government opponents tend to disappear or fall to their deaths from police-station windows. The luckier ones live but often end up in jail because when the cops call they inevitably find guns and tiny stashes of narcotics. Others seem above the law. Living standards in Uzbekistan have deteriorated but Tashkent has become the money-laundering centre of the region's heroin trade and small towns in the towering mountains are awash with late-model Mercedes. Customs officials acquire palatial mansions, and one intelligence report, from a French drugs agency, has it that 'the nouveaux riches revel in dream cars and girls on tap'.

The next dossier on Gafur Rakhimov was opened in the Moscow office of the Chief Directorate for Fighting Economic Crime, a division of the Russian Ministry of Internal Affairs, which has access to KGB files on the long-time gangsters of the Soviet black economy. It paints a broader and darker picture than the FBI file. Few, it seems, are richer or more powerful in Central Asia than Gafur Rakhimov. And, the Moscow crime-fighters warn, Gafur's gone international. He operates in Moscow and London and spends long periods in America. 'He is a personal adviser to the Uzbek president, Islam Karimov,' they say, 'and performs his special, delicate tasks, including the relationships with the Russian leadership.'

Rakhimov has his own Moscow office and 'enjoys unique influence in the Uzbek embassy, whose employees refer to him with fear. He has very strong influence in the economic and political leadership of Uzbekistan and is also influential in other Central Asian countries of the former Soviet Union. Without his unofficial sanction no single major economic project starts in Uzbekistan.'

The crime-fighters traced his extraordinary links to the Moscow powerbrokers. As well as having influence in the Kremlin, through Pavel Borodin, Yeltsin's administration chief, Rakhimov was well connected to Yeltsin's rivals in the camp of Moscow's mayor, Yuri Luzhkov.

The front for Rakhimov's illegal operations, they say, is the Uzbek cotton trade. He's a global player, claiming to buy – and sell – the entire Uzbek cotton harvest, the world's third largest. In secret, according to his Moscow file, 'Gafur Rakhimov is one of the leaders of Uzbek organised crime and his main speciality is the organised production of drugs in the countries of Central Asia.' He is, 'a major figure in an international drug syndicate. He keeps very close connections with Afghan traders of drugs.' The dossier claims that Rakhimov exports his heroin through Turkey, Chechnya and the Balkans.

Rakhimov has to fear that his assassin may lurk around the next corner. His Moscow file notes that he is a one-time associate of Sergei Timofeyev, leader of the Orekhovo crime family, who was taken out by a car bomb in the early 1990s. Rakhimov had helped broker a peace deal between Timofeyev and another alleged Uzbek crime boss known to the Moscow authorities.

Rakhimov's reputation went global in the autumn of 1997 when researchers at the Paris-based Geopolitical Drugs Watch flushed him out in their annual report on world narcotics distribution – and posted it on the internet. They named Rakhimov as one of Uzbekistan's top three mafia bosses, heavily involved in the drugs trade. Gang warfare raged in Tashkent, they said, and one rival 'was cut down by machine-gun fire at the bottom of the Chimgan ski slopes as he was about to take guests on a moonlight ride on the ski lifts'.

Rakhimov was already operating in Paris. In the year of the Atlanta games he'd set up an import–export business in avenue Hoche. In January 1998 Rakhimov flew into Le Bourget airport, near Paris, in a private jet owned by the charter company Air Entreprise. He arrived from Zurich with a ninety-day visa for the Schengen countries of the European Union, travelling with eight companions, several of them Russian-born emigrants to Israel. They were waved through by immigration officers; maybe it helped that Rakhimov's ninth travelling companion was Monsieur Georges de Charette de la

Contrie, whose cousin Hervé de Charette was France's foreign minister.

It was only after the party had left the airport in an 'immaculate' black Rolls-Royce, a Volvo and Renault Safrane that immigration officers looked in their files and discovered they had three different sets of records on Rakhimov, all warning that he was considered 'a leading member of the Uzbek mafia and posed a grave threat to public safety'.

The happy party glided comfortably into Paris and during the following week Rakhimov and his business partner Artur Martirossian were photographed with two men who planned to build a new business with them in Tashkent. One was Georges de Charette, a director of Air Entreprise. Standing next to Rakhimov, bespectacled and serious, and also a director of the charter company was His Royal Highness, Prince Jean of Luxembourg, son of the IOC's Grand Duke Jean, and younger brother of the Prince Henri who in four weeks time, at the Nagano games, would be appointed to take over papa's seat on the Olympic committee.

Prince Jean has not responded to my attempts to ask him about his dealings with Gafur Rakhimov, but Monsieur de Charette was most helpful. 'We were planning to set up an air charter company, similar to our own, in Tashkent, providing air limousines for whoever needed them,' he told me. 'At one stage Rakhimov told us that he was short of money because he had just purchased the entire Uzbek cotton crop – he was playing the commodity markets. After this very damaging picture was published in France – we had known nothing about what was being said about him – we had no more to do with him.' Did Mr Rakhimov ever talk about sport? I asked. 'Oh yes,' said de Charette. 'He said everything is dishonest, even in sport.' And what do you remember of him? 'He has freezing eyes.' To the relief of immigration officers Rakhimov returned to Le Bourget a week later and flew home to Tashkent.

Big hugs, kisses and hearty handshakes followed seven weeks later when Rakhimov was welcomed in Lausanne, where he arrived with an Uzbek Olympic delegation. Such visitors may expect a warm embrace from Samaranch at the Château de Vidy. Maybe little presents were handed out. What else happened? Try asking the avowedly New! Transparent! IOC. My questions about Samaranch, Rakhimov and Uzbekistan have been treated with all the enthusiasm you'd expect if you asked them for a picture of Juan Antonio giving his straight arm salute. (After the first month's silence I caught up with Samaranch mouthpiece Franklin Servan-Schreiber on the terrace at the Olympic Museum and asked if I was ever going to get any answers. 'But of course my dear Andrew,' he answered loftily. 'It's just a question of finding time to look in the records.' Four months later he hadn't called.)

The next day, 20 March 1998, Rakhimov flew to Paris from Geneva, again by private jet. His pilot was another man with a curious life story, a man who laundered slush-fund money between European heads of state, is a close associate of President Samaranch, a remarkable wheeler and dealer . . . we'll learn more of him later.

This time the immigration cops at Le Bourget did their job. How pleasurable it must have been to bring down the 'Cancelled' stamp on Rakhimov's visa when he arrived soon after eleven in the morning. Seven hours later Rakhimov was up and away on the long flight through four time-zones to Tashkent.

*

240

As Rakhimov had arrived in Lausanne for his meeting with Samaranch, he was under attack in Denmark. The very same day the respected Copenhagen daily *Politiken* disclosed, under the headline 'Beer Giant Co-operates with Mafia in Corrupt Country', that for the previous eighteen months Carlsberg had been negotiating with Gafur Rakhimov to take over and modernise an ageing Uzbek brewery. Journalist Bjørn Lambek was first to report a series of anonymous faxes to the media, claimed by Rakhimov to have originated at a rival company, another big European brewery.

Carlsberg's beer had sold well in Uzbekistan since the country opened to the West. Then the Karimov government killed the business with an import ban. Hello boys, said Gafur who just happened to have a sizeable share of the old brewery at Kibrai and was looking for investment partners. According to the faxes, Rakhimov was dealing with the cream of western capitalism. The European Bank of Reconstruction and Development (EBRD) was considering putting up money but, when I called them to check, an agitated press officer refused to admit there had been any meetings. 'We don't keep minutes of these sort of meetings, if they happened at all,' she said. It seems they did happen. I have a letter from Rakhimov to boxing's president, Anwar Chowdhry, dated January 1997, in which he says, 'I have programmed a meeting with representatives of the European banks in Tashkent.' Eventually the European Commission confirmed EBRD involvement but warned that it would 'continuously evaluate whether the necessary prudence is employed'. Then they pulled out.

Six months later French television's *Le Vrai Journal*, revealed that Rakhimov had been doing business in Paris and was eventually refused permission to enter the country because of his alleged Mob connections. Producers Pascal Henry and Stefan Ravion had acquired the reports of the French, Russian and American governments. To their astonishment Rakhimov sued. Of all the lawyers in France he chose the high-profile Jacques Verges, defender of Carlos the Jackal and Klaus Barbie, the war-time Butcher of Lyons. Mr Rakhimov, wrote the lawyer, was most upset. His honour had been questioned. He was sitting at home in Apartment 13, 9 Chimkentskaya Street, Tashkent, feeling deeply wounded. In August 1999, after further allegations in the French media, Rakhimov's lawyer filed papers abandoning the case. Four months later BBC Television's *Panorama* named him as a mafia boss. He demanded compensation for the damage to his reputation, which he valued at $20 million.

When I contacted Mr Rakhimov's Tashkent office in the summer of 1999 I got a call back from a gravel-voiced aide who told me, 'Mr Rakhimov, 'e say 'e don't want you to write this story.' Er, well, I put to him, it was going to be written and I'd be most appreciative if he would answer some questions. Off went my fax and back came Gafur's.

In bold type, and underlined, he asked me to 'hold to the answers and not to interpret them to the best for your advantage. Moreover, I reserve my right to claim for libel if any hints about connections between Mafia and drug trafficking take place.' He wanted me to know that his lawyers were taking action against his critics in France. Three days later he withdrew his Paris libel case.

I asked about his dealings with Carlsberg, and did he pay for the re-election of Anwar Chowdhry? No he didn't and when it came to cheating in boxing, 'I always come out and condemn.' He sent me a letter about himself, written by Mr M. T. Khaitov, director of the National Central Bureau of

Interpol in the Republic of Uzbekistan. 'Please be informed,' announced Mr Khaitov, 'there is no data about above mentioned person in our criminal records.' I called amateur boxing's general secretary Loring Baker, elected on Rakhimov's list in Antalya, and asked what he thought about the FBI having a file on the chairman of boxing's business commission. 'A man is innocent until he's been proved guilty. Ah would not make it an issue myself,' ruminated Loring (it came out 'maahself'). 'Ah don't have the highest regard for the FBI as far as ethics and so forth goes, anyway. So the fact they would have him on a list would not have any weight whatsoever. Ah put no credence in it whatsoever.'

When Gafur Rakhimov, on his way from Olympic discussions in Lausanne to business in Paris, accepted a free flight on 20 March 1998, his pilot was André Guelfi, a close associate of Samaranch, a daring entrepreneur. They'd met before, at the Atlanta games in 1996.

Within months of their touchdown in Paris, Gafur's generous pilot crashed into the headlines as Europe's most notorious money-launderer. André Guelfi knew the secrets of Europe's most powerful politicians. He knew where the money came from to win elections, he knew enough to spark Europe's biggest political scandal since the end of the second world war.

French investigators picked up the trail in the mid-1990s. At first Guelfi wouldn't talk, but he was a man in his seventies and a few weeks in jail changed his mind: in secret he began to unburden himself. He reportedly talked about dirty money being laundered through Olympic bank accounts, about payoffs to politicians in Africa and Latin America, about channelling at least $40 million in bribes from the late French president François Mitterrand to former German chancellor Helmut Kohl. At the time of writing, Guelfi's disclosures have disgraced Kohl and shattered the Christian Democrat Party, which ruled Germany for sixteen years. Many politicians and business people wait nervously to discover if their pasts will catch up with them and send them to jail. 'Every tree in the forest could fall,' said the *Washington Post*, comparing the Mitterrand–Kohl scandal to Watergate.

The scandal was born out of President Mitterrand's fear that, if Kohl's Christian Democrats failed to wrest control of eastern Germany from the left-wing parties, reunification's pace would slow, damaging both leaders' standing. Money would help. The evidence is growing that Mitterrand instructed the French state-owned Elf oil company to buy a dilapidated refinery in former East Germany for a hugely inflated price. This created a wash of money, a slush fund which Kohl could deploy secretly to fund his electoral machine.

The story unravelled through 1999 into 2000 and Guelfi, having tasted jail, could not stop talking about his exploits. He said a lot about how his Geneva-based companies were used to launder the political bribes and began to talk about his intimate business and personal relationship with the Marqués de Samaranch.

In the early 1990s Elf, casting around for new oilfields, learned that rich reserves might be found in the new republic of Uzbekistan. Acquiring drilling rights would be tricky. The man they chose to smooth their path to a deal with President Karimov was flamboyant Moroccan-born French entrepreneur André Guelfi, who handled their negotiations with Boris Yeltsin in the Kremlin. Fifty years earlier, Guelfi, in his twenties, had made his first fortune, running a fishing fleet off the Atlantic coast of Africa and earning the nick-name 'Dédé the Sardine'. He socialised with the royal family in Morocco and with leading French actor Jean-Paul Belmondo. He became a friend of the chief of France's intelligence service, competed in the Le Mans 24 Hours race, flew his private jet around the world, acquired a sports company and sponsored Tour de France winner Bernard Hinault and tennis player Arthur Ashe. Life was wonderful.

Guelfi bought himself a Lausanne villa overlooking Lake Geneva in the early 1970s, just as Juan Antonio Samaranch was plotting his rise to take control of the IOC. They were introduced by a man who became their close personal friend, Horst Dassler, owner of Adidas and the most influential businessman in sport. Guelfi had earned a reputation for turning round ailing companies and the French government invited him to rescue the sports-clothing manufacturer Le Coq Sportif.

Soon after moving into the company in 1977, he discovered a remarkable asset, the commercial rights to exploit the Adidas trefoil logo and three stripes within France. He talked to Dassler, a business relationship evolved. Dassler acquired Le Coq Sportif and then, together, they branched into sports marketing, selling rights to the 1980 Moscow Olympics. Guelfi supplied funds to launch Dassler's International Sport and Leisure Company, ISL. Through Dassler's contacts with sports leaders, ISL went on to acquire the marketing rights to the Olympics, to soccer and world track and field.

Guelfi says Dassler introduced him to Samaranch in the late 1970s when the latter was Spain's ambassador to the USSR and that they worked together to make the Moscow games a success. And, Guelfi says, he and Dassler collaborated to help line up votes behind Samaranch in his successful bid for the IOC presidency in Moscow in 1980. During 1999, when Guelfi's name became a byword for scandal, Samaranch insisted to the *Wall Street Journal* that he didn't meet the entrepreneur until well into the 1980s.

Another valuable contact was a close Samaranch ally, Russian IOC member Vitaly Smirnov. 'We've known each other for nearly thirty years,' says Guelfi. 'Vitaly has been a faithful friend.' When Guelfi was jailed for thirty-six days in 1997 by magistrate Madame Eva Joly, investigating the Elf affair, Smirnov wrote to her pleading that whatever Guelfi might have done, he did it for France.

For three decades Elf functioned as a secret slush fund for French governments to bribe foreign politicians. The company, set up in 1962, was first controlled by a former French intelligence chief. African leaders visiting Paris routinely paid their respects to its chairman before calling on cabinet ministers. Elf's huge income from oil 'took care of everyone', wrote a former company chairman in a secret memo before being cast into jail for six months by the investigating magistrate, who hoped the experience might refresh his memory enough to name everybody who had been 'taken care of'.

One politician said to have been exceptionally well treated was Foreign Minister Roland Dumas. His mistress was given a sweetheart 'consultancy', a credit card without limits and a Paris apartment valued at nearly $3 million. The press published pictures of her in alluring swimsuits and she too was jailed (for five months), emerging to write her life story, starkly titled *The Whore of the Republic*.

*

When Samaranch gazed along the lake shore from his Olympic headquarters at the Château de Vidy in the mid-1980s he must have liked the view. At Ouchy, beyond the yacht marina, was the perfect site for the Olympic Museum that would for ever be his memorial. Unfortunately somebody had already built a villa there. Fortunately the owner was his friend André Guelfi and $4 million from Olympic funds eased him out and the builders in.

Theirs was a seamless relationship, sharing business, Olympic and otherwise, between old friends. When Vitaly Smirnov nominated St. Petersburg as a candidate to stage the summer Games of 2004, Guelfi hurled himself into action. Always, he had a deal in mind. 'I don't ask for a cent from St. Petersburg, or from anyone,' he told *Newsweek*. 'If I succeed I want to be the one who chooses all the companies to do the major construction projects.' The commissions and intro-duction fees would do nicely. Just about everything in St. Petersburg needed renovation – the Hermitage museum, the subway, the roads, telecommunications. Old sports venues needed rebuilding, at least twenty new stadia would have to be constructed. The Russian government pledged one billion dollars. Then there'd be profits from sales of television rights. The potential explosion of business opportunities around the Olympics was breathtaking.

Would André behave himself if the bid won – or would he try to tempt Vitaly, Juan Antonio and other Olympic insiders to share a slice of the action? Everywhere Guelfi turned there was another Olympic friend and another Olympic opportunity. The IOC's evaluation commission examining the Russian city was led by German member Thomas Bach. Surely André remembered Thomas, the ambitious young lawyer who'd worked for Dassler's international relations team in the mid-

1980s, five years before Samaranch presented him with a seat on the Olympic committee.

The world sports community treated St. Petersburg's bid as a joke, but everybody made something out of it, except the poor Russian taxpayers who funded it. In charge of invitations to visit the city was Olympic official Aleksandr 'Sasha' Kozlovsky. 'Please feel at liberty to bring any family, friends, or associates from your Federation who may wish to accompany you,' wrote Sasha to Professor Chowdhry, another Dassler Old Boy.

Sasha often leads the singing round the piano in the Lausanne Palace bar. One night in October 1999 I plucked his sleeve and asked him, 'Do you know Gafur Rakhimov?' Sasha visibly paled, dropped his voice, whispered, 'He's as big as Berezovsky' (one of Moscow's biggest tycoons) and moved away from me smartly. (When scandal hit the IOC Sasha was one of the first people Samaranch called to sit on the body he set up to recommend reforms.)

Guelfi could see opportunities for himself where others saw only disaster. He'd cut his teeth on Olympic bidding a couple of years earlier when he'd promoted the silliest candidate ever. Straightfaced, he backed Tashkent for the 2000 Summer games. The bookmakers wouldn't offer odds on success. 'The Tashkent bid was a joke, a publicity stunt,' Guelfi later admitted. 'You have to be crazy to think you could have the Olympic Games there.' It was just a favour he'd done for President Karimov, helping to raise his and Tashkent's profile in the world. Guelfi claims he'd become a trusted adviser to Karimov, introducing not just Elf but also French aerospace giant Thomson and many other businesses.

André Guelfi's private jet, a thirteen-seater Falcon 900, was just what the Marqués de Samaranch needed to help him do business with his new friends in Central Asia. Samaranch had bestowed his official recognition on the new Uzbek national Olympic committee and seemed keen to meet them, again and again and again. Guelfi flew frequently to Tashkent for Elf, lured by the promise of fabulous commissions. He says that on at least three occasions he flew Samaranch into the arms of the welcoming Uzbeks. Samaranch, he insists protectively, 'never knew what I was going to ask heads of state when I had meetings with them'.

It's hard to imagine why the Olympic president should make room in his tightly packed schedule to jet off with Guelfi, time and again, to a distant land on the outer reaches of the Olympic movement. Samaranch's spokesmen find it hard to explain.

'Guelfi made it very difficult in some respects to say no,' said IOC media whiz Franklin Servan-Schreiber, offering no evidence for this absurd suggestion. 'It was a free plane ticket to a very difficult place to reach. It allowed the president to rope in several new countries.' Young Franklin's boss, François Carrard, said: 'Guelfi was happy to go to Uzbekistan with Samaranch because Samaranch was treated as a head of state. We have no idea what Guelfi was doing in Uzbekistan.'

Monsieur Carrard should ask the respected Paris-based intelligence newsletter www.intelligenceonline.com. In June 1999, as French media disclosures about Elf and André Guelfi reached frenzy point it reported that Gafur Rakhimov had established 'close relations' with Samaranch. There was more; the newsletter claimed Guelfi had told investigating magistrate Eva Joly that he had, 'transferred secret commissions from big French companies through the bank accounts of various Olympic committees in the region.'

Samaranch's urge to ingratiate himself with tyrants seems boundless. As the Uzbek jails filled up, living standards for most people slumped and the heroin traffickers flaunted their brash new wealth, he bestowed the Olympic Order on President Karimov. He got a bauble back and, on one visit, they attended the inauguration of Tashkent's Olympic Hall of Fame which Samaranch described as 'undoubtedly one of the best of its kind in the world'. In September 1998 he gave the Olympic Order simultaneously to Helmut Kohl and to Sabirzhan Ruziyev, president of the Uzbek national Olympic committee.

Meanwhile, André Guelfi was becoming a worried man. There were rumours that the benevolent Elf boss who'd promised him fat commissions, 5 per cent of all profits from the Uzbek oilfields, was about to be sacked. Guelfi wasn't close to President François Mitterrand, who would take the decision, but he knew somebody who was, and turned to novelist Françoise Sagan. He later told investigating magistrate Mme Joly that he offered Sagan £900,000 to persuade Mitterrand to keep Elf's boss in place. Ms Sagan denies taking money, but admits she did speak to Mitterrand and urge him to visit Tashkent, which he did.

When Guelfi got out of jail, he gave interviews to the media and published a rambling but hugely enjoyable account of his extraordinary life, *L'Original*. It contains two remarkable pictures. The first shows President Karimov, Guelfi and the Elf boss Loïk Le Floch Prigent relaxing in a garden, sharing a joke. The caption said this was a happy time, before the gendarmes took an interest in his affairs.

Below it is another picture, and Guelfi's caption says how happy he is to be out of jail and reunited with his friends. The picture shows a Kremlin reception with, from left to right, a hazy-looking President Boris Yeltsin, a beaming Mr Guelfi and, simpering into the camera like a schoolboy allowed to stay up beyond bedtime, IOC president Juan Antonio Samaranch.

During 1999 *Newsweek* magazine, the *Wall Street Journal* and several German papers published prominent articles linking Samaranch to Guelfi and the Elf scandals, yet IOC members and the board behaved as though nothing had happened. They like to compare themselves to multinational corporations, but in any business whose boss was found courting a money-laundering jailbird, and an alleged mobster, the board would swiftly tell him to clear his desk.

Samaranch appears at ease prostituting Olympic Idealism to benefit his friend Guelfi, who fondly remembers their trip to Beijing. Amid the Olympic back-slapping, he secured a meeting with no less than Chinese prime minister Li Peng to discuss a joint venture to build passenger airlines. Being an intimate helped. 'When I'm with Samaranch, and I request an audience with somebody, I get it . . . we are the masters of the universe,' says Guelfi.

Chapter 16

Robbery in the Ring

The Professor spoons more yoghurt into his mouth. He's pleased with himself. Houston's Mayor Lee P. Brown has declared that 27 August 1999, the last day of the world boxing championships, is Anwar Chowdhry Day. Indeed, each new day brings good news. He's had a letter from Judge Mbaye, head of the court of arbitration. The judge says he would be honoured to have President Chowdhry as one of his mediators: 'The mediator is a person with high intellectual and moral values.'

That reminds me: 'Why isn't Mr Rakhimov here in Houston?' I ask. Chowdhry has appointed him chairman of the business commission; he's the link man with sponsors. The old man slides lower in his low armchair, gazes around him conspiratorially, leans towards me and mutters, 'He can't get a visa for France!'

'Why?' I ask. The Professor waves to his son-in-law who has sat silently through our meeting. I am handed a soon-to-expire diary and shown the door.

At the boxing hall I bump into Turkey's executive committee member Caner Doganeli. He's in cheery mood. Where is Mr Rakhimov? I ask him. Surely he wouldn't want to miss the worlds? 'Mr Rakhimov has family problems, he couldn't get a visa for his young son,' Doganeli tells me. 'He's in petroleum and exporting electricity from Uzbekistan and he's a lovely, lovely man.' He looks at me sideways and adds, 'We in boxing are a family of interesting people.'

It's odd that Chowdhry has appointed a chairman of boxing's business commission, Mr Rakhimov, who is excluded by the immigration officers of many prosperous capitalist countries as a danger to society. It's hard to imagine the bosses of the big Olympic sponsors jetting to Tashkent to sign contracts because Mr Rakhimov has problems coming to call at corporate headquarters.

The cavernous, windowless, concrete George R. Brown convention centre in downtown Houston is home to boxing's 1999 world championships. The show is put together by the hosts, USA Boxing and Doganeli, chair of the technical and rules commission. It's chaos, angry coaches and team managers tell me, the worst-organised worlds ever.

I paid a visit to the restroom nearest the ring. Between the occupants of the cubicles and the men at the urinals, half a dozen naked young boxers stood washing blood from their cuts in the hand-basins. It didn't seem right, these noble young fighters robbed of their dignity – quite apart from the danger to their health. 'This is a disgrace,' one visiting official told me. 'No showers, no clean towels. It probably breaks every rule in the Houston City hygiene regulations.'

The boxing ends around nine in the evening and our leaders are chauffeured away fast in their air-conditioned limousines, back to their hotel. I wait with hundreds of fighters outside the loading bay at the back of the convention centre. The coaches are always late and too few. The first night I am sandwiched between a couple of Olympic gold medallists pouring sweat in the steamy night – it's 104 Fahrenheit and humid on the Gulf of Mexico. A coach draws up and we scramble for it. Too late. We're turned back to wait for the next one. The Houston cops are there to make sure we keep our cool.

When we get back to the hotel complex I take a peek into the dining room and see our leaders emptying their dessert bowls and wiping their mouths. Through the windows in the half-light, assuming they can be bothered to look, they'll see boxers sitting on the kerb eating their specially catered meal – cold snacks from brown paper bags. After four days more of brown bags and protests, a cheap no-options hot buffet is provided in a dining room.

The fight I was waiting for was the rematch between Félix Savón and the man who stole his heavyweight title two years earlier in Budapest. It came one hot August afternoon in the quarter-finals. The Uzbek Ruslan Chagayev, sturdy and muscular, started well and landed one big punch on the Cuban. Savón clouted him back and that was the end of Chagayev's hopes. These bouts were fought over four rounds and Savón, using his left to keep the Uzbek at bay, swung repeated high rights to the head, giving the upstart a 9–1 lesson in Olympic-style boxing. Budapest was avenged.

Savón's victory brought Cuba no comfort. Two days after the fight, the Cubans came calling on Chowdhry, led by team manager Raúl Villanueva. Four Cubans had fallen to what their government later called, 'unjust and shameful decisions by a group of unscrupulous referees and judges'. Villanueva handed Chowdhry a written demand that seven named judges should not officiate again in Cuban bouts. 'We've suffered four outrageous decisions already,' he said. 'Please, no more.'

All through the tournament, sitting at the ringside were Scotland's Frank Hendry and Wales's Terry Smith. On a small table in front of them was a cardboard egg-rack packed with numbered ping-pong balls. Each ball represented one of the pool of judges and referees. Every time a new bout was announced Terry and Frank reached for a ping-pong ball. I asked General Secretary Loring Baker if this system might be perceived as open to corruption and he replied, 'Anything is possible . . . but Ah don't think it was too probable.'

Baker was eager to tell me about the new tough rule his leadership had brought in especially for the championships. Any referee or judge found to be incompetent or biased would be suspended for a minimum of four years or a maximum of life. It didn't seem much of a deterrent to the Armenian judge, who, just before a countryman was due to fight, approached other officials offering them watches and, pointing at his man's rival, whispering, 'He's dirty – he uses his head.'

The five ringside judges used the two-button computer system Chowdhry boasts has eliminated corruption. On a pad in front of them are two buttons, one for each fighter. Judges press the appropriate button every time they see a blow landed, and a point is recorded. But they count towards the final score only if three judges register the same blow within a space of one second. Still, the system is only as honest as the man hitting the button. A dishonest judge can keep whacking away at his favoured boxer's button and register nothing for the opponent.

Transparency in judging would give fighters more confidence that bouts were not being fixed; even the IOC wants judges' running scores to be displayed during the fight. Chowdhry prefers those individual scores to be seen only by officials viewing a monitor on the presidential podium. The temptation to peek was too much for one Uzbek judge who lurked behind the podium, noted the scores while an Uzbek was competing, then slipped them to a Kazakh judge at the ringside. Had the judge wanted to massage his score to deliver victory, this would have been vital inside information. The Uzbek fighter won the bout.

The finals are spread over two evenings and to celebrate the first night Chowdhry is helped up the steps to the ring; he clambers awkwardly through the ropes. It's the first award of the championship, some civic bauble, and, whatever it is, it's being presented to our president by a trim man in a boy scout uniform. I and two other British reporters leap to our feet, shouting, 'Show us the money!' but Chowdhry can't hear the words and the louder we bellow the more benignly he smiles in our direction.

The boxing begins. Six of the twelve title fights are on tonight and the Russians have three would-be world champions stepping up into the floodlights, the Cubans another three and America two. There's an Uzbek as well.

First up is America's light flyweight hope, Brian Viloria. He's a good fighter, brave, hard-working, world-class. But he faces Cuba's Maikro Romero, reigning Olympic, world and Pan-American champion. Less than a quarter-hour later it's over. 'Mafia,' Romero whispers to the judge nearest him. Then he circles the ring, shaking his head, smiling, saying it again, 'Mafia, Mafia, Mafia, Mafia,' to the other four judges. Defeat is one thing, somebody has to lose – but by the crushing score of 9–2? That's robbery.

The slim, pretty girls in their tight black dresses, carrying flowers and medals, slip elegantly between the ropes and hold the fixed smile throughout the ceremony. They tiptoe back down to earth and wait to do it again, five more times tonight.

Next is the first Russian hope and his dreams of the world bantamweight title are speedily destroyed. Up comes the second Russian and he's bashed into submission by Cuba's lightweight Mario Kindelán. Humiliation looms for Moscow. Two years ago, at the last worlds in Budapest, the Russians shared the top of the medals table with Cuba, taking four titles each. In the next contest their man Timur Gaidalov, seeking the welterweight title, is their last hope of a gold. A faint hope too, looking at his rival, the prodigious Juan Hernández, a Cuban who took silvers at the last two Olympics, three world championships and two golds at the Pan-American Games. He is formidable.

Hernández scores at will with right jabs and big left hands to the body for three rounds. The Russian rallies briefly in the fourth and final round but the six-foot-two southpaw demolishes him. It's all over and the jury of AIBA executive members who have been watching their monitor screen know the result immediately. They don't look at all agitated and why should they? There can't be any doubt who won. That jury is made up of Ugandan IOC member Francis Nyangweso, Mexico's Ricardo Contreras, Australia's Arthur Tunstall OBE and Chowdhry's long-time friend from Singapore, Kriskrishnapillai Thiruganasothi, all under Emil Jetchev's leadership.

These men have watched the fight from their ringside table and utter not a word of disagreement with the judges' scores. Up on the podium Chowdhry and Baker, Gary Toney and Caner Doganeli, with the very best view and their own monitor, are content with the result. The referee hears the compère's voice booming the scores through the loudspeakers and lifts the victor's hand.

The rage begins at the ringside, Cuban officials gesticulating, shouting and soon their anger is echoed in dozens of languages by furious male voices, all the way up into the darkest, furthest seats. Hungarians in green and red shiny tracksuits, Italians in blue, the French, everybody, even Americans, are jeering, slow hand-clapping, bellowing, 'Cuba! Cuba! Cuba!' and their own expletives. Whatever the words, the sounds scream: cheat, fix, outrage!

Hernández is dumbfounded. Everybody in the hall has seem him overpower the Russian. The judges have given the gold the other way. Cuban officials shout an order to Hernández, who does as he's told and sits down, dejected, in the ring.

In the pool of light round the ring cops muscle their way in front of Cuban officials protesting to Chowdhry and Baker, huddled on the presidential podium. 'Stay back, sir, don't push sir, I'm warning you, sir.' The minutes pass, Hernández sprawls in the ring until Chowdhry assures the Cubans that the gold medal will not be awarded to Gaidalov until the jury has reviewed the Cuban protest. They scratch around, find the $100 protest fee and retire to the back of the hall. We're told they're speaking direct to Fidel, by phone, in Havana.

The Venezuelan judge gave it to Hernández, so did the Argentine. The Russian from Estonia and the Bulgarian gave it to Gaidalov. The fifth judge was Mongolia's Batbileg. In his opinion the Russian was a mighty slugger, smashing home fourteen scoring blows to the Cuban's puny three. It's Roy Jones all over again. And again boxing's leaders sit back and let it happen.

The last bout of the night: the heavyweight title contest. Defending is Félix Savón, who's won the title at every world championship since 1986. That's six titles and he took golds in Barcelona and Atlanta. He's fought four hundred and two fights and lost only seventeen.

His opponent, Michael Bennett, is a champion on his own

turf. Three times he's taken the heavyweight title in different prisons in Illinois. He's been out of jail for a year after serving seven years of a fifteen-year stretch for armed robbery. He worked hard in the gym and hard on the road to turn his life round. His street-fighting skills and coaching in Olympic-style boxing got him into the US team and now, after only three international bouts, all in the last week, he's about to fight for the world title.

We're half blinded by the bright lights on the gantry above the ring but something's happening in the gloom at the back of the hall. Heads turn; we all stare; there's a group of men standing in the shadows. It's the entire Cuban team and at its head towers the champ, swathed in towels, flanked by his handlers.

Félix Savón, awaiting the call to fight for his seventh world title, should be shadow-boxing, weaving and feinting, but he stands rigid, tall, unmoving, and we're drawn to his eyes, wide and burning from under his blue headguard. Head coach Alcides Sagarra, one of the world's greatest, holds Cuba's red, white and blue flag with single star in both hands and strides off down the aisle, his team in tow. The police block them but Sagarra, Savón and two more slip through and jog towards the ring, singing amid the crowd's din. Savón, traumatised, by-passes his corner, and now we can guess what instruction has come from Havana.

There isn't going to be a title fight. The Cubans won't go along with this sham: they're going home. Savón keeps moving around the ring, neck stiff, head high, he disappears through the black ceiling-to-floor curtains. America's Michael Bennett clambers up into the red corner and waits under the lights. The referee orders him to put in his mouthpiece, the bell is rung. Two minutes tick by, Bennett stands there looking

259

awkward, Savón's a no-show and Bennett is declared world champion by a walkover.

'We were assured by Mr Chowdhry that other problems would not occur,' said a grim-faced Raúl Villanueva at Cuba's press conference after the walk-out. 'Our boxers have been unfairly deprived of victory, therefore we will withdraw from the tournament immediately.' Next to Villaneuva is Félix Savón's mentor, heavyweight Teófilo Stevenson who notched up three Olympic golds in his career and rejected millions of dollars to turn pro. Next to Stevenson, who has had his hand pumped hundreds of times by strangers over the last few days, is Loring Baker, impassive as ever. Baker looks on as Villanueva spits: 'Nothing that AIBA does now will be able to clean the dirt that has been thrown on this tournament by the judges and the referees.'

The Cubans wanted a decision on the Hernández–Gaidalov fight before Savón climbed into the ring, he says. Chowdhry denied them, and that's why they're going home. They leave the convention centre and Baker takes over. The reporters are angry; the robbery was shameless, yet all Baker can say is 'Ah don't know' and 'Ah can't comment on that.' He tells us that he cannot prejudge the appeal jury's decision because he will be a member of it. We must come back tomorrow. Bored by the stonewalling I leave the press conference. Outside I bump into the television producer from the ESPN sports channel who will be transmitting highlights later. 'When do you think we'll get a verdict on Hernández?' I ask him. 'Don't you know?' he says. 'They already changed the verdict and gave him the fight.' Shame they didn't tell Loring.

'People just don't understand the sacrifices I make to make the weight,' Juan Hernández told reporters as he packed to go home. 'After all that hard work, then this happens.' I went looking for President Chowdhry. I knocked on the door of his suite and was dismissed by his son-in-law who told me, 'The president is not available to the press. He has gone to a party.'

I caught up with him at lunch next day and asked if he would be meeting with the press to talk about the previous night. Chowdhry looked at me as if I were demented. The very thought of it, talking to reporters, on the record, about corruption in his sport! He went back to eating.

Loring Baker assured us: 'Mr Chowdhry and I were enraged when we looked at the scores. The decision obviously was a bad one, and we've done what we could as swiftly as possible.' The three judges, from Bulgaria, Estonia and Mongolia, who made Gaidalov the winner were suspended. They might be out of the sport from four years to life, according to the new rule which Baker had boasted of earlier in the week and which had failed to prevent the worst boxing scandal since Seoul.

To keep them company, out of the door went the Argentine judge who had voted for Hernández. Apparently he had been too generous to the Cuban! Here was a signal to other judges who might register punches for Cuban fighters. Loring never did get to explain why he and the leadership could see nothing wrong with the verdict until the Cubans protested. Reporters gave up asking questions of a man who could only repeat, 'Ah don't know'.

Then came the hit. Cuban coach Alcides Sagarra and another Cuban official had been suspended from international sport. Why? Oh, said Baker, smugly, had we forgotten the other new rule they'd created, just before the championships? The AIBA 'would tolerate no public displays on the field of play, and violators would be dealt with severely'.

In my mind, that closed the circle. I'd been tipped off a

couple of months earlier that the Cubans would be shafted in Houston, that a conspiracy was being plotted. What a great game, to drive the Cubans mad with crooked decisions then punish their officials for reacting!

The IOC's sports director, Gilbert Felli, turned up in Houston for the second night of the finals, representing the self-styled moral leadership of world sport, and sat on the podium with Professor Chowdhry. After America's Ricardo Juarez won the featherweight title the evening degenerated into more of the previous night.

French light welterweight Willy Blain looked to have dominated his bout against the Uzbek Abdullayev – but he lost the decision. French fans booed, hissed and waved their arms but held back their rage; no-one wanted to make problems in the light heavyweight final for their John Dovi against America's Michael Simms.

The final score was a 3–3 draw, the decision going to Simms for landing more blows. That was enough for the French, who felt they'd suffered one robbery and then a close decision. They marched round the ring shouting 'Mafia' at each judge. The cops rushed in. Simms said: 'In some ways I knew it was close because we did so much toe-to-toe fighting. He was tough and pretty smart, but the officials saw it my way.'

Oh what a sweet night it was, to be savoured by Loring Baker and Gary Toney. Their new global strategy had triumphed! America had four gold medals! Four world champions! Winners of the team title – The Best Boxing Team in The World! Twice as many golds as the Cubans! Turning the knife in Cuba's wound, AIBA announced on its internet site, 'Veteran observers noted that the level of competition at the World Championships was the best ever and suggested

Cuba may be having difficulty accepting the fact that its dominance in the sport is eroding.'

Ten days later Chowdhry's circus pitched up in Johannesburg for the African Games. The African boxing nations hadn't been in Houston but they passed a resolution anyway expressing, 'unreserved confidence in Prof. Anwar Chowdhry'. Thirty-three nations, all the big hitters, from Benin to Guinea, Gabon to Rwanda, condemned 'the unacceptable behaviour of the Cubans'.

The next month, October 1999, the Professor was welcomed again in Uzbekistan. His friends hosted another event and had another bauble for him – now he was an honorary citizen of the city of Gulistan! Uzbek fighters won the light flyweight, bantamweight, featherweight, light welterweight, light heavyweight, heavyweight and super heavyweight titles.

This boxing tournament, like Johannesburg's, ended on an uplifting, moral note, condemning the Cubans for having the audacity to complain to Samaranch about, 'injustice and corruption at the highest levels of the AIBA'.

'Asia, with disgust, condemns the malicious remarks by some Cuban officials about Prof. Anwar Chowdhry', announced the Asian Boxing Federation, 'as the most childish, irresponsible and personal attack against the President who was unanimously elected by a vast majority of countries. We in Asia cannot and will not condone such irresponsible behaviour as it defeats the whole purpose of sportsmanship, thus bringing disrepute to our sport.'

'I also worry about problems of bribery and agreed fights,' Gafur Rakhimov told me in a fax sent from Tashkent before the Houston world championships. 'And the problem of [the] possibility of removing boxing from the Olympics takes my heart and all my free time.'

True fight fans may be alarmed and saddened to learn that Mr Rakhimov and other alleged Mafia from the East have become serious players inside the Olympic Games. Chowdhry shrewdly gambled that he could get away with cheating his athletes in Seoul – and Samaranch stood back and let it happen. When my disclosures forced the IOC to investigate the Jones scandal, Judge Mbaye and François Carrard, with the entire executive board's support, buried it again. All the signals from the IOC have been, before and during their own corruption scandal, that crooks and spivs inside and outside the organisation can get away with anything, so long as the public don't find out and make a fuss.

The Americans – Loring Baker and Gary Toney and the US Olympic Committee – could have taken Chowdhry on. They could have joined the Western European nations, and the good guys in other continents, pressured IOC members, worked to expose corruption in boxing. They could have saved their sport from Olympic oblivion. Instead Baker and Toney tolerated the company of corruption and sleaze and allied the name of American sport with alleged heroin-traffickers and sports officials who trade medals for bribes.

The Professor and his friend Emil Jetchev selected the officials for the Sydney Olympics. Jetchev would chair the same jury that found no fault with the Hernández defeat in Houston, and judges and referees would likely come under even more pressure. Gafur Rakhimov told me that Ruslan Chagayev 'will bring glory to Uzbek amateur boxing in future', which sounded like gold in Sydney.

One of the stunning achievements of Muhammad Ali was to loosen the Mob's grip on professional boxing. Smart and independent, Ali never fell under Mob control, and when he beat Sonny Liston he beat the gangster, Frankie Carbo, who controlled him. There's a new Mob coming from the East. They're brutal, rich, criminal, and determined to acquire gold medals for their boxers and relaunch them as pros. The Mob is making a comeback.

Chapter 17

Tantrums and Tussles

March 1999, and it was springtime for Samaranch! Armed with his vote of confidence from the membership, and back in the driving seat, he felt his standing in the world rise again. He sent Anita to take the flak for him in April at McCain's Senate hearings and concentrated on associating himself with success. He had work to do, changing his shirt yet again, casting off the autocrat's and putting on the spruce, bright shirt of reform. Enter Juan the Reformer! Leading the Olympics into a New Era!

Inside the Lausanne bunker, of course, nothing had changed for Samaranch and his retinue. They'd listened to Dick Pound banging on about how sponsors would quit if they didn't vote for reform. They'd voted, under duress. They'd expelled dear old friends like Agustín Arroyo, and they didn't like that one bit. They recoiled from those thrusting young men in big suits who strode around bragging about 'strategizing' and 'working synergistically' and presuming the right to determine who should speak for the Olympic family. Who were these Hill and Knowlton people claiming they knew how to communicate Olympism? What did they know about it?

For nearly two decades, there'd been one voice, one opinion at the IOC and it was the voice of Juan Antonio Samaranch. For the first time, in recent months, he'd felt his authority, his methods, his loyal retinue under serious threat. Long years of survival had taught him what to do about that. Wait. Watch the enemy. Wait a little longer. Then strike back.

Director-general François Carrard was the man who'd signed that first contract with Hill and Knowlton. He knew there was trouble coming, so donned sackcloth and ashes for the June executive board meeting in Seoul. He owned up that he alone had made the decision to employ them, and 'due to the urgency of the situation', he had informed the president and Kevan Gosper, chair of the press commission, after the event. They had done good work, he said: 'The initial target had been to change the media's perception from "very bad" to "neutral", which had already been achieved.' He went on: 'They did not expect the media's attitude to be "good" yet', and thought this would be 'difficult to achieve' before the IOC's reform commission did something tangible.

Samaranch had waited just long enough. He made his strike. No-one who witnessed it would ever forget the presidential tantrum. The minutes are embargoed for ten years, but we have them and they tell the story. 'The issue was not whether Hill and Knowlton were doing a good job,' Samaranch snapped. 'He was furious that he had not been consulted about signing a contract worth $1.5 to $2m. He hoped that this would never happen again. Initially he had been told that one of the vice-presidents had approved the decision, which he could have accepted since urgency was of the essence. However the vice-president in question had denied having any knowledge of the contract which made him take a very serious view of the matter.'

For Dr Kim it was nice to see someone else in trouble for a change. And how delightful that it was that goody-goody François Carrard who had driven him mad with rage at the session back in March and very nearly experienced a kick in the teeth from the president of international taekwondo. Dr Kim 'wished to know for how long the contract had been signed'. He was poking a stick into a wasps' nest. Samaranch ranted again. 'Hill and Knowlton had already cost the IOC $1.5 million to $1.6 million' and, what's more, 'he had made it clear to the head of the firm that the contract would not be extended beyond the end of the year'.

Carrard tried to placate the president. He was 'willing to take the blame for signing the contract, but repeated there was absolutely no commitment beyond the 30 days' notice which could be served on Hill and Knowlton at any time'. Samaranch was not remotely placated by that. He 'could not accept that such a contract had been signed without his being consulted. He had been in his office in Lausanne every day.'

Old men piled in to back him. Judge Mbaye, who had previously owned up to ignorance about the world of communications, 'had his doubts about the usefulness of Hill and Knowlton', the minutes record. 'What were they doing exactly? Were they really effective? Did he really need to be told how to deal with journalists? After all he had become used to talking to the press over the past 50 years. In fact, he was dumbfounded by the whole business. As far as he was concerned, they were signing contracts for vast amounts of money for nothing.' Marc Hodler agreed with Judge Mbaye that the company, 'were not doing anything useful'.

Dick Pound could see all his careful work slipping away. They still didn't get it! With the combined weight of Samaranch, Mbaye, Kim and Hodler against him, he had to measure his words carefully. He 'did not want to sound like an apologist for Hill and Knowlton, but he believed the decision to hire the firm had been the right one. He thought that the

IOC would not have survived the media firestorm without the assistance of Hill and Knowlton. They had organised a good response, made contact with the media, and he believed that they had got the best possible support from a very good organisation. He would have made the same decision as the director-general.'

Plucking up courage, Gosper agreed that, 'they had done a good job of coping with what was a world-wide press operation'. Their strategy, he tried to explain to the numbskulls, had been to get IOC spokesmen to talk to the press and demonstrate that they were in control of the situation.

Pál Schmitt, a member not on Hill and Knowlton's list of approved spokesmen, complained: 'As first vice-president he had never received any advice or support from Hill and Knowlton about media relations. He had some serious doubts about the effectiveness of the firm.'

Mbaye 'wanted to know exactly what Hill and Knowlton had done. He had not noticed anything. He genuinely believed that it was now time to stop throwing money away and was sure that the $2 million already wasted as far as he was concerned could have been better spent.'

Since he'd started working alongside Hill and Knowlton, Franklin Servan-Schreiber's confidence and prospects had soared and he couldn't resist showing how much he had learned in the two whole months since they made him director of communications. 'Press coverage was now generally positive,' Franklin asserted. He 'felt this was to a large extent due to the involvement of Hill and Knowlton'.

Samaranch brushed him aside like a flea. The president 'did not agree that press coverage was positive. There were some positive pieces but there were still many negative articles being written about the IOC. He had read in the previous day's press that Senator Mitchell recommended the USOC should, "take two aspirin and go to bed", and that the IOC "should have brain surgery".' Samaranch had made his point; the younger members and Hill and Knowlton had better not forget it. He was in charge, and, however much they all might talk about democracy and reform, Samaranch remained the supreme power.

Juan Antonio genuinely didn't understand how the sweet press he had so long enjoyed could have turned sour. Why didn't these people do as they were told? Hill and Knowlton understood and were busy altering states of mind with their proven techniques of planting positive stories, flattering helpful reporters, trying to convert the critical and badmouthing those who resisted persuasion.

The *Wall Street Journal* was behaving as if readers needed to know the truth about the IOC. It's the business paper, the sponsors' paper and there it was, month after month, running entertaining and increasingly hostile Olympic stories. It even ran a positive front-page profile of me, the man Samaranch once tried to have jailed. Researching that piece writer Craig Copetas underwent a revelation and he told my co-author Clare Sambrook about it. Craig's a veteran reporter, handsome and wily, who brings wit and passion to his work.

'When I went to London to meet Andrew Jennings at home I arrived half an hour early to see him looking goofy,' he admitted. 'I thought, this guy is kind of clownish, maybe the IOC is right about him. Then I saw that he is this incredibly professional archivist and I thought, well, maybe he is a little bit gonzo, but that's what you have to do to sell books.' Copetas still couldn't work out why I seemed gripped by the story. Then he called IOC member Alex Gilady of NBC Sport, 'a big cheese, a global executive, someone a *Wall Street Journal* reporter would go to as a solid source of commentary.' Gilady told Copetas: 'Jennings had an uncle who lost his life in the Spanish civil war. That's why he goes after Samaranch.' Everything fell into place for Copetas. 'I went, Oh, that's the reason Jennings is doing this. It's this personal vendetta because a member of his family was killed. I got back to Paris, called him up and, in my best *Wall Street Journal* voice, I put it to him. Andrew howled with laughter, and said, "My uncle was an accountant – the only border he ever crossed was into Wales." I went back to Gilady, said, "What you told me wasn't true," and he smiled.'

'That's when I knew the IOC was capable of more than obfuscation,' Copetas said. 'One had to wonder how many powerful individuals Gilady and others had said that to over the years. In my opinion what Gilady said about Andrew is hard evidence of a campaign of disinformation.'

Not long after Craig's story about me appeared in his paper, strange things started happening to him. In February he took curious calls at the office from men with no names telling him: 'Lay off the IOC,' and 'Why are you looking at Samaranch? You should be looking at Kim.' Then, one day at his Paris apartment, 'my wife took a call at home. They said to her, "Lay off Samaranch," and hung up.'

Nursing a bout of flu in March, Craig travelled to Lausanne to write about IOC members expelling the Greedy Six. He booked in at the usual Olympic press hotel, the Continental. 'One night at 2 a.m. there was a pounding on my door,' he said. 'Three or four drunk Africans screamed at me in French, saying I was responsible for Ganga being removed from the IOC.' Eventually they left. The following night, 'I got back to find my hotel room had been broken into and rifled.'

Curious about Samaranch's fascist past, Craig and his colleague Roger Thurow travelled to Barcelona to meet historians of Franco's regime and find relatives of Salvador Puig Antich, the young man executed after a trial in one of Franco's kangaroo courts. By early December, days before Samaranch was due to testify before Congress, their front-page story was ready to run. It wasn't helpful. Hill and Knowlton had been busily 'positioning' Samaranch as Juan the Reformer, and here was the newspaper that sponsors respect devoting thousands of words to a story about judicial murder and Juan the Fascist, and drizzling scorn on his late conversion to reform. The headline: 'IOC Scandal Has A Familiar Ring For Mr Samaranch: Olympic Imbroglio Reflects President's Francoist Past'.

CyberMan had come a long way since those horrible first days in the press office when the lynch mob harangued him down the phone and made him feel something less than adequate. He'd been a diligent apprentice to Hill and Knowlton's wizard press adviser Michael Kontos. Come April, Franklin Servan-Schreiber got a promotion and could type the words 'Director of Communications' at the top of his increasingly preposterous letters to the press.

'We regard with curiosity your two articles dated 30 September and 5 October about the IOC's anti-doping policy,' Franklin told *Suddeutsche Zeitung*'s Thomas Kistner, one of Germany's most highly regarded sports writers. Then, he reeled off a list of Positive Facts, 'that can be added to at your convenience'. Perhaps CyberMan had learned his communications skills during a long stint in short trousers as a school prefect. 'I think it would be fair that you take these facts into consideration and put them into perspective,' he sniffed.

'The same applies to your repeated polemical judgments about various IOC members.'

Kistner told me what happened next. 'Before long, Franklin was on the line, demanding to speak to the sports editor. When eventually he got through, he started firing off questions about me. Was I a freelance? Did I just write comments? Franklin wanted the *Suddeutsche* to know that he was not at all happy with my work. "Well, why don't you just speak to Kistner?" said the sports editor. "No, no, I want to speak to you," Franklin replied. "Can we meet?" "The only way is if you come to Munich," said my boss, "but Kistner will be at the meeting." "Can't you come to Lausanne?" Franklin said. "Will you come for the reform meeting?" "No, that will be covered by Kistner." That was it. He found there was no way to attack me through my chief.'

Franklin spotted someone else who wasn't playing the IOC's game. Natasha Bita is an Australian reporter with a posting that sounds too good to be true. From her base in Florence she covers the IOC for Rupert Murdoch's News Limited papers in Australia. Franklin noticed that Natasha wasn't helping. She asked some questions about Samaranch's fascist past and despite being given the usual reassurances she wrote a story about it. She covered a meeting of the IOC's reform commission and failed to grasp the story as Franklin perceived it: how fantastically the reform effort was coming along. He fired off a letter to her boss.

'I was deeply disappointed by the coverage of the IOC 2000 meeting by Natasha Bita,' he complained. 'The only two stories she apparently filed were the tickets and a really far-fetched story on the Ethics Commission and Phil Coles. That last piece was stretched so thin that it was disgraceful. I thought you had given the word to your staff that the Olympics, and

especially the IOC, should not be treated as a circus. There are
enough stories out there to entice the public without having to
make new ones out of thin air,' he whined, libelling the
reporter with each new sentence yet failing to point out any
errors in her stories.

'In the past I have given to Natasha wide access to the IOC
upper echelon, including the exclusive interview that the
President granted her last September,' he pontificated. 'I can
tell you again that I feel terribly disappointed that this open-
ness has been repaid with carelessness.' Delighted with his
work, he copied it to Hill and Knowlton's Michael Kontos, to
show what a very fast learner he was.

A Murdoch executive wrote back. He was 'disturbed at the
tone' of Franklin's missive and dryly informed CyberMan that
'the interests of public relations and journalism don't always
coincide'. Franklin's tacit suggestion that access to the IOC
upper echelon was conditional on writing stories the way he
wanted them written did not go down well. The executive
added that he admired Bita's professionalism and her stories.

We wanted to talk to Hill and Knowlton about their work for
the IOC. Surely, they'd be delighted to talk about what they
were doing. My colleague Clare e-mailed their Olympic man
in London, Theo Chapman, asking if she might drop by his
office for a chat. Theo, a languid floppy-haired young fellow,
was more helpful than he intended, inadvertently sending her
some of the internal correspondence about her inquiry. He
suggested she talk to 'Ron Harwigh' in California, who turned
out to be Ron Hartwig, a man so candid that the minute Theo
alerted him to Clare's interest, he fired off a message to Dick
Hyde, the big boss, a veteran of influence wars Bhopal and
Three Mile Island. Ron squeaked, 'I need your help here if I'm

contacted by the reporter.' Clare contacted Ron. He didn't reply.

Later in the year, when Samaranch was due to testify on Capitol Hill, Clare tried Gary Hymel in Hill and Knowlton's Washington office. Perhaps he could find some time to meet her after Samaranch's appearance? Sure, said Gary's secretary, Laurel, he'd have lots of free time in the two days after the hearings. Just call before you leave London. Clare called; evidently Gary hadn't caught on that she was working with me; and then he got it. 'I don't know my schedule, and I would suggest you give me a call when you get in, how about that?' he said. She did, again, and again, and again. Eventually a gruff Gary Hymel came on the line and said, 'We don't talk about what we do for clients – it's up to the client to talk about what we do.'

Chapter 18

A Rebel in the Family

Closing time at the Shopper's Drug Mart and Donna Tewksbury cashed up in a hurry. She drove to the family's four-bedroom bungalow, prepared the evening meal, changed her clothes, got back in the car, and drove out to Calgary's Stampede racetrack to count money until late. Back home by eleven, she had one last chore before bedtime. 'My mum used to make seven sandwiches at night,' recalls her son Mark, a teenager then, 'one for my brother Scott, one for my sister Colleen and five for me.'

Donna was up again at dawn, packing eight muffins in a brown paper bag for Mark's mid-morning snack. Husband Roger woke the boy, wrapped himself up against the sub-zero chill, warmed up the family's Chevy Chevette, scraped ice from its windscreen, and prepared to drive Mark across the city to his first swim of the day.

'My mum worked two jobs to put me through swimming,' Mark told me. 'Financially it was difficult, always a juggle. My brother and sister had to put up with us billeting athletes from various cities. There was of course a huge impact on the family.' As Mark's talent grew, the family budget stretched to cover airfares for competitions across Canada. Roger and Donna didn't mind the sacrifices. 'My parents were thrilled that I found something that I wanted to be a part of within the amateur sport world,' Mark explained. 'Our family came out of an environment that believed sport was important to the development of youth. When I was eight the Montreal games came on television. Our entire family sat down to watch the opening ceremonies. From that moment on, I was hooked.'

On the other side of the television screen, another boy who'd caught the Olympic dream young was all grown up and powering his way through the water to win four golds and one silver in Montreal. 'He seemed so relaxed and smiling and enjoying himself,' said Mark. He was the American legend John Naber, and four Olympics later Naber watched Mark Tewksbury beat the world in the 100 metres backstroke to take gold in Barcelona.

Mark lived his Olympic dream to the full. In his twenties, with his gold medal behind him, he had a comfortable home in Toronto, enjoyed national celebrity, built a nice living in motivational speaking and put his name and good looks to work in his own line of branded menswear, which sold across Canada. The Olympic family loved him and groomed him for IOC membership, sending him around the world with a special commission assessing sites for the 2004 games. Mark had a taste of the IOC lifestyle: gifts, flattery and privilege came his way wherever he went.

St Petersburg was the first stop. Mark had been there many times as an athlete and recalled tough living conditions, poor diet, real hospitality and comradeship. 'Part of the beauty and charm of that world cup circuit was that you got to experience cultures and live how the people of that country lived,' he told us. Visiting St Petersburg IOC-style was an entirely different experience. 'We stayed at the most luxurious hotel that I had ever stayed at in my life. I had two bathrooms and a sitting room and this glorious big bedroom and I thought, "Oh my gosh!" We had a private tour of the Hermitage, a private tour of the Summer Palace, going behind the scenes, walking where the tsars had walked. I remember coming out of this room and running into the hallway and expecting all the people to be out there going, "Wow! Look at the room!" and I was the only one. Every night in St Petersburg I would come back to the hotel and there would be fresh caviar and a bottle of vodka and champagne and fresh cut flowers and caviar to take home, and books on the Hermitage and CD Roms, and just endless things arriving.

'What was so remarkable was how quickly you become a part of that because it's really difficult to fight it, you know, it was amazing. By the third or fourth city I came to expect that. If there weren't fresh cut flowers in my room or there wasn't a gift in the evening I guess I thought subconsciously, "Gee, are these people really serious?" It doesn't take long and I'm not proud to say I certainly became a part of it.'

As the only athlete on the IOC commission he enjoyed special attention. 'I was always positioned as being the most important person,' he said, 'I would hear it every city we'd go to.' But it didn't escape his notice that every other member was responsible for a specific category – accommodation, marketing, finance, whatever. 'I didn't have any one of them and everyone else did.' Athens won the games for 2004 and Mark was left wondering if he'd spent three months of his life touring cities for nothing. 'I felt the result was predetermined . . . you can't help but see enormous politics. Then all of this scandal broke and we really had a chance finally to come clean and say, "You know what, we're all a part of this, maybe we need to re-evaluate and honestly look at what's important here."' Mark waited for someone bigger than him in the Olympic family to make a move. He waited, and he waited.

*

Anita DeFrantz earned a reputation for speaking out when she was a young rower. Her eight-woman crew had to make do with bronze in Montreal in 1976 and she ploughed her disappointment into passion for gold next time. A few thousand painful training sessions later, fit and ready with only months to go before vengeance in Moscow, Anita was furious to learn that President Jimmy Carter had ordered American athletes to boycott the games in protest at Russia's invasion of Afghanistan. 'What do you think of the fact that we are boycotting?' a *Sports Illustrated* reporter asked. 'What do you mean *we*?' Anita snapped. 'Where were *we* when I was on the lake in the winter freezing my butt off?' A lawyer, she fought the boycott, sued the government, lost the suit and with it her last chance of gold. But the fight transformed her life. Samaranch gave her a bronze Olympic Order, Anita was offered a place on the Los Angeles Games organising team and moved to LA and a starring role on the international sporting stage.

By the age of thirty-four she could afford to feel sanguine about being robbed of that gold. Who in the world can recall the names of winning eights? Anita, in 1986, was appointed to the IOC, the first black woman in its history, tipped to be its first woman president, a member of the world's most exclusive club with all its privileges until she turned eighty. People would remember her name.

She was building power and influence in her adopted home state too. She'd been made president of the Amateur Athletics Foundation, a charity that had $95 million of the Los Angeles games surplus to spend on encouraging kids to play sports. Her dream job gave her a swiftly rising salary package that leaped to $230,000 by 1998. Her contract says she's paid to work a forty-hour week. She also flies around the world to do the IOC's business on several busy committees. The charity lives in one of LA's finest buildings, Britt House, designed in the Colonial Revival style and known for its grand white portico with vaunting fluted columns. Walk around and enjoy the Italian marble, imperial porcelain and Flemish oak woodwork – it's an impressive HQ, with a fine sports memorabilia collection and splendid research facilities. Anita's charity gives grants and runs programmes to help youngsters experience what she calls, 'the magic of sport'. She and her board have managed to grow the assets from an initial $95 million to $187 million in 1998.

On the charity's board, among others, are three former athletes, one oil company chairman on $2 million a year, one sticky-labels magnate on $1.7 million a year, a Walt Disney executive and an on-line-sports-retailer president. There's one movie producer (credits include LA games opening and closing ceremonies) and another movie producer (credits include *Congo* – killer apes run rampant in diamond mine). Plus the aluminium multimillionaire Jim Easton.

We left Mark Tewksbury waiting for someone in the Olympic family to speak out against the caviar culture. It wasn't going to be Anita. 'You can only boil a frog if you put him in cold water and you turn up the heat,' John Naber replied when I asked him why he thought Anita did not speak out. These days John is president of the United States Olympians – all the athletes who have made the Olympic team; he earns his living as a public speaker and spends his free time working for drug-free sport and dreaming up metaphors. 'If you toss the frog in hot water he realises it's hot and he jumps out,' John explained. 'If someone has a lifetime appointment they sit in cold water at first and they are not aware of the subtle changes in temperature, whether it be ethics or protocol or whatever that gradually take place. So, Anita DeFrantz wanted to join an IOC that wouldn't have scandalous behaviour but once she's in there she's not as keenly aware of its effects as those of us on the outside.'

Mark Tewksbury was one frog who felt the heat. Two months into the crisis, still no senior Olympian had called for serious change. 'Personally, if I wanted to be able to look myself in the eye it was time for me to speak out,' he said. Mark resigned all his Olympic posts, on the Canadian Olympic Association, the international swimming federation and Toronto's team bidding for the 2008 games, throwing away any hopes he had of becoming an IOC member one day.

'This was an extremely difficult thing to do because I wanted to serve on the IOC,' he said. 'I knew I didn't like the culture but as an Olympian and someone who is a very big idealist, of course I wanted to keep serving the Olympics.'

One day in late February 1999 he was due to have lunch with a business contact Keith Stein, bushy-haired communications director of Magna, an international auto-parts group. 'I'd been thinking about Mark's stand,' Stein told me. 'I don't like bullies and people who abuse other people. I admire what athletes do. And for their achievements to be tainted by a bunch of old guys in Europe, I found that upsetting. Generally I don't like bullies and I don't like corruption.'

Over a plate of risotto in Mark's neighbourhood Italian restaurant, Keith made a proposition. 'Why don't we create an organisation so all these voices out there in the world can come together?' Magna came up with the funding and Tewksbury hit the phone. Ann Peel, international race-walker and a long-time activist, the rower Heather Clarke, gold medal Paralympian André Viger, Susan Auch, speedskating silver medallist, and Mark's business partner Jacques Legris came together. 'The core of us just hammered this thing through,' says Mark. Eighteen days after the risotto went down, OATH – Olympic Advocates Together Honorably – hauled up its standard in Lausanne. Mark and his team gate-crashed the IOC's reform and expulsions party, and the press, who'd been writing non-stop for months about sleazy old men, were glad to have some athletes and idealism to lighten the mix.

'As a public, we have expected the IOC to be guardians of the Olympic spirit,' Ann Peel told the press. 'And they have protected it well from external threats, such as war and terrorism. But today the threat comes from within. The closed nature of the IOC and its lack of accountability have undermined the Olympic spirit, and that can not continue. As athletes and the keepers of the spirit, we are here to reclaim it, for the public to whom it belongs.'

'Congratulations on your belly flop,' an acerbic Dick Pound told Keith Stein later that day in the Palace Hotel bar. Back in his hotel room, Stein had a late night, anonymous call, 'something to the effect of, "Don't come back to Europe, don't come back to Switzerland," it was a male voice.' Next morning, after breakfast, Mark Tewksbury and his partner returned to their room to find another surprise, and it wasn't champagne, vodka or caviar this time. 'All of our video footage since leaving Toronto was stolen, press conferences, behind-the-scenes meetings, everything,' Mark said. 'Not the camera, just the footage. Nothing else was touched, no passports, no airline tickets, no cameras were taken, just the film and the computer disks – all of our information. Then we wanted to get out of there. We felt, we're up against a pretty big force here.'

Mark says he reported the break-in to the hotel, but not to the police, nor the press: 'We didn't want the story to get out because we didn't want athletes to be afraid to join us.' The story leaked anyway and Dick Pound remarked, 'I'm surprised that anyone would take the time to do this to such a marginal group.'

Bright and early one June morning in 1999, Australia's Dawn Fraser led the running pack out into Central Park, New York. Two hundred schoolchildren of all shapes and sizes, taut, lean athletes and Michelin kids, happy and laughing, ran after her. Among them you could spot the long limbs, toned muscle and familiar faces of some of the world's finest athletes.

Dawn Fraser was easy to identify: sixty-two years old, white-haired, laughing and wielding a torch. Dawn is the first woman to have swum the 100 metres freestyle in under a minute. She won gold in three games, rubbing up against humourless sports officials all the way: she celebrated her third 100 metres gold in Tokyo with a midnight raid on the Emperor's Palace to steal a souvenir flag. Australians loved her and voted her into the New South Wales parliament as an independent in 1990.

It wasn't just the kids who were awe-struck. 'One of my favourite moments was running behind Zola Budd,' said Mark Tewksbury. 'I was just going Wow! And then on one side was speedskater Johan Olav Koss and on the other side was Pete Carruthers the figure skater and Franz Weber the downhill skier. It was just extraordinary.' Tewksbury couldn't resist surging ahead of Budd. 'She said, "Let's do three more laps."'

Carla Qualtrough, blind runner, kept a nice, easy pace, André Viger whizzed by in his wheelchair, Britain's swimmer, Sharron Davies was there too, and long-jumper Lynn 'the Leap' Davies, all running among kids enjoying a side of the Olympic family that's not part of the official presentation. There was nothing pompous about it. Everyone had fun, it was a laugh.

Then the athletes and fellow thinking academics got down to work on OATH's first international symposium, and the serious business of trying to bring some fairness and joy back into the Olympics. For all the IOC's attempts to diminish them as a bunch of self-seeking Canadian marginals, OATH had managed to draw together at short notice in New York delegates from Germany, Ireland, Austria, the Netherlands, Jamaica, Australia, Zimbabwe, South Africa and China, thirty-six Olympians, twenty-three Olympic medallists, and a special guest, Senator George Mitchell, who came to wish them well.

I should declare an interest. They flew me to New York and gave me a medal for 'integrity in reporting'. I shared the stage with one of my heroes, Dawn Fraser, who got hers for embodying the 'spirit of sport'.

'We all came together to recognise that there is a crisis in the Olympic values . . . the IOC have strayed from their own values,' Ann Peel told the press, summing up the weekend. They'd agreed that the world's sports governing bodies needed a counterbalance and OATH should be it. They had a vision, 'that sport is ethical, and contributes to the peaceful fulfilment of human potential', and their mission was to restore the Olympic spirit, 'promote ethical guardianship, responsible governance and effective management of the Olympic Movement'.

Willie Banks, three times Olympic triple-jumper, welcomed, 'a tremendous working opportunity for all of us . . . and I hope and pray that this will continue to go forward.' 'We don't want a piece of the pie,' said John Naber. 'We just want to make sure that the pie tastes as good as the recipe intends it to.' Grace Jackson, the 200 metres runner who won silver for Jamaica, said it was nice, for a change, that smaller countries had a voice. 'We are very rarely heard in forums such as these. Sometimes we get lost in a sea of big fishes.' She had hopes for the athletes' commission, which, as it stood, had a chairman hand-picked by Samaranch and no voice on the executive board. It needed to 'open up opportunities for teaching our athletes to be leaders, to be on the governing bodies of sports', said Grace. As revolutions go, OATH's was pretty tame – bloodless, cheerful and intent on *not* seizing power. What could the IOC have to fear?

Whatever it was, when Mark Tewksbury and Dawn Fraser flew to Seoul to visit IOC members at their session, 'we hit a brick wall,' Mark recalls. 'They kept marginalising us and saying just meet with the athletes' commission, just meet with the athletes' commission.' By the time Canada's Charmaine Crooks called up to say that she and a few others from the commission could spare OATH half an hour, a jetlagged Dawn Fraser was sleeping like a baby. Mark set off across Seoul for the IOC's hotel, the Shilla.

He met in the bar with Crooks, a silver medal 400 metres runner, German rower Roland Baar, and Bob Ctvrtlik (pronounced Tssvertlik), the US volleyball star. 'It was a very, very antagonistic meeting, they just couldn't understand why OATH was around, what we were doing, it was as if they're doing everything that needs to be done,' said Mark. Before long an IOC official broke it up. 'She came in and said, "Charmaine and Robert, the president is waiting," because

Samaranch I guess was starting the athletes' commission meeting. And I had never seen two people run so fast. They ran so fast they forgot to pay the bill. The bar guy went chasing after them. It made me realise the complete and absolute power Samaranch has over these athletes and that while they're sitting here saying they don't understand the need for an athletes' organisation, their actions spoke volumes. It gave me a shiver down the spine.'

Some friends of the Olympic Movement did what they could to undermine OATH and Tewksbury. Reporters profiling him said their editors received calls. 'He's a faggot,' said the friends. That might work as a slur among bigots and fools, but it was hardly hot intelligence. Tewksbury is openly gay and received good reviews for his one-man stage show, *Out and About*.

Anita must have felt like a boiled frog by the time Samaranch sent her out flak catching again, this time before Congressman Upton in October 1999.

'Were you ever in a position where you saw cities come to you and offer gifts that exceeded the $200 gift rule?' Upton asked her.

'Mr Chairman, I had a particular approach to this,' Anita replied. 'I believed that my responsibility was to find from every bid city what they were going to provide for the athletes, so I always ask for technical information. Gifts were of no interest to me. I paid no attention to them and indeed I usually left them in the room if they came to me.'

'Yes or no?' said Upton, 'Were you offered gifts that exceeded $200?'

'I don't know,' replied Anita, 'because I didn't accept the gifts.'

Upton persisted. 'You accepted no gifts but the question was were you offered gifts? Were there gifts that were offered to you that you might have turned down that were in excess of $200?'

'Mr Chairman, it is difficult for me to answer,' Anita said. 'If I did not open a box or look at a gift I can't tell whether it was over $200 or not but I can tell you that I do know that the rule was that gifts were OK so long as they were under $200.'

And so it went on.

'She certainly wasn't helpful,' the committee's spokesman, Steve Schmidt, told us. 'She was very careful in answering, she was very artful in answering so the members were frustrated that for all those years she saw no evil and heard no evil.'

Then Upton's people got their hands on an investigative report on the Salt Lake scandal, and spotted one footnote relating to the Big Birthday Party. Members had been laughing about it soon after Anita joined the IOC, and when she asked them to explain, they said that during 1986 as cities vied for the 1992 games they showered IOC members with presents. Anita had told the Salt Lake investigators that much.

'It looked like she may not have told us the whole truth,' Schmidt said. Anita spent three hours with Upton's lawyers. 'She maintained her statements that she knew nothing, that she got in the IOC when she was thirty-four years old, and she was just oblivious to it. She had heard rumours, but she doesn't play in rumours.' The lawyers scoured the transcripts and decided she had no perjury case to answer. 'Her answers were very Clintonian,' said Schmidt. 'It was the Olympic equivalent of it depends what the definition of "is" is.'

Later it came out that Anita had accepted an 18-carat gold necklace, a pendant of Olympic rings inset with garnets on a 16-inch gold chain, from the wife of Japanese IOC member

Chick Igaya. The gift came in Tokyo in 1990 as the Nagano team cranked up their bid. When the gift was revealed in February 2000 CyberMan said: 'Mrs Igaya wanted to do something nice. It was her gift. I don't know who paid for it, but it was clearly a personal gift.'

Personal? You had to be an IOC voter to get one. 'It would stretch it to say it is directly related to the bid,' he said.

Mark Tewksbury and his team had been meeting congressmen and senators through the spring and summer of 1999 – and feeling more despondent each time until Senator John McCain gave them an hour and a half and told them he would reopen his hearings and invite OATH to testify in the autumn about doping.

Swimmer Nancy Hogshead cut short her honeymoon to be there. Nancy had left the Los Angeles games with three golds and a silver, then built a successful legal career. Moments before she testified, an official from the other side strolled over and warned her, 'Whatever you do, don't blow it.'

Nancy Hogshead delivered a steaming attack on the IOC's 'terribly late, inadequate and inconsequential' response to the doping crisis; she unveiled OATH's practical proposals for accountable, transparent and independent testing – and for democracy within the IOC.

Then she made an impassioned appeal: 'to those who watch the games and encourage their children to strive for excellence, those who drive their kids to swimming practice at six every morning. It's a call to those who profit from the games, to sponsors and the media, to care for their investment . . . a call to governments that invest public funds in sport, the games and bids for games and to those who support the Movement through favourable tax arrangements . . . a call to

partners to help the Olympic Movement be the best it can be.'
That's what McCain wanted to hear.

Those OATH people were becoming an embarrassment to
the IOC. Next time they threatened to upstage the client, Hill
and Knowlton would be ready for them.

Chapter 19

A Real Soldier Joins the War on Doping

The general who led the 24th Infantry deep into Iraq, driving Saddam Hussein's army back to barracks, doesn't seem too worried about the belligerent noises coming from the glass and marble bunker in Lausanne. In spring 1991, while Samaranch was grooming himself to accept homage from Nagano and Salt Lake City, General Barry McCaffrey was winning medals in the Euphrates Valley with Desert Storm. He keeps a photograph of himself with his then commander-in-chief, George Bush, on his office wall.

There's a British policeman's hat up on one shelf, a leadership award from the National Association for the Advancement of Colored People, and a ball presented to him by Major League Soccer. Not on display are his two Distinguished Service Crosses, the nation's second highest award for bravery, and three Purple Hearts for combat wounds. He learned his combat in Vietnam – on one occasion, single-handedly, he took out a machine-gun emplacement with a pistol and a couple of grenades – and retired as the youngest and most decorated four-star general in the army. Now Barry McCaffrey has a new title and a new boss. From his window he can see the White House; on one wall, above photos of his wife and grandchildren, is a framed copy of the solemn document appointing him a member of the Clinton cabinet. He's director of National Drug Control Policy: America's drugs czar.

Liberals don't like McCaffrey because he's a hard-liner,

opposed to needle exchanges and the legalisation of marijuana. The Mexican drug cartels like him even less and reportedly have a rocket-propelled grenade with his name on it.

Today the general-turned-director sits immaculate by his desk: he's lean, has economy-styled white hair, and it's hard to look away from his milky-blue eyes. 'I don't think the international community will tolerate the destruction of integrity in the games,' he says. 'They are too precious to us, and there is too much money tied up in them.'

McCaffrey picks invisible bits of fluff from his pristine navy trousers. 'We're focusing our efforts on fifty-six million American schoolchildren. Last year over half a million of them used steroids. They're looking to our elite athletes as role models, and we don't want them going down the road of performance-enhancing drugs.'

The director fiddles with his cuticles as if he's trying to line them up to attention. 'Do we really think it's an intractable task to take on, reassuring athletes that you don't have to use chemical engineering to compete?' He has a firm, dry way of speaking and now he changes up a gear and he's leading the infantry again. He's horrified at the 'disgraceful performance of the IOC in Atlanta and Los Angeles and the allegedly dirty urine samples which were never released'. Ah, so he knows about the Samaranch cover-ups. 'But it's not just an IOC failure. We've all lost it. I went to the Olympic village and talked to one of our weightlifters who said, "I've been competing fourteen years. I've never gone beyond number three. I'm drug-free. What are you going to do?"'

Over in Lausanne for thirty years they haven't stopped talking about their war against drugs. Most of the time they claim they are winning it. Brass-faced, Samaranch declared the Moscow games drug-free. Los Angeles detected a fistful of positives which might have wounded IOC profits, and didn't tell us. Seoul and Barcelona were said to have suffered cover-ups after results left the labs, Atlanta went sour when it was disclosed that, as in LA, positive results were suppressed.

Samaranch's retinue backed him and not one rank-and-file member cried, 'Stinking Fish!' And all the time we heard the muted, poisonous hiss from Lausanne that disqualification periods for athletes caught doping should be cut. The excuse was that civil courts would not uphold suspensions; many suspected Samaranch was playing the old game of reducing the penalty to make the crime seem less grave.

Samaranch – and many of his sponsors – never stopped chafing that Beijing had lost out to Sydney for the games of 2000. Australia is a mature market for the consumer-products corporations that buy the rings; China is the great voluptuous virgin they all want to penetrate. Despite brazen evidence of doping programmes, Samaranch baldly announced, 'China is clean.' That nonsense had to end.

Public servants, from junior police officers to government ministers, started in 1998 what the Olympic world should have done many years before. Australian customs found vials of human growth hormone (an undetectable drug) in the luggage of the Chinese swimming team arriving in Perth for the world championships. In mid-year French customs officers arrested a trainer with the Tour de France Festina team. Bertie Voets had a car boot full of drugs. The cops and magistrates took over and riders and officials found themselves tossed into jail like common criminals. Some lied, others confessed, and seven of the twenty-one teams pulled out.

Samaranch saw his 'winning the war' illusion shattered, and tried plan B: define the problem out of existence. He told a

Spanish newspaper that the list of banned drugs was too long and should be slashed back only to substances that were 'hazardous to health'.

The reaction could not have been more hostile if he'd goose-stepped up to the Olympic Museum and given the straight-arm salute to the Olympic flag. Every shade of opinion from politicians to athletes to scholars to the media erupted at the suggestion that performance-enhancing drugs were OK if, in some way, they didn't harm health. Samaranch was mocked the world over as an idiot.

He hastily announced the usual panacea – a conference to study the issue six months hence, in the new year. Hopefully public opinion would be diverted, only reliable reporters would turn up and the 'war' could resume. Might even get it all over before lunch.

Thanks to Marc Hodler, the biggest gang of press and radio reporters, television crews, satellite trucks, scientists, ethicists and physicians ever to cover an IOC meeting turned up in Lausanne in February 1999. Even worse, most European Union countries sent their sports ministers and teams of civil servants. But the biggest group of all was the Americans, a brigade-strength column of government haircuts and, leading his troops, Barry McCaffrey.

The Olympians were staggered, especially by McCaffrey's army, who set up a war room, a bilat room (that's a suite for cutting deals with other governments) and a full-service office manned round the clock by embassy staff. There were public-affairs people, logistics people and a squad of armed US marshals. Amid the purple velvet comfort of the Palace Bar, members whispered: 'Have they come to arrest us?'

Languid, foppish Alexandre, Prince de Mérode joined the IOC

in 1964. He lists his main occupation as president of Belgium's Genealogical and Heraldic office. When time allows, he is also president of his country's Royal Association of Historic Residences. A student of classics, philosophy, arts and law, he was the obvious candidate in 1967 when the IOC's new medical commission needed a chairman to lead a war against drugs. He has presided over the suppression of positive tests and the explosion of doping and cheating that has all but destroyed sport's integrity.

Mérode is a joy to reporters because he sometimes speaks out of turn and when he glided to the podium on day one of the Great Dope Congress, reporters grabbed ballpoints and pencils.

Eyeing the rows of politicians and government officials at the Palais de Beaulieu convention centre Mérode inquired: 'Why has no one ever thought to test ministers at the end of a parliamentary session?' If there was any hope of an early accommodation with McCaffrey, Mérode had just blown it. Hard-nosed public servants looked around, saw the Benetton-style posters of youngsters with the word 'Doping' across their chest and a black strip across their eyes, and dubbed this the See No Evil, Speak No Evil Congress.

Reporters had arrived to find an agonised press release from Samaranch exploding a few myths. He never requested large limousines, hotel suites, red carpets and champagne from bid cities. And another thing: he had asked people years ago to desist from calling him 'Your Excellency'. The convention began and for three days speakers from his Olympic family who hadn't heard the new orders, stepped up and began with a deferential 'Your Excellency'.

The IOC proposed setting up a new, 'independent' anti-doping agency. In the chair would be an independent

Samaranch, who proposed to appoint the independent Mérode as chief executive. The agency would be bulked out with more Samaranch appointees, people from national Olympic committees, Olympic sports federations, some carefully selected scientists and, of course, representatives from pharmaceutical companies and the sponsors. As the congress hooted at this try-on, Anita DeFrantz suggested replacing 'independent' with 'international'. That didn't rate much discussion.

Although this was not a full IOC meeting, what looked like a majority of members were in town, enjoying the good life, some calling on their girlfriends and dropping by the convention for a free lunch.

When McCaffrey's turn came at the lectern he told his hosts that they could not succeed in the fight against drugs unless they had 'credibility, legitimacy and transparency'. How would they achieve that? McCaffrey told them, 'I quite clearly call for the IOC to consider institutional reform: open books and financial records, open recorded votes, a code of conduct that is published and enforced, and probably most importantly an elected membership that is accountable and responsive.'

British Sports Minister Tony Banks said: 'Their internal system of organisation and election must be based on democracy, accountability and honesty . . . The British government expects the IOC to clean up its act.' European Union ministers piled in to agree and German Interior Minister Otto Schily said Samaranch should go. His Excellency was having his backside kicked again and again. They were queuing up like kids at a fairground.

That night I followed Kevan Gosper into the bar at the Palace Hotel and heard him splutter to a fellow member, 'Who do these sanctimonious politicians think they are to tell us what to do?' Mérode made it worse for them the next day, helpfully telling reporters that he had proposed an anti-doping agency ten years ago. 'Samaranch opposed this . . . as did practically the whole executive committee,' he said. 'It was shot down by ninety per cent of the people who favour it now.'

The biggest single fight at the congress was over the length of suspensions. The overwhelming consensus was two years for a first offence. This was resisted by soccer and cycling, the sports with the richest athletes most likely to wage legal battle if barred from working. OK, said nearly everybody, we'll chuck them out of the Olympics. Let them sue us. The IOC has the money to face down these dopers. We must treat all cheats equally. Samaranch was aghast. That would be bad for business.

Delegates listened in dismay as Samaranch, backed by Judge Mbaye, caved in to soccer and cycling and said the IOC would impose two-year suspensions on all athletes found doping – except in 'specific exceptional circumstances'. Government delegates and most of the international federation people looked glum. Samaranch rushed the meeting to a close: 'Can I have approval?' There was lukewarm applause from his supporters and that was that. Franklin Servan-Schreiber started beating the drum, and out went news of the wonderful 'Lausanne Declaration'. The governments acknowledged that Samaranch had out-manoeuvred them. What would McCaffrey do now?

Dick Pound got the job of creating a world anti-doping agency to which most of the real world objected. The Americans, the Australians, the Canadians and most of Europe watched as Dick went through the motions. Two months after the Lausanne Declaration, Dick brought together a bunch of institutions with little experience in sport. The Council of Europe sat down with Interpol, the World Health Organisation and a United Nations committee on drug control. The IOC was in charge and brought along some of the family, old friends from the Arab states, Africa and the national Olympic committees, most of which rely on IOC handouts. Some athletes came along too. As the year went on they held four more meetings, all of which they said were 'positive and constructive'. Canada's internationally respected anti-doping official Dr Andrew Pipe was asked in the summer what had happened since February's conference. 'I have heard nothing since,' he replied.

General McCaffrey made the occasional intervention calculated to enrage the Club of Lausanne. He went to Salt Lake City and said he'd 'never seen anything like' the IOC, 'a group of self-appointed people hiding behind a myth', led by 'a former fascist . . . now exercising unilateral authority'. In Washington he met visiting politicians and accused the IOC of stonewalling, and being in 'neutral cycle . . . the energy is going to have to come from the European Union and the rest of the global community.'

In mid-September Pound dispatched an angry letter to Washington and displayed it on the IOC's internet site. 'I was surprised and, I must confess, quite disappointed with the remarks you appear to have made regarding the work we have been doing to establish the World Anti-Doping Agency,' it began. 'I can only hope that the position you seem to have taken is the result of less than complete information that may be at your disposal.'

Pound recited the names of the organisations he'd recruited to fill his meetings and dug out some old Samaranch press releases about the IOC leading the fight against doping for the past thirty years. The IOC 'has used its position of moral suasion to build a consensus that culminated in the outcome of the World Conference in February'. Others recalled that Samaranch had screwed up terribly trying to play down doping and the conference was his way of trying to save face.

Pound said American sport was awash with drugs and suggested the director came up with a solution for sports federations who feared being sued by wealthy dopers. Washington wasn't shaken. 'If they build a bad car, why would we want to be a passenger?' asked McCaffrey aide Rob Housman. 'That's what they are offering us: come be a passenger in our lemon.'

The general decided to send in the big guns. He'd met Henry Kissinger soon after Kissinger had agreed to join Samaranch's reform effort. It was time to write Henry a letter. Do you realise these people are trying to marginalise us? That was the gist of it. Henry called Juan and strongly advised him to deal with the General.

Pound and McCaffrey met in Washington when Senator McCain staged his autumn hearing on doping. Athletes and American officials backed McCaffrey, who said that IOC efforts to crack down on drug use were 'more public relations ploy than public policy solution'. Samaranch and his chums were 'literally in denial'. Jaws dropped when Pound argued, 'Frankly, I think our track record over the last thirty years has been pretty good.' He went home and announced that the IOC-dominated World Anti-Doping Agency was imminent; they called it the WADA.

'I've never seen anything like it,' McCaffrey remarked. 'They just announced a unilateral solution, isolating the US. This isn't the way these operations are done.' He reminded the IOC that America put around $2 billion into the Olympics every four years, and that the IOC needed US tax breaks. Then he carried on building his alliance with the Europeans. In London, cabinet minister Mo Mowlam gave him soup, sandwiches and an assurance of Britain's support.

Before leaving Europe McCaffrey speculated that WADA 'won't in fact be independent, probably won't achieve the results and won't have credibility with the world's athletes'. Lausanne had to do something to shut him up.

Anita DeFrantz cleared security and made her way through the White House on the afternoon of 4 November 1999. She walked through the Mess, past cabinet ministers taking lunch, past smartly dressed navy stewards and oil paintings of naval victories, and stepped into the wood-panelled Ward Room for the meeting she'd secretly sought with President Clinton's closest aides. They were the only people who could rein McCaffrey in, tell him to shut up, stop upsetting the Olympic family. It was a great idea; go and lobby Doug Sosnik, Clinton's right-hand man, one of his closest policy and strategy advisers. IOC members expect to be able to pull rank this way.

With Anita were one of the IOC's expensive Washington lawyers, Jodi Trepasso, and a senior Hill and Knowlton man who had worked on Clinton's first election campaign back in 1992. That was a master-stroke, bringing in a guy who was cosy with senior Democrats.

Waiting for her with Sosnik, as expected, was Thurgood 'Goody' Marshall Jnr, a close Clinton aide who co-chairs the White House Olympic Task Force – and the savvy son of a former Supreme Court judge. And there was another guest, Rob Housman, one of Director McCaffrey's top strategists. He had a problem. Perhaps Anita could help and show him where, in the IOC's plans for the WADA, were the words guaranteeing its independence? Where did it confirm what she claimed, that they really wanted to see America in a leadership role? Mmmm, well it's not actually been written into the draft, she said, but you can trust us.

Was Doug Sosnik paying attention? He was sitting back, quiet, even distant. People who know Doug say that's when he's at his most formidable. You're at hazard if you try to pull something over on him. He sees right through it. Doug sprang to life. 'Let's go through who exactly sits on this board. Please, will you take me through the numbers again, who is from what organisation?' He made them repeat the numbers, say who was from the IOC, who was from sports federations, who was from national Olympic committees. Doug jotted the numbers on a card. When Anita had finished, he looked up and said, 'It's about power. These people have the power.' He placed his piece of card on the table and stabbed his finger at Anita's entrenched group, controlled tightly by the IOC. He said it was the government's view that the US and other countries were being excluded.

There was something else Doug wanted Anita to know about the Clinton administration. There was not one view on the IOC in the White House, Doug told her, there was a spectrum. And it just so happened that General McCaffrey wasn't a hard-liner, he was pretty much a centrist and there were others, far more hard-line than the director. They might just like to bear that in mind as they considered who they wanted to deal with. There was a hint in the air that Doug himself might be one of those hard-liners. The man who had the president's ear.

There was a subtext: just don't ever try to make an end run around one of the president's trusted cabinet ministers. That's what they call it in American football.

The atmosphere in the Ward Room changed. In the past, when the director and his aides had raised their concerns about how WADA's board was being filled, they'd felt the response was dismissive. Not now. Anita and the lawyer and the Hill and Knowlton man started back-pedalling fast. Well maybe we could do this, they said, and maybe we could do that.

Rob Housman saw his chance and seized it. He and McCaffrey had been urging Pound and Samaranch to hold back from the formal announcement that the WADA would soon be set up under Swiss law. Housman put it to the IOC team: Why do you have to rush into this? It's only a PR thing. You want to show that the WADA is really moving forward, but we don't want the structure you want.

We're off to Australia soon, said Housman. We are meeting twenty-five other governments who are as concerned as we are about what you are doing. Why not hold back until after our meeting in Sydney? Or, if you feel you have to set up a foundation, we know the law, and you don't need to be specific about the board representation at this stage. Come on, let's take this opportunity to negotiate something.

Oh we can't do that, said Anita.

McCaffrey's man and the president's advisers had assumed that Anita and her folks had the power to cut a deal. You just don't walk into a White House meeting with high-powered presidential aides unless you have the power to cut a deal. 'We were a hair's breadth away from laying into them,' someone in the room told me later.

Anita had inadvertently hardened the government's resolve in its most decisive intervention in world sport since the botched Moscow boycott.

Three very clear signals went out from the Ward Room that

afternoon. The US government wasn't joining on Samaranch's terms; if they didn't fix the problems with the WADA they'd suffer the consequences of America walking away; and don't ever try again to divide us. 'It would have been ugly on both sides,' says my contact who was there in the room. 'But we were ready for that. They blinked.'

Uh-huh, said Anita. Before you take a very hard-line position, give us a chance to get this right. On that note, she and her team left the White House. But she didn't get it – or maybe Samaranch wouldn't listen to her – because the IOC insisted on going ahead anyway and setting up the WADA. Anita got back in touch with McCaffrey's office trying to charm them into signing up and was told, as bluntly as in the Ward Room: we are not joining your photo-call, we are not coming to play in your sandbox. You need us more than we need you.

Pound had been jibing to reporters that the IOC was putting up $25 million of its 'own' money. Where was America's? Bob Agresti, a senior adviser to the general, told me, 'Their offer to talk was like an armed robber saying, "We can discuss what happens with your cash and credit cards after you hand over your wallet."'

'There has never been any question of the IOC controlling the agency,' said Franklin Servan-Schreiber, as he announced on 10 November 1999, that the WADA had been established. In the chair was Dick Pound and alongside were five other IOC members, Arne Ljungqvist, Alexandre, Prince de Mérode, Jacques Rogge and Hein Verbruggen. Hein was president of cycling, the dirtiest sport in the world. From the athletes' commission was Finland's sixty-two-year-old Peter Tallberg, a yachtsman and IOC member of twenty-three years' standing.

America's volleyball hero Robert Ctvrtlik, who always

seemed to see the best in the IOC, was on the WADA too, along with Manuela di Centa, an Italian cross-country skier whose sport is plagued by blood-doping scandals, and Johann Olav Koss, Norway's speedskater. These three former Olympic athletes were thirty days short of being recruited to IOC membership. Not on the IOC were Finland's culture minister, Ms Suvi Linden and Mr Awoture Eleya of the Supreme Council for Sport in Africa. And Anders Besseberg, president of biathlon, a minority sport in which skiers fire guns at woodland targets.

Two days later McCaffrey wrote to Samaranch 'to begin the process of improving WADA'. The world is waiting for you to get in line, he said, not the other way around. McCaffrey offered to begin talking immediately and attached a list of seventeen points that had to be addressed.

There had to be seats for governments, and membership could rotate between them. Meetings must be open to the public, information transparent, conflicts of interest declared and observers allowed to speak at meetings. WADA must be independent and accountable. Samples must be stored in the hope that currently undetectable drugs could be traced in years to come, and sanctions must be common to all sports. That was code for soccer, cycling and tennis to get in line – or get out. His aides dispatched this letter as the general flew over the Pacific on his way to the twenty-six-nation doping summit, hosted by the Australian government.

He took along the army that had swept fear through the bars of Lausanne, and a few special guests: Donna de Varona, the US swimmer and activist who'd been considered too feisty for IOC membership, Dr Gary Wadler, one of the world's most respected sports doctors, and Mickey Ibarra, a close aide of Bill Clinton, a co-chair of the White House

Olympic Task Force and physical proof, if anyone needed it, that McCaffrey's mission had the US president's full support.

McCaffrey landed to find himself banned from setting foot in any of Sydney's Olympic venues. This order came from a Mr John Coates, president of the Australian Olympic Committee, who took exception to US threats to end IOC tax breaks. 'General McCaffrey is not a friend of the Olympic movement,' said Coates, who had ploughed his own and lots of Australian Olympic money into a casino, part-owned by Austrian IOC member Leopold Wallner; the investment went belly-up. 'He may be a four-star general, but he does not even rate one star in the drugs-in-sports arena.' The ban succeeded in one thing: it seized the media's attention, guaranteeing coverage of McCaffrey's every move.

Kevan Gosper told a reporter: 'I think that the United States has not really kept fully in touch with developments that have taken place.' McCaffrey and his friends from the governments of Britain, Canada, China, Finland, France, the Netherlands, New Zealand, Norway, Poland, Portugal, South Africa and Sweden burned through their three-day sports summit and at the end, set themselves up as the Sydney Consultative Group on Anti-Doping.

Sensing he was being sidelined, Samaranch issued a press release begging McCaffrey to travel to Switzerland, 'as early as possible', for talks about the WADA.

Rob Housman observed, 'Traditionally we agree with the view that government shouldn't politicise the Olympics. But when the problem is corruption within the house of the Olympics, governments have a responsibility to fix it, and we weren't the only people with that view, it was twenty-six nations.

'We played a sophisticated, multilayered game of statecraft, bringing great leverage and resources to bear,' Housman explained. 'We sent out instructions to our ambassadors around the world requiring them to make our case with other governments at the most senior level.'

McCaffrey kept up the offensive, asking how it was possible that Dick Pound, the IOC member responsible for bringing in the television and sponsors' billions was now presiding over the WADA, which, if it did its job properly, would unearth dopers and damage the commercial value of the Olympics.

The Australian summit demonstrated the hollowness of IOC claims that McCaffrey's efforts were ill-informed and isolated in the world. Finally, the penny dropped that the Olympians were up against superior force. Slowly, they began their retreat. Behind the scenes McCaffrey met Gosper and secured the IOC's agreement to support the summit's declaration.

Pound moved swiftly to build bridges to Washington and the rest of the world. At the beginning of December he went to Washington and took lunch with McCaffrey, in the same White House Ward Room Anita had visited three weeks earlier. The general took him through the Sydney agreement and Pound agreed to everything, including a promise that at future Olympics there would be no hiding of test results and that all would be made public as quickly as possible. That should end decades of mistakes, misinformation and occasional deception from the IOC.

The deal was made public in Washington the day before Samaranch testified before Congress. Incorrigible, and while he still had time, Samaranch hastily added two more IOC members to the WADA, Britain's Craig Reedie, supposedly representing national Olympic committees, and Mustapha

Larfaoui, president of world swimming. Five more officials from various branches of his Olympic family were added, giving the IOC a total of sixteen seats to the six held by outsiders.

McCaffrey, Australia's justice minister Amanda Vanstone and Canada's sports minister Denis Coderre travelled to Lausanne in early January 2000 to eyeball Samaranch on behalf of the Sydney group. Samaranch prepared for mega-phone diplomacy, seating himself at one end of a long, long, table, and the general far, far away at the opposite end. The rest were placed with Samaranch's usual regard for protocol, miniature national flags and place-markers. Someone suggested they all gather around one end of the table. Offences against protocol rank higher than doping at the IOC, but Samaranch had to give in. Then he took more humiliation. Canada's Coderre warned that if he didn't deal with doping, that would be the end of the Olympic movement. 'We told him it was a case of either you're part of the solution or part of the problem,' Coderre said later.

After more than three decades of the IOC betraying the public trust and failing sport, someone else had to start clean-ing house: it was the public servants just doing their job, the customs officers in Perth who pricked the Chinese bubble, the gendarmes who arrested souped-up cyclists, and civil servants in two dozen countries. Ordinary people who take their kids to soccer practice, cheer them on in the sack-race, and swell with pride when they do well, want drug-free sport, and for years the IOC had failed them. The people's servants made a start of pushing the IOC aside.

Chapter 20

Juan the Reformer!

'We promised to clean the house. We did it,' Samaranch declared after six expulsions had been agreed in Lausanne in March 1999. 'We promised reforms. We did it.' On cue Hill and Knowlton wheeled out some sponsors, McDonald's and UPS, the parcels people, to give Samaranch the public show of support he needed.

Encouraged, he announced there'd be a Reform Commission – that had a nice ring to it – headed by the man best qualified for the job. It took nanoseconds to appoint himself; selecting the appropriate people to join him would take longer.

There would be an Ethics Commission too – that sounded impressive and would be easier to assemble. Within three weeks Samaranch had found exactly the people he needed who would bring a New! Independent! Ethical! dimension to the troubled IOC. Ringing the changes . . . Judge Kéba Mbaye, who had been voted into the IOC twenty-six years earlier by the likes of Jamaica's Tony Bridge (who persuaded the Atlanta boys to carry $15,500 into America for him), Vitaly Smirnov, ('serious warning' over his role in the Salt Lake scandal), Louis Guirandou-N'Diaye ('serious warning'), and Agustín Arroyo (expelled). And, of course, Samaranch.

Mbaye, in the chair, was joined by IOC executive board members Kevan Gosper (twenty-three years travelling in comfort) and insurance salesman Chick Igaya (seventeen years). Samaranch then selected four 'distinguished individuals' known for their 'independence and strong ethics'. All were retired politicians. From Switzerland came former president Kurt Furgler, from America former Senator Howard Baker, and they were joined by former UN chief Javier Pérez de Cuéllar and France's former minister of justice Robert Badinter. Later in the year I heard M. Badinter murmur to a colleague, 'Some of the criticisms of the IOC have been excessive.'

Just in time someone spotted they were all men well past sixty, so in came Jamaican-born Charmaine Crooks, who'd run for Canada in five Olympics. Charmaine was already a cherished member of the Lausanne family at the IOC's Culture Commission, and before the end of the year she was co-opted on to the IOC, making the balance of membership of the independent Ethics Commission four insiders and four outsiders.

Mark Tewksbury, Dawn Fraser and the other athletes at OATH pointed out – although the IOC had long ago put its fingers in its ears – that none of these ethicists were trained in ethics. 'The IOC does not really recognise that it faces a crisis in ethics and values,' they said.

The first grand scheme, according to director-general François Carrard in the spring of 1999, was for Dick Pound to abandon his investigations and hand the files over to the new ethics panel. That's what Kevan Gosper thought, too, when he announced one bright day in May, in Lausanne, that new allegations about Kim Un-Yong and Phil Coles would be examined by him and his friends on the ethics commission. No, no, said Howard Baker, that's not right, Kevan and I and our friends on the ethics commission don't have jurisdiction, so we've pushed it back to Kevan and his friends on the executive council or whatever they call it. I'm sure President Samaranch will take care of everything.

Kim and Coles were duly dealt with by their friends on the executive board and given new and serious warnings.

Judge Mbaye took off on his own ethical odyssey, announcing that allegations against around thirty members made by former bidding cities would be handled not by him at the ethics commission but by him at the executive board. 'In the information we got from the national Olympic committees, you can't say that there are really many of what you could call cases or affairs,' explained the judge. We had to take his word for it because he wouldn't show us the letters of complaint.

Six weeks passed and near the end of June the executive board handed down its judgment on twenty-seven members, all accused of dubious activities by cities that had campaigned for the Olympics. 'None of them was as serious as to merit a warning,' said the executive board's Pál Schmitt, closing the inquiry.

That intrigued me. Two rip-offs that happened in Manchester, the ticket scam and the 'Help-My-Room's-Been-Burgled-Give-Me-$20,000!' racket, could have landed members on criminal charges. Yet they didn't merit so much as a warning. Perhaps the British Olympic Association had forgotten to tell them. I called the BOA and asked for a copy of whatever they'd sent in response to Samaranch's request for bid naughties. Surely, in this new era of transparency, they'd be happy to fax one over.

'We didn't take copies of anything,' trilled their press office. What? I said. Are you serious?

'If we do have a copy it doesn't belong to us, it's just something the IOC requested and we facilitated,' they burbled.

I wondered where the British Olympic Association thought their loyalties lay, with the British people who backed Manchester's bid, or with the IOC who were so relaxed about their members ripping off Britain? So I asked the BOA. 'We have written to the IOC asking permission to make the inquiry documents public,' came the reply. 'If and when we get this permission we will be in a position to make them available.' I heard no more from them.

The next case to cross the ethics commission's desk was Atlanta. Come September, in came the investigative report prepared by some Atlanta lawyers for Billy's boys after Fred Upton threatened to send gun-toting marshals to seize the archives. It told of silverware gifts and healthcare and flights to Disney World and all sorts of things that might give a tough, independent ethics commission cause for concern.

Judge Mbaye said he needed time to study the report; if he found 'anything meaningful' he would submit it to the full commission for review. 'This shows the IOC is serious about reforms and the ethical practice of its members,' said a spokesman.

Mbaye had some ethical dilemmas judging anything to do with Atlanta. According to one of those confidential file notes by the Atlanta bid team, Mbaye had said he was grateful to Andrew Young who, when American ambassador to the UN, pushed for Mbaye to get his dream job at the International Court of Justice at The Hague. Young went on to become co-leader of the Atlanta bid with Billy Payne. And Mbaye was a member of the golfing party that had a high old time, thanks to the Atlanta boys, in Augusta – a perk that was quite simply priceless, because you couldn't buy your way on to its exclusive fairways if you tried. And wasn't his fellow ethics commission member Chick Igaya on that dream freebie too?

How could any of the IOC members on the ethics committee approach the matter of Mrs Samaranch's single-minded freeloading across the South without burning their fingers?

Would Mbaye do the ethical thing, step back at the start and hand the whole thing over to someone else? Er . . . no.

The following month Howard Baker issued a statement saying, 'I am pleased by the progress of the IOC Ethics Commission.' Nothing more was heard about the Atlanta shenanigans. 'It is just another case of a US "inquiry" in which the opinions of only one side were canvassed,' opined Dick Pound, another of the Augusta golfers.

The judge called a press conference in mid-December to say that they didn't want to look at existing allegations and weren't keen to initiate new investigations. Before Hill and Knowlton's minders could get a sack over his head, Mbaye attacked Congressman Fred Upton, who would be quizzing Samaranch soon in Washington, for alleging there was an IOC culture of corruption. 'If there were just one honest man in an organisation,' said the judge, 'I think that would be sufficient not to cast a shadow on the entire organisation.' Was Mbaye positioning himself as the one honest man at the IOC?

Case number three came in by a very peculiar route: my letter box. One morning in January 2000 a slim parcel of documents arrived on my doormat, detailing somebody's jaunts, seemingly at Salt Lake's expense. There were three pages of spread-sheets, with details of air travel, and a Christmas holiday in a luxurious ski lodge during Salt Lake's second bid campaign. There was information about ski clothes, a trip to the Utah resort of Lake Powell, tickets for a Billy Joel concert – and photographs of Kevan Gosper and his wife, Judy, having a good time in Utah. Many of the expenses that appeared to have been incurred by the Gospers had been paid by Tom Welch, Dave Johnson and another member of the Salt Lake team, and none of this had come out in public before.

I sent a detailed e-mail to Kevan, asking who had paid these holiday bills and were the visits within IOC rules? His reply flashed back a few hours later, all sixteen words of it: 'I refer to your email of today. I have receipts to cover whatever you are alleging.'

I wasn't alleging anything, only asking some questions. I e-mailed back, asking Kevan as a member of the executive board, the ethics commission, and chairman of the press commission, and in the new spirit of IOC transparency, if he had the receipts, could he please ask his secretary to pop them on the fax machine.

That's when Kevan said a very odd thing: 'To respond directly on such matters, would seem to me to disregard the very purpose for which the Ethics Commission inquiry was convened.'

Twenty-four hours later he was back on my screen. 'It's important you don't think I'm being unfriendly or unco-operative. I will send you some more information in response to some of your questions on Monday.'

I'd also asked Kevan about another matter. As part of his campaign for the IOC presidency, Kevan, who used to be Shell Australia's boss, has often talked about the need for the IOC to adopt management skills (like Kevan's) and once, when I told him how well journalists get on with his main rival, Dick Pound, he spluttered, 'Yes, but he's a lawyer. He's never run a big company!' (Unlike Kevan). Then I learned something that made me wonder about Kev's head for business.

It concerned Lloyd's, the insurance market that used to draw its capital from some of the finest families in English society. Prince Michael of Kent was a member; also, a brace of dukes, a dozen earls, and a pile of peers. Then, with dreadful losses just a few years away, Lloyd's embarked on a sudden, massive expansion and Kevan joined, in 1985. A few nice cheques came in, then the losses, and like so many outsiders Kevan ended up with a mighty share of the loss; it's likely he was hit for about £150,000. I wanted to check this account with Kevan. He said he'd joined and left Lloyd's, but wouldn't go further than that: 'I am puzzled by such a question,' he remarked, and that was the end of it.

Early on Monday I was woken by the first of a stream of calls from Australia. Kevan had published a press release, announcing that he'd referred himself to the ethics commission, said the Salt Lake boys' expenses claims were 'believed to be false' and 'fraudulent' and asserted I had a source which gave me 'questionable information'. He confirmed his wife, Judy, and two children had taken a trip to Utah in December 1993, but didn't explain why he involved Salt Lake bid people in this private holiday. Two years later Kevan and Judy visited Utah for his official visit; he had little to say about this, either.

Kevan insisted that the ethics commission was 'an independent forum' and forecast it would establish 'there was no improper behaviour on our behalf'. He added, 'No documents in my possession concerning my young family's private visit will be released.' But documents *were* released, to selected reporters, on condition they did not disclose the source, which was . . . Hill and Knowlton.

They showed that Gosper had written to Tom 'n' Dave insisting that he would pay the entire cost of his family's holiday – but there were no receipts for their stay in a luxury lodge or for meals and clothing which appeared to have been bought for the family. A few weeks later the SLOC people released all one hundred and fifteen pages of Gosper-related documents they could find in their files. There were no receipts or repayment records.

While waiting for the Ethics Commission to rule on Gosper's complaint against himself, I leafed through a review copy of his imminent autobiography *An Olympic Life*. It was a part of his campaign for the presidency, co-authored by Murdoch's *Sydney Morning Telegraph* reporter, Glenda Korporaal. A reference to Judge Mbaye, chairman of the ethics panel, caught my eye. Mbaye, said Kevan, is 'as close a friend as I've got in the IOC'. I e-mailed the judge, asking if he thought he should remove himself from judging Kevan. There was no reply.

But there was a shock for reporters when they arrived in Lausanne on 6 March, 2000: Gosper had resigned from the ethics panel and an independent investigator would be appointed to report on his case.

The Lords still couldn't get it right. 'The IOC's ethics commission only perpetuated its ongoing struggle with credibility,' commented Associated Press, reporting that panel member Pérez de Cuéllar 'ruined any semblance of objectivity when he downplayed the accusations, saying the panel already considers Gosper innocent'. The Ethics Commission's ruling, which did not appear before this book went to press, was widely expected to clear him.

There was one titbit in the records divulged by the SLOC. In October 1993 Gosper was one of five IOC members attending a dinner hosted by Salt Lake bid officials at Le Cirque, one of New York's finest restaurants. The bill for the evening, including limousine service, totalled more than $4,200. Tucking in were, among others, Anita DeFrantz, Dick Pound, Nigeria's General Henry Adefope and Walther Troeger from Germany. IOC director-general François Carrard and marketing director Michael Payne also dined. Living so lavishly on Olympic business is perfectly ethical.

JUAN THE REFORMER!

You are so welcome to Lausanne, we do value your contribution, we couldn't undertake reforms here at the IOC without generous outsiders like yourself giving up your valuable time to strengthen our commission. Isn't it lovely up here in the sunshine on the museum terrace, such an enchanting view across the lake to Evian and the Alps. The flowers are at their best in early June, we're so glad you could come. A small glass? Yes, we keep a fine cellar.

One of the joys of our Olympic way of life is that we can come here to have our serious discussions about reform while around us parents and children imbibe the rich culture of Olympism, enjoying past games on the video screens, reminding us of our sacred trust to stage the games for the young people of the world. Some might think we haven't got so much very wrong over the last century. Olympism, as you'll enjoy discovering, is the harmonious blend of sport, education and culture. That's what we're about.

Those marble columns over there, they were donated by the Greek government. It is a magnificent building, isn't it, and it's good to know we retain the confidence of our sponsors. A tasteful touch, don't you think, that gently curving granite wall behind the indoor pool with their names carved on individual blocks. We're very proud we can exhibit Baron de Coubertin's original study with his desk and pens and close by find an aesthetic way to thank Asahi Breweries, Sapporo Breweries, Kirin Brewery, Suntory whisky, Coca-Cola, Daimler-Benz, Mitsubishi and other dear, dear friends.

Have you been to see the baron's grave? Very impressive, surrounded by cypresses, it's near the Château. Olympism was his life, you know, and when he died, at his request they cut his heart out and buried it in Olympia near the site of the ancient games.

This first weekend is going to be so exciting. Together we'll be creating an International Olympic Committee for the next century so we are calling ourselves the IOC 2000 Commission. It's wonderful you could be part of it. And you must stay in touch when it's over. We'll be looking out for the right kind of people who feel they have more to give to Olympism. You might be just the sort of person to bring on to the committee. I expect you'll be wanting some tickets for Sydney, let me know later, I'm sure something can be arranged. Come and meet some of the other members of our Great Reform Commission! They're pretty impressive people.

That's Paul Allaire over there, he runs the Xerox company, they do wonderful things to make our Olympic communications work so well, and they pay a fortune to be an Olympic partner. You know we're proud to say that it's our big sponsors who help keep the Olympic dream alive for the athletes. He's talking with Gianni Agnelli, wonderful chap, his family runs Fiat, and I can tell you Gianni's got his fingers crossed for Turin to win the winter games of 2006, he gives so much support to sport, he puts his heart where his money lies, his family owns some wonderful ski resorts.

Good to see Nick Hayek could join us, he's the gentleman from Omega and Swatch, they do a lot in sport, timing events, that sort of thing. We're hoping he'll take the plunge sometime soon and become one of the top sponsors. The Americans are here at full strength today, they're the biggest single group on the reform commission. I wonder what Dick Ebersol is cooking up with Bill Hybl? Dick runs NBC Sport and I can tell you, Coca-Cola and Visa and

McDonald's and Kodak pay us in millions of dollars, but Dick's NBC pay billions. Bill runs the US Olympic Committee and a charity in Colorado, gives away a fortune, people hang on his every word I can tell you.

There's Anita DeFrantz and Seb Coe with Professor John MacAloon, great scholar, wrote a wonderful book about the Olympics, we like him and wanted him here because during our troubles he was so wise, he said, 'This will turn out to be a tempest in a teapot.' We were worried he might be upset we have seventy-two men and only seven women on the commission – you know how academics can be. But it's so hard to find the right type of woman, the type who understands we are forcing the pace of change and these things take time. The Professor looks happy enough. He's here, that's the main thing.

Sorry, it's no good looking around for Oscar Arias Sánchez. We do so like Nobel laureates but he couldn't make it, so he won't be playing any part in our deliberations. He was busy in Costa Rica but we've left his name on the list to show how seriously we're taking reform. Think of him as 'playing a symbolic role as an honorary member of the group' – that's what we'll say if anybody asks. This is a very ethical congregation, you'll want to meet Judge Kéba Mbaye, he was at the International Court of Justice, you'll find him with Kevan Gosper and Chick Igaya, they're playing a guiding role in the reform process. Chick comes with Mr Mizuno, he's another of our sponsors, they give us all those wonderful warm coats to wear at the winter games, I'm told their running shoes are very good, a lot of the stars wear them.

A word of counsel: whatever you do, don't ask Olegario Vázquez Raña about his brother Mario – or vice versa.

They're both here but they're not close. That's family, isn't it? Here in the Olympic family we like to be a family, so once Mario was co-opted to the IOC, Olegario had to be too. Then we set up the reform commission and Mario has to be on it so we had to ask Olegario as well. They are very rich, there are some very rich people in Mexico. Mario's so generous. He lends his private jet to our president and looks after the association of national Olympic committees. They love him you know, he's re-elected every time and he's gathered good people around him like Professor Chowdhry, Jacques Rogge from Belgium, he's a chevalier – a very honourable title – Kevan Gosper, Dick Palmer from England and lots of IOC members. It's the third leg of the Olympic movement, along with the IOC and the international federations. Talking of federations, Olegario's a president of one, he's run international shooting for nearly twenty years. Good Olympic sport. Baron Coubertin thought shooting was important. I think that's got you started, you'll soon get to know people. We're all in this together. Oh, look over there, coming through the door with our president. He's here. There's Henry Kissinger!

Henry Kissinger, whose gnomish features are instantly recognisable to over-thirties across the planet, has only to enter a room to cause ripples of excitement and awe. He exudes power and authority. He shaped American foreign policy for Presidents Nixon and Ford, planned the secret carpet-bombing of Cambodia, then picked up a Nobel Peace Prize for his trouble. Love him or hate him, there's no disputing the man is a star.

He has plenty in common with Samaranch. They're of the same generation, virulent anti-communists and firm believers in the notion that age should be no barrier to the exercise of power. Since leaving public service, Kissinger has traded his international celebrity and political connections for cash in the corporate world. His Kissinger Associates is the ultimate influence broker between corporations and governments across the globe. Among the many companies he's helped is Freeport-McMoRan, the mining company that digs gold in Indonesia and does business with local IOC member Bob Hasan.

It's a small Olympic world. Samaranch plotted for a decade to take the games where the sponsors most wanted – to China. Hill and Knowlton worked for the Chinese government and Air China. Over the years Kissinger's work has brought him into contact with leading Hill and Knowlton strategists. Henry Kissinger smoothed Olympic sponsor Coca-Cola's path into Beijing and spoke up against sanctions after the massacre of students in Tiananmen Square. Samaranch completed the circle of commercial desire by riding a bike across the notorious square in 1993, smiling for the cameras and doing his best to help them defeat Sydney for the games of 2000. Beijing lost by only two votes.

'You asked if Dr Kissinger had been remunerated for his work and he answered, No,' said an assistant at his New York office. Kissinger didn't need money from the Olympics. Samaranch had something infinitely more valuable to offer. In the power and influence-peddling business it's no use being yesterday's strong-man; you have to keep your pulling power in the public eye. The Olympic movement was in trouble and look who they'd called to help them out of it. Kissinger to the rescue!

Former Republican Senator Howard Baker was refreshing his international profile at Samaranch's ethics panel. He served as minority and then majority leader of the Senate for the best part of a decade, then the revolving door from public service to private enrichment spun for him too. His law firm ranks among the ten most powerful influence-peddlers in Washington. The firm offers clients privileged access to the lawmakers and, according to its advertising, 'thoroughly monitors the legislative process to identify existing opportunities and to create new ones for providing the client's message an effective forum'.

Kissinger and Baker had joined a battle to save the Olympics for the corporate world.

Senator George Mitchell, a younger man, a Democrat, and hero of the Northern Ireland peace negotiations, had made scathing comments about the IOC's dubious culture in his influential report for the US Olympic Committee. He's another public servant who has spun through the revolving door into influence-peddling and corporate riches at his Washington law firm. They're even richer than Baker's outfit! They made $19 million in lobbying fees in 1998. George sits on the boards of many big companies, including Walt Disney, Federal Express, Unilever and Olympic sponsors Xerox.

Juan Antonio Samaranch went to work on Henry, Howard and George with his most potent weapon, the personal charm he reserves for very important people. Kissinger, Baker and Mitchell, the Holy Trinity of American public life, national icons, international statesmen, men who understood the corporate world, were locked into a process which ultimately would endorse the IOC and their event as safe for sponsors to invest in.

On pleasant weekends through the late summer and early autumn of 1999 the Marqués de Samaranch convened 'working parties' at the Olympic Museum. The press releases made them sound awfully purposeful. Out in the wider world there was derision for Samaranch's reform commission. Of the eighty or so members – you could never be sure who turned up to meetings – forty-five were IOC members and most of the rest drawn from Samaranch's wider Olympic family, dependent on him.

'What they're saying is, we only trust people with our own DNA,' jibed their most consistent critic, David D'Alessandro, chief executive of the Boston-based John Hancock insurance company, one of the top Olympic sponsors. 'It's all about Olympic cousins. What's happening here is what usually happens when you marry your cousin. You get cross-eyed results.'

I met the offspring in late October when the Marqués called his 'Plenary Commission' meeting at the museum to finalise what his parties had been working at. Hill and Knowlton presented us with 'Fifty Reforms'. Here in this thirteen-page document were the Tough Constitutional Changes that would tackle, head-on, the IOC's culture of corruption and lack of democracy and accountability.

'A substantial travelling exhibition of the Olympic Movement and Olympic history to be installed in host cities' was one root and branch reform, buttressed by another demanding 'Greater recognition of the educational importance of the flame relay'. The Fabulous Fifty continued with radical measures like 'During the Closing Ceremony of the Olympic Games, the Elected Athletes [on the IOC Athletes Commission] should be recognised by their peers and by all the Olympic Family.'

On and on went the cross-eyed proposals. The IOC should 'reinforce its capacity to advise on and control the preparation of the Olympic Games', there should be more humanitarian projects, more information centres, and the IOC's Culture and Olympic Education Commissions should be merged. And there was a bright new suggestion to help deal with scandals; the president and senior executives should have their own spokesperson. More expensive, but easier than gagging Marc Hodler.

The Marqués opened this plenary meeting and told us, with all the drama his dry-as-a-stick demeanour allowed, that a new IOC will rise as a phoenix from the ashes of the old. As he droned on, the metaphor seemed more and more inappropriate. From the contented look on the faces of his friends around him, the IOC hadn't been singed by the flames of scandal, never mind destroyed by fire.

It took a while to reach the issue at the top of the Marqués's list of priorities, his campaign for a Nobel Peace Prize. Recommendations forty and forty-one called for more publicity for his Olympic Truce. A clause was read out: 'During the Olympic Games the IOC should implement the proper measures to symbolise or enforce the Olympic Truce.' At this point Kissinger, sitting to one side of the room and smaller and baggier than I remembered him, stirred. Enforce? The IOC was going to 'enforce' a world truce during its sports event? Images of Samaranch ordering the US Army back to base dissolved as a Germanic-American voice croaked, 'Conservatives in America will go crazy when they see this.'

Samaranch was thrown off balance. It was dawning on the several hundred reporters that The Leader, The Kissinger and most of The Reform Commission hadn't scrutinised the text. They'd supposedly been honing these proposals for five months yet hadn't noticed this idiocy. Samaranch agreed, hurriedly, to drop 'enforce' but like a petulant child who won't admit it is wrong, insisted that back in 1998, at the Nagano winter games, his call for an Olympic Truce persuaded Clinton to postpone bombing Iraq. Everybody in the room looked embarrassed; we all knew that America still bombed Iraq, like it bombed Belgrade. Doesn't he read the newspapers?

The pain wasn't over; up perked another of Samaranch's headline acts who also seemed to be reading the reform proposals for the first time. 'Are you going to define conflicts?' inquired the patient voice of former UN secretary-general Boutros Boutros-Ghali. 'Do you mean big wars or small wars?' More red faces on the podium and, embarrassed, Samaranch admitted they had better redraft this proposal. Mr Boutros-Ghali graciously offered to do it for them. He's very quick and within a few minutes had a new draft. 'During the Opening Ceremony of the Games the President should mention all the actions undertaken by the IOC in favour of promoting peace.' Relieved, everyone nodded. It shouldn't delay the start of the sport. Reporters noted in their stories that the reform panel spent as long discussing the truce as it did finances and doping.

Working overtime to register his importance with the distinguished guests is Mario Vásquez Raña, king of the national Olympic committees. At one stage he bounces out of his seat on the podium, squeezes past the dignitaries, and theatrically delivers A Very Important Document In A Big Envelope to an irritated Samaranch. Mario won't say what's in it but does tell us that he held a meeting with his cronies in Paris a few days ago and they demanded that members retain the right to remain on the committee until they reach eighty years of age. I imagine that running under Mario's image on the monitor screen is the caption 'Admired for my devotion to Olympism, not because I give rides on my private jet'.

There are eight mentions of transparency in the proposals

– and they seem to think that's as far as the revolution needs to go, thank you very much. The organisation specialises in quick-change routines and never faster than when the question 'What Are You?' is raised. Most of the time they pose as a charitable organisation run by unpaid volunteers.

In Britain our laws require charities to declare the number of employees earning more than £40,000 a year and list them in upward bands of £10,000 a time. They're even tighter in America. Every non-profit foundation must fill in a tax form disclosing the pay and perks of the top five earners. That's how the public – and financially hard-pressed athletes – discover that every four-year Olympic cycle Anita DeFrantz pockets nearly $1 million from her Los Angeles Olympic foundation.

So how much do the senior IOC paper-shufflers like director-general François Carrard and marketing director Michael Payne pocket from the Olympics? Ahhhhhhh! Now the IOC is not a charitable foundation. It's a commercial organisation which publishes a bunch of figures 'in accordance with international accounting standards'. That's code for 'We're a private business, what we take out of the Olympic goody jar is none of your business.'

Which makes you wonder if they've awarded themselves the kind of salaries, perks and pensions that go with their preferred lifestyle: the biggest Mercedes, five-star hotel suites and wide leather seats with complimentary champagne. The only clue is their published accounts showing a wage bill of $10.5 million a year.

There's a bit of a tussle over whether they are going to ban visits to bidding cities – the free holidays that brought them down in Salt Lake. A few members whinge but Samaranch knows the American reporters are watching this one most

closely and he has to be seen to be 'responsive, if not accountable', as one of his aides whispers to me. Up speaks Judge
Mbaye. 'We are trying to protect members from the bidding
cities,' he claims, and it seems they're still in denial.

Anita DeFrantz is on-message, as ever, announcing: 'To
give people vacations is not a good way to spend our money.'
Later that day, she is reminded that visiting Sydney in 1991
she was happy to be a member of the 'Holidays 'R' Us' club,
telling reporters, 'Already I have played tennis, been wind-
surfing, rowing and I am going sailing this afternoon.' She
ponders for a moment, then says, airily, 'It was wrong.'

During a break I chat over coffee with Marc Hodler. 'We
don't need to visit,' he tells me. 'IOC members can learn all they
need to know if they spend three hours reading the detailed
reports we prepare on each city.'

'How many members do this?' I ask. 'Maybe ten or twelve
per cent,' he replies.

For some of us, the freeloading in bidding cities, college
scholarships, ticket rackets, shakedowns for gifts and hospitality for members' extended families were only a symptom of the
problem. The physical corruption was the offspring of their
fundamental moral corruption, their refusal to tolerate democratic elections to their ranks or make themselves accountable
to sport.

Since the Baron de Coubertin gave them their legacy of
elitism at the end of the nineteenth century the world has
changed dramatically. A century later, the ballot box has
spread from sea to shining sea, across all Europe, from Riga to
Vladivostok, Latin America has rejected its military juntas,
South Africa defeated apartheid – but the IOC wasn't having
any of this nonsense.

For ten decades their practice had been for the executive board to present names to the annual session – and see them co-opted by acclamation. What would the new process be? Here it was: the executive board would present names to the annual session – and see them co-opted by acclamation. If anything, the process was more sinister than before. Now there would be a selection committee to 'evaluate the quality of candidates'. Secret reports would be prepared to help the executive board decide who to recommend to their colleagues. 'The principle of cooptation is a guarantee of independence,' said the reformers on their very first page.

At the press conference I asked the star of the show about the document they had agreed. 'Dr Kissinger, how will the word "cooptation" play in Washington?' He seemed puzzled for a moment. 'I think an attempt has been made to try and subject each member to some election process. I haven't read it carefully, is the word "co-opt" in?'

Two weeks before Christmas the IOC members travelled to Switzerland, were welcomed at a special reception desk at Geneva airport, chauffeured to Lausanne and installed in their usual comfort at the Palace Hotel. Next morning Samaranch embraced them from the platform of the convention centre at the Palais de Beaulieu. 'You have faced harsh criticism, very often unfair,' he told them. 'You have gone through undeserved suffering and pain. Myself, as president, I have suffered too. We have all suffered. I express my admiration for your dignity.'

Then they adopted the 'massive reform programme', as they called it. There were tough new term limits on membership. The bad news was they would all have to go after eight years. The good news was they could vote themselves back in for a further eight years, do it again, and again until they were eighty years of age. Younger members, like the Prince of Orange, would be forced out eventually . . . in 2047.

As the occasional vacancy came up they would admit a few more of their friends from Mario's club of Olympic committees and from the sports federations, assuming they satisfied the selection committee. But they would have to quit at seventy. To distract the reporters and the American politicians, there would be Athlete Members! Samaranch just happened to have a few hanging around the corridors, all 'elected' at the Atlanta and Nagano games, without any real campaigns or policies, to the athletes' commission. The athletes were instantly appointed to the IOC and, as intended, this device captured most of the headlines.

I caught up with one of these new members, American volleyball player Bob Ctvrtlik, surrounded by reporters in the lobby. Face glowing, arms pumping, Bob's enthusiasm for his new pals was touching. 'One of the good things now is that I can introduce athletes to IOC members,' he gushed. Easing forward I asked, 'Bob, what do you say when you introduce them to Bob Hasan?' (the rainforest logger). Young Bob looked puzzled. 'Bob who?' he asked me. No wonder they liked him.

As dusk fell over Lausanne, television reporters lined up in front of their cameras and the message went up to the transponders that the IOC had kept its word and passed Fifty Stunning Reforms. His eyes misting, Franklin Servan-Schreiber looked in the direction of the Marqués and said, 'He is a great parliamentarian, the Churchill of the Olympic movement.'

Chapter 21

Mr Samaranch goes to Washington

A worried little man hovers close to the police officers in the austere lobby of the government building and looks about him. It's Samaranch, trying his best to be invisible. To his right, half a dozen TV cameras wait in ambush. To his left, twenty, maybe thirty, boisterous reporters browbeat a policeman. 'If you would please stand in line, folks,' the officer pleads. They won't. Everyone wants to be first through the hearing-room door to get the best view of Samaranch when he testifies, to see, will his hands tremble, will his brow sweat?

This is a new experience for Mr Samaranch. Usually, on his visits around the world, people treat him like a head of state, motorcycle outriders clear his way through traffic, people call him 'Your Excellency'. Always and everywhere he encounters deference. He does not hang about in public lobbies seeking refuge among police officers who don't even know his name.

Samaranch knew from the start that this trip to Washington would not be his kind of party. The IOC's stock on Capitol Hill hit a low during the Salt Lake scandal, and kept on falling. In April 1999, at Senator John McCain's hearings, there'd been the Anita DeFrantz and Jim Easton fiasco, prompting a realisation on Capitol Hill that these clowns were not America's representatives but Samaranch's, accountable only to him and the IOC. Samaranch's own failure to turn up caused deep offence. Then Fred Upton, a youthful Congressman from

328

Michigan got interested, went digging in Atlanta, exclaimed, 'Holy Cow! This has got to end,' and started his own hearings through his commerce investigations committee whose mission is to 'go after fraud and abuse wherever we find it'. Anita turned up with her see-no-evil-hear-no-evil act in October and the ioc's stock on the Hill sank deeper.

When Upton invited Samaranch along, it was made clear that, if he refused, some day when he set foot on American soil, whether for a fine dinner in New York, a spot of skiing in Aspen or to visit Coca-Cola, he would find himself welcomed with a subpoena. Samaranch agreed to appear, not in October when they wanted him, but in December, when he would have reforms to show them.

For weeks before the hearing, as Samaranch scrambled together some reforms, Hill and Knowlton worked to salvage a little dignity from the occasion. From his office on Washington's New Hampshire Avenue, just a few blocks' walk from Upton's offices, Gary Hymel, grey-haired, sixty-six years old, and a Hill and Knowlton hard man, started throwing his two hundred and ten pounds of weight about.

'What Hill and Knowlton wanted to do was have Samaranch bond with the members,' said Steve Schmidt, the committee's spokesman. 'They requested for Samaranch to hold a little briefing prior to the meeting and maybe have, like, tea and doughnuts with all the members for what they originally requested was an hour prior to the hearing, so that they got to know the real Mr Samaranch, not the person they'd been reading about in the press.

'It's not appropriate and we denied it,' Schmidt said.

Hill and Knowlton do not give in so easily. They requested private meetings for Samaranch with Fred Upton and another senior member. Schmidt explained why they said no: 'This is an investigatory committee and the rules of procedure are strictly adhered to. The witnesses aren't friends of the members. It's not a folksy thing.'

Next they wanted Samaranch and his retinue, in their fleet of limousines, to drive directly to the doors of the Rayburn building where the hearing was held, along a restricted area called the Horseshoe where no US citizen may drive; they walk up from the street. Er, no, said congressional staff. You can have one limousine on account of Mr Samaranch's age; that's all.

'They wanted to come in early and sit in an anteroom reserved for members so that he would avoid all international press and so that he did not have to come through the public doors of the committee room,' said Schmidt. That request, too, was denied.

So there he was, worried little Samaranch in the pell-mell of the public lobby hovering round the policemen and their metal detectors, getting his first taste of something he'd avoided all his life: the democratic process and all the dreadful indignities it held for him. Once his retinue caught up, they showed what they thought of the democratic process and its petty little rules. 'They just marched through to the anteroom and at that point we were not going to stop them,' said Schmidt.

Some things had gone Samaranch's way before the hearing. Over the months, he'd courted Henry Kissinger, Howard Baker and George Mitchell, he'd shown them his gentle side, his new passion for reform, and it looked as if he had won their confidence. That was a coup; the Holy Trinity of American politics would be here today to support him.

That very morning in the *Washington Post*, Amy Shipley, a

young woman who sports tweed jackets, sensible skirts, flat shoes and thick white stockings, reported that Samaranch would testify that the IOC had already implemented the most important reforms. Her story was headlined 'Samaranch: Reforms are in Place'.

The old man had a few tricks to pull on the day. He would testify in Spanish, despite the strong command of English his aides used to boast about. Everything would be translated, back and forth. That would slow things down, give him time to think. And there was another device, a special Hill and Knowlton device which would swing the day's fortunes heavily in Samaranch's favour. The old fascist was on hostile ground. Of course he had the wit to come armed.

Samaranch walked briskly to the witness table, tossed his notes in front of him, straightened his documents, undid his jacket button and took his seat. Either side of him sat his interpreters. Behind him scowled Dick Pound, big and rangy in red tie, grey suit and tasselled loafers, and Anita DeFrantz in a green floral dress and green tweed jacket. Jim Easton wore his unfortunate furtive look and Bill Hybl was there too, flashing charm on and off like neon lights. They'd brought some athletes along.

The big brass clock, high on the wall, said ten o'clock, the members took their seats on the dais, Upton, boyish, tired-eyed and lean, wielded his gavel and immediately started laying into Samaranch's hastily concocted reforms.

'We are here because the Olympic Games are too important to allow a culture of corruption to be whitewashed and perpetuated by a piece of paper called reforms,' he said. 'The record is riddled with evidence of over a decade's worth of blatant abuse which was ignored by those who consistently,

arrogantly, unbelievably, turned a blind eye to the ugly truth.'
Samaranch sat, rocking and nodding, head cocked towards the
interpreter on his left.

Next up was the kind of woman Samaranch can't stand,
sassy, bright, aggressive, impervious to his charm, and a
Democrat. Diana DeGette of Colorado gave him a tongue-
lashing: 'I fear that these reforms will be cosmetic and purely
to mask the aristocratic aura that has formed around the
organisation,' she said.

California's Henry Waxman, with deep brown eyes, round
spectacles, dark eyebrows and moustache, looked like a
cleaned-up Groucho Marx, but he wasn't playing for laughs.
Waxman, the IOC's enemy number one on the Hill, introduced
a bill back in the spring that might hit the IOC where it hurt,
prohibiting American corporations from providing any
financial support until the IOC adopted George Mitchell's
reforms.

Now he told Samaranch, 'Without a genuine change in
attitudes, no amount of enforcement will be enough.' He was
struck by some IOC reaction to the reform plan, by the Italian
member who said, 'Our vote was mostly a vote of confidence
for Samaranch. Many, many people were against some of the
proposals, but we decided almost unanimously that we would
support the president.'

'Even more incredible,' said Waxman, was the Pakistani
member who said bid cities had used 'Satanic methods' to prey
upon IOC members and claimed the IOC was, 'unnecessarily
suffering from a guilt complex'. 'This is another IOC member
who doesn't get it,' said Waxman.

As more committee members pitched in, opinion ranged all
the way from contempt to even more contempt and
Samaranch faced something rare and rather dangerous on

Capitol Hill, bipartisan consensus. Joe Barton, the Republican from Texas, was curious about Mrs Samaranch's $13,000 holiday, courtesy of the Atlanta bid people.

'I have a wife too,' Barton said with his long, wide Texan vowels. (The 'I' came out close to 'Aaahh', just as wife came out 'waaaf.') 'She likes the high society. She likes to go shopping and when she goes shopping I pay for it.' Samaranch's head wobbled, he twisted a piece of paper between his fingers; it looked like a wounded butterfly. 'I would like you to announce today that you will resign,' said Barton.

Upton invited Samaranch to take the oath. He stood up smartly, raised his hand, and for a moment, the briefest moment, there was just a chance he might forget himself under the pressure, raise his hand a touch too high, extend his arm, click his heels and like Peter Sellers's Dr Strangelove, ('Mein Führer, I can walk!') perform the fascist salute from the good old days. It didn't happen. Samaranch simply swore to tell the truth, the whole truth and nothing but the truth, and took his seat to deliver his statement.

'I promised the IOC would institute fundamental reforms. I can now say the IOC has kept its word,' he said, reading from his script, in English. The reforms would result in a 'renovated IOC – one that is more transparent, more accountable, and more responsive', he went on. 'We have elected ten active athletes to our membership and banned visits to bid cities,' he went on, and on, and on.

Perhaps he'd been reading the *Arabian Nights*, and the king's wife, Scheherezade, who devised a cunning way to put off her execution, had given him an idea. Samaranch wasn't about to captivate his audience with gripping stories though; he was boring them into paralysis. He took us on a trip back into history, to 1894, explained the IOC structure, and its legal status under Swiss law. It made teeth ache.

Briefly, a buzz circulated the room. Heads turned and we saw that there was a star among us. Henry Kissinger was in the house. (More than that, Samaranch knew, and everyone would soon discover, his Prince had come).

On and on Samaranch droned, about the history of IOC visits, the escape from financial crisis twenty years ago. On and on, six thousand words, twenty-five minutes of mind-numbing blandness. Reporters slumped in their seats, pens ran out of ink, audio tapes needed changing and batteries ran flat. Up on the dais, congressional eyes glazed over. Still Samaranch trudged on, through the precise structure of his IOC 2000 Commission, listing all the prestigious international names everyone already knew.

It was a wily speech, as anyone who stayed awake the whole time could tell you, alighting on positive keywords at every opportunity: 'athletes' made fourteen appearances, 'youth' another seven, words to do with 'trust' popped up half a dozen times. The people, the public, not usually high in Samaranch's priorities, scored another six.

He had two pages of thanks to read out, he wanted to express appreciation to the IOC 2000 Commission, to Jim and Anita, various other people and the IOC members who'd made everything possible. Perhaps he'd forgotten he'd come to apologise for a discredited regime, not to pick up an Academy Award. Someone should have stood up and shouted, 'Oy! Juan! You forgot to thank your mum!'

Probably the guys at Hill and Knowlton had calculated precisely how much of the committee's time Samaranch could kill. He'd just wasted twenty-five precious congressional minutes and he was about to burn more.

Fred Upton and his team asked questions in rounds, racing

against the red light that flashed on when time was up. They knew, and were not happy, that Samaranch's insistence on using interpreters would effectively halve the time available for questions, but they could surely have no inkling of the old man's magical ability to make time evaporate.

The questions started off well enough. 'In the words of a famous senator sitting in the front row I want to know, What did you know and when did you know it?' asked Upton. 'When did you personally become aware that bidding cities were giving excessive inducements and gifts to IOC members in violation of IOC rules?' He was referring to Howard Baker, who'd put that famous question to Richard Nixon during the Watergate hearings. Had Nixon possessed Samaranch's talent for waffle, he might have stayed president.

Samaranch answered with a leisurely trip around the houses that took in, among other highlights, the history of the Los Angeles games, its financial success, the good works it funded. Outside in the crisp sunlight, little creatures lived out their entire lifespans and died. Inside, the brass clock ticked on, people grew a little older, and Samaranch relayed in minute detail the rules and regulations the IOC had introduced in the past. ('Play up the IOC's history, accomplishments and successes in judiciously addressing alleged improprieties over the years,' Hill and Knowlton had been urging from the start.)

Upton wanted to know why Samaranch hadn't acted on the Toronto report that warned IOC members as long ago as 1991 about gifts. Samaranch embarked on the long and weary story of his encounter with Toronto's man and topped it off with his routine response, 'Never did he submit a single name. Had they given us names we would have been able to take action.'

The red light shone for Upton and at least one representative began losing patience. 'Mr Samaranch, as you see the red light goes on really fast in this committee and I would appreciate short answers if possible,' said Diana DeGette. She fixed him in her steely gaze. 'All right?'

'Right,' said Samaranch, with a cheeky smile.

DeGette wanted to know if the ethics commission would be able to compel testimony from members. That seemed simple enough.

'The ethics committee is totally independent,' Samaranch replied. 'I am sure Senator Baker will be in a position to provide assistance.'

'So you as president don't know whether or not the commission will be allowed to compel testimony by subpoena or other means from IOC officials?' said DeGette. 'Yes or no?'

'To give you a short answer, yes,' said Samaranch. Back and forth it went from English into Spanish, from Spanish into English and the big brass clock ticked on.

DeGette: 'You *do* know?'

Samaranch: 'Sí.'

DeGette: 'And *will* they be allowed to compel testimony?'

'They are fully independent and they will act as they find advisable,' said Samaranch.

DeGette's voice thinned and moved up its range. 'So is that a *yes* they *will* be able to compel testimony, or a I don't know whether or not since they are independent.' She blinked twice, raised her eyes heavenwards, sighed and put her hand to her chin.

'As I say again the ethics commission is independent,' said Samaranch.

'Yeah, yeah, Mr Samaranch,' said an angry DeGette. 'Will

the ethics committee be able to compel testimony or not? If you don't know we will ask someone else.'

Samaranch, at last, replied: 'I do know and the answer is yes.'

DeGette did her best to extract from the president some detail about how the ethics commission would work, but she was swimming through treacle. She thrashed about for a while on the new reforms' vague rules on gifts.

'The rules you call vague was one of the rules of the ethics committee,' explained Samaranch. 'But that problem is no longer with us. It has disappeared completely, no visits, no gifts.'

'But that's the problem,' said DeGette. 'The new gift rules say only gifts with nominal value in accordance with prevailing customs. What happens if someone says a gift of $500 or $1000 is in accordance with prevailing customs? What's to prevent this under this new rule passed by the IOC this weekend?'

'I think that gifts were closely related to trips,' said Samaranch. 'The article you refer to would no longer be valid today. I will have them remove it.'

DeGette looked up, astonished: 'You'll have them remove the gift provision?' For all Samaranch's protestations about the independence of the ethics commission, there he was, autocratic as ever, asserting he'd have them strike out one of their rules. DeGette hadn't got any further when the red light signalled the end of her round.

Richard Burr was one of several members concerned that Judge Mbaye was chairman of the ethics commission as well as vice-president of the executive board, which would rule on any sanctions recommended by the ethics commission. Isn't that what's generally known as a conflict of interest?

Not at all, said Samaranch. 'He is Supreme Court justice of

Senegal, [former vice-] president of the International Court of Justice in The Hague. I think these credentials are sufficient for us to place our trust in him.' He might have added that Mbaye had a nifty golf swing, as anyone who'd seen him on his Olympic freebie in Augusta could tell.

Waxman spotted two more gigantic conflicts of interest (both revealed for the first time in my *The New Lords of the Rings*). Waxman laid out his facts. Without inviting any competing bids, the IOC granted the NBC television company a contract to cover five consecutive Olympics. At the time an NBC executive had an IOC seat, and shortly after securing the contract NBC made a $1 million donation to Samaranch's Olympic Museum in Lausanne. 'And I have to tell you that looks to me like a quid pro quo,' said Waxman. 'But even more incredibly a Japanese company gave a $20 million contribution to that museum at the same time as the IOC was considering whether to award the 1998 games to Nagano Japan! I'd like you to respond to these allegations.'

'We are very happy with the NBC contract. They have been with us for a long time now,' said Samaranch.

Waxman coloured a little. He took a deep breath. 'The appearance is that when a highly lucrative television contract is let to one network, and the other networks don't even have a chance to come in and present to you an opportunity to do as well if not better, and then money is donated by the winner to a museum that you've been very involved in, doesn't that appear to be a conflict of interest, an impropriety?'

No, it did not. And in any case, said Samaranch during another time-consuming excursion, 'The museum is not my personal initiative. It is the home of world sport.'

Waxman's colour turned a darker shade of angry. 'Look my time is up. We're going to have Bonnie Blair [American speed skater] testify before us today. She didn't win her gold medal because the Olympics were comfortable with her . . . She did it solely on her merits. She competed against others who wanted that gold medal as well. But here the IOC gives a contract to a network and the others were not even allowed to compete! . . . The Olympics should be about real competition and the IOC ought to make these decisions based on competition and not something that appears to be a conflict of interest, an impropriety, a sweetheart deal.'

Samaranch's head wobbled. That was all.

The laid-back Joe Barton reminded Samaranch that he was on oath, reminded him that he was on record as saying he'd first become aware of improprieties a year ago and reminded him of something he might prefer to forget, that Swedish Olympic secretary-general Wolf Lyberg complained to Dick Pound in 1986 that an IOC member had demanded sex from a woman on the Swedish bid team. 'Were you aware of this letter?'

'We asked them for names and they did not come up with any,' said Samaranch amid another exhausting reply.

'So the fact that the secretary-general of the Swedish Olympic Committee sent a formal letter – you didn't consider that a formal request?' retorted Barton.

'The letter that we received contained no names,' said Samaranch.

'Did you make any attempt in your office to follow up on this letter?'

'We continued trying to find out who that member would be, but no success.' Samaranch's memory must have failed him. I have the confidential minutes of the IOC meeting where he said he wanted to take action – against the Swedish Olympic official who first revealed the demand and as good as named the culprit.

Barton moved on to Samaranch's hotel suite, which, he'd read in *Sports Illustrated*, cost the IOC half a million dollars a year.

'Is that true?' he asked.

'No, this is not true,' Samaranch replied.

'What part of that statement is not true?'

'The total, the half-million dollars,' said Samaranch. 'I live in a hotel in the city of Lausanne. I have two rooms. One is my bedroom, the other is a small salon, it is not very large, that costs approximately two hundred and fifty dollars a day, and days on which I am out of town like today, I pay seventy dollars for them to keep the reservation, the room available to me. Let me assure you it is far from being a luxurious suite.'

Barton wasn't giving up: 'Do you maintain personal effects in the two small rooms in Lausanne, Switzerland, in the Palace Hotel, your personal artefacts that are only yours, that stay there when you're not there?'

Visions of the presidential Y-fronts, toothbrush and talcum powder, perhaps even a truss, came to mind.

'As I said earlier, sir, when I am not in town the IOC pays seventy dollars a day.'

Henry Waxman had done a time swap to have one more go at Samaranch. He was curious about why Nagano had burned the records on what IOC members had got up to.

'What are we to make of that?' he asked.

'I don't know. You should direct your questions at Nagano,' said Samaranch.

That did it. 'The reason I'm asking you is the IOC does not appear to have done much investigation about any of the potential abuses by other cities except to send some letters and asking them whether they knew of some abuses and accepted what they had to say.' Waxman drew breath – he was too cross for punctuation. 'It seems to me that the IOC if you really cared to know what abuses took place in the past would have demanded records and called the people from Nagano on to the carpet to find out why they destroyed their records. We in the US have held up Atlanta and Salt Lake to scrutiny. It looks like we care about it. I'm not sure the IOC cares about it.' Henry Waxman left the room.

Joe Barton wanted to know more about Mrs Samaranch's visit to Atlanta.

'They insisted on inviting her,' said Samaranch. 'I said that she should accept the invitation and visit Atlanta. My wife is already advanced in years and she can not travel on her own. I am not going to tell you how old she is because she might be angry with me.' That drew a generous laugh from the IOC contingent. 'She accepted the invitation. She was very well treated. I wouldn't call it an official visit but it was a visit by the wife of the IOC president. With your permission I have in my hands a letter that is very significant. I'll ask that the interpreter read it.'

It was a letter from Dan Quayle, then American vice-president, telling Bibis what a pleasure it was to meet her in Atlanta, and hoping she was able to 'sample the warm hospitality for which the South is famous'.

'What formal purpose if any was served for the good of the Olympic movement by having the Atlanta organisers spend at least thirteen thousand dollars to have your wife visit Atlanta, Charleston and I believe Orlando on that trip?' asked Barton.

'This is what the letter says, which is that the South is famous for its hospitality,' said Samaranch.

'I agree with that. I'm from Texas,' Barton drawled. 'I understand that we're famous for our hospitality . . . I think it's well and good if she wants to visit the South and have that hospitality, but I don't think the Olympic movement and host city should have to pay her expenses.'

'You are probably right, sir,' said Samaranch. 'This is probably of the organising committee. This was an invitation based on friendship and this is all I can advance.'

It was close to one o'clock. Stomachs grumbled.

Samaranch, single-handedly, had consumed two hours of congressional time and left no-one any wiser. It was a kind of achievement. Upton excused the witness, who stood up and walked into the arms of Henry Kissinger. Henry gripped Juan's left arm and held him close. Juan gathered Henry into the warmest of hugs and grinned all over his face as if they might waltz off into the sunlight together. It was an unsettling scene, two men of one generation, the elderly Jew who had escaped the Holocaust embracing the elderly fascist whose country kept Hitler's Wehrmacht in smart grey uniforms throughout the War.

Up on the dais, the politicians looked physically sapped, and now they had to face the Holy Trinity of American politics, Henry Kissinger, Howard Baker and, if not George Mitchell himself, who was held up by fog in Michigan, his representative on earth, Ken Duberstein.

All three men praised the reforms. Kissinger, bizarrely, shared his unusual take on the Hitler Olympics of 1936 as an occasion when Jews enjoyed a brief release from Nazi pressure. He had 'enormous confidence in the ethics commission', and before Mitchell's man had got a word in, Kissinger assured the members, 'I talked to Ken Duberstein at least once a week and I have the impression . . . that what we proposed was consistent with the wishes of the Mitchell commission.' Kissinger praised his own role in reconciling the conflicting approaches of the IOC and the White House towards the drug problem. Evidently he'd done another splendid job.

Actually, Duberstein wasn't entirely happy. The IOC, he said, had fallen short of Mitchell's recommendations when it came to electing members, term limits and, as for dismantling the interlocking relationships between IOC members, national committees and the rest, they hadn't done that at all.

But Duberstein's reservations somehow melted in the air. Someone mentioned this was the last congressional session of the century and it certainly felt as if we'd all been there a very long time. The representatives on the dais seemed drained by Samaranch's curiously hypnotic performance, fading through lack of lunch and dizzied by the intoxicating whiff of power-celebrity coming off Baker and Kissinger. When they put their questions this time, they were loose, floppy, easily deflected.

What about extending the reforms to the president? Barton asked Kissinger.

'Well, I frankly hadn't focused on that,' said the Great Man. 'I would certainly expect the president of the IOC will set an example to others for meticulous adherence to the letter and the spirit of reform.'

Kissinger had to leave early, tightly scheduled as ever, to catch a train to his next appointment. He had just enough time for some hugs. Anita stepped forward. Kissinger offered her first one cheek then the other and slapped her hard on the back as if he were burping a very big baby. And he was off, leaving his old friend Howard Baker to finish the job.

Which he did, in spades. Baker, easy and languid, was so reassuring it was tempting to yawn, curl up on a hearth rug somewhere and go to sleep. Sure, there were a few things missing from the ethics code, but take it from me, he was saying, it'll all work out. Don't worry.

One member asked, would the ethics commission's recommendations about sanctions be made public? 'I don't believe it's dealt with any place in our bylaws or in our code but I believe so, yes,' drawled Baker. No-one dared ask him, well would they or wouldn't they?

Sensing a power vacuum, Baker stepped in to fill it and started giving answers to questions that hadn't been put. Like, 'Tell us, just how terrific is Judge Mbaye?'

'I must say I am mightily impressed by him,' said Baker. 'He's careful, he's deliberate, and he's determined to see that this undertaking works. That he's also a member of the executive committee doesn't bother me.'

'Senator Baker, how warm is your regard for President Samaranch?' was another question nobody was asking.

'I could not have asked for more co-operation than I have had from President Samaranch,' Baker said. 'I have talked to him privately. I have talked to him in groups and I came away convinced that he was fully dedicated to the matter of trying to clean this up so to speak.' Nobody stopped him, so he rolled on: 'I have a very high regard for President Samaranch and I know he's testified effectively this morning . . . I really don't have any fear of undue influence by President Samaranch . . . I think he's well-meaning, he's dedicated. I think he's given distinguished service and I really have no reason to think that this will change.'

It was time for the next session, which didn't matter much: it was only the athletes. Samaranch made his way to the exit. Amy Shipley stepped forward and offered him her hand. Samaranch took it and held it for a moment. They stood close and smiled into each other's eyes.

Franklin Servan-Schreiber had come a long way from the Cyber Office to the Congress. He strutted about. He actually touched Henry Kissinger. He issued instructions to the media. He called a press conference and cancelled it. He said, 'The last question is for Amy.' This was CyberMan's finest hour.

Outside in the lobby Samaranch consented to speak to the press. It was back to the usual not very tough questions.

'How do you think the testimony went?' someone asked.

'I think the testimony went very well,' he smiled.

'Is the scandal over?'

'I hope so.'

'Mr Samaranch, are you indispensable?'

He didn't answer, left the building, stepped into his limousine and glided away.

Baker went before the news cameras. My colleague Clare asked him: 'Mr Baker, you've been very warm in your support of President Samaranch. Does it worry you at all that the leader of the world Olympic movement is a former fascist?'

'No it doesn't,' drawled Baker. 'I judge by what President Samaranch is doing now and what he is now and if you start looking that far back into the past it is absolutely fruitless.'

And that was that. The press ran off to write their stories. Amy reported: 'Displaying occasional humor and unshakeable calm, IOC president Juan Antonio Samaranch testified for three [actually, two] gruelling hours . . . on Capitol Hill.' Samaranch the Reformer. With a little help from his friends, he had changed his shirt and saved his skin again.

Back in the hearing room the athletes performed to a nearly empty house. Big, bouncy, puppyish volleyball star Robert Ctvrtlik showed the qualities that had got him chosen as the very latest United States IOC member the previous weekend. 'Something somewhat magical happened when athletes took the floor,' he enthused of his first IOC meeting. A beatific smile lit up his face. 'As opposed to sleeping, people seemed to sit up and listen . . . From day one, I had the feeling that world leaders and IOC members seemed to pay special attention when one of the athletes would take the floor.' Before one athlete could say a word at today's hearing, world leaders and IOC members had fast-legged it to the door.

Then, one speaker started making sense. John Naber, tall, dark and handsome, the legendary swimmer and member of OATH, had come armed with a metaphor and lashed into the reforms. 'Giving the ethics commission the responsibility to eliminate the perception of IOC misconduct without giving them the power to do so is like finding a man drowning twenty feet from shore, tossing him a fifteen-foot rope, proudly claiming you've met him more than halfway.'

As for drug testing, 'A "zero tolerance" attitude is believable only from a truly independent testing body.'

On elections, he warned, 'the possibility of the same group voting for each other year after year, is both disturbing and real.' Athletes should be allowed to vote for who they judge will represent their interests, not just fellow athletes within eight years of their last Olympics. And to hold elections during the games 'when athletes' minds must necessarily be on more pressing issues' was 'sadly ill-timed', he said.

Samaranch had been asked whether the US drive for Olympic reform might trigger retribution. Not at all, he'd replied. Naber disagreed: 'How can we not think somebody out there is not going to hold this discussion or others like it against us?'

That's what Naber said, that's what the committee expected him to say and that's why they'd invited him to testify alongside Kissinger, Baker and Mitchell in the session that was heavily reported by the media. Instead, Naber spoke in the graveyard session when the press table was empty. And here's why.

'Hill and Knowlton had called us the previous week, it was Gary Hymel, incensed that John Naber would be placed on that panel with Kissinger, Mitchell and Baker, demanding to know which member had requested that witness,' Steve Schmidt told me next morning, still fuming. 'Lobbying started. The day before we had a heated discussion with the chairman. Fifteen minutes literally before the witness list was to be public a call came through from the chairman that said he will be removed and it is not debatable. So Naber, whose comments were very, very good, and specific, was lost yesterday.'

As the room emptied, Hill and Knowlton's Gary Hymel strolled over to Upton's counsel. 'That was just a great hearing,' he smiled.

'You won one on me, Gary, and I'm never going to forget it,' she replied.

'I'm not going to admit to anything,' Hill and Knowlton's man said.

Acknowledgements

The Great Olympic Swindle could not have been written without my co-author Clare Sambrook. She helped shape the themes and tone of the book, came up with the title and wrote five chapters. The curtain-raiser on Anita DeFrantz is hers as are 'Call Hill and Knowlton', 'Tantrums and Tussles', 'A Rebel in the Family' and 'Mr Samaranch goes to Washington'. Clare researched Kissinger, Baker and Mitchell, interviewed General McCaffrey and Marc Hodler, secured the Atlanta documents and edited the text.

We owe a big thank you to readers who bought the first two *Lords* books, many of whom sent encouraging messages asking for a third. And we're indebted to many sources who can not be named; they know who they are. Within the sports establishment and on Capitol Hill people went out of their way to offer documents, insights and leads.

Among the athletes Mark Tewksbury was especially generous with his time. Thanks also to John Naber, Dawn Fraser, Ann Peel, Nancy Hogshead and all the athletes, scholars and administrators from OATH.

We owe a considerable debt to sports editor Jen Jensen and Dan Melchior of *Ekstra Bladet* in Copenhagen who commissioned investigations around the world on sports politics, money and corruption – and the Mafia.

For all the reporters who take a kicking in this book many more fine journalists offered advice and kindness. We are grateful to Michael Gavshon, Carolyn McEwen, Ian Bent, Craig Copetas, Steven Downes, Albert Knechtel, Paul Lashmar, Thomas Kistner and Jens Wienreich.

And additional thanks to Alan Abrahamson, Elliott Almond, Olav Skaaning Andersen, Jens Sejer Andersen, Mihir Bose, Frank Brandsas, Frank Deford, Kevin Flaherty, Jane Lee, David Leigh, Erskine McCullough, Ulf Nilsson, Brendan Pittaway, Randy Starkman, Matthew Rose, Melissa Turner, Sue Turton and Matti Virtanen.

The new pictures of Samaranch in fascist uniform came by way of old friends Victor Saura and Jaume Reixach at *El Triangle* in Barcelona. Paul McGeough at the *Sydney Morning Herald* and Tom Smart at the *Deseret News* in Salt Lake City kindly provided pictures, and Paul Bellinger helped capture IOC luminaries testifying in Washington.

John Hornewer allowed us to choose from his ringside pictures in Houston and let us pick his brains on the sport. Thanks to Rob Fleder and Craig Neff at *Sports Illustrated* who commissioned the Houston trip and to Steve Bunce, Ornulf Hansen, Ken Jones, Paul Konnor, Pat Putnam, Rod Robertson, Heidi Steiger and Karl-Heinz Wehr for a fast education in amateur boxing.

Boxing led to the Mob and we could not have got to grips with the story without help from Peter Dewhirst, Leonid Finkelstein, Michael Gillard, Pascal Henry, Pierre Hurel, Bjørn Lambek, Kirsty Malcolm, Nick Anning, Stefan Ravion, Paddy Rawlinson and Toby Sculthorpe. Photographer Morten Bjørn Jensen of *Ekstra Bladet* got the shots that mattered in Antalya.

Once again Jim Ferstle was generous with his time and his expertise on doping.

In Australia and on the road we've had welcome assistance

from Natasha Bita, Kimina Lyall, Jane Cadzow, Jacquelin Magnay, Pamela Williams, and old friends Greg Hunter, Graem Sims and Ross Coulthart.

In Utah we had the benefit of guidance from Katharine Biele, Howard Berkes, Dean Derhak, Mike Gorrell, Linda Fantin, Alexis Kelner, Wes Odell, Lisa Riley Roche and Ivan Weber.

In Japan Monica Nakamura provided bed and board, time and translation skills, and introductions to the refuseniks of Nagano. Haruo Nogawa, Mitsuo Ohno and Eiichiro Tokumoto opened other doors. On Bob Hasan help came from Jeremy Bristow, George Aditjondro and Gerry van Klinken.

Charles Lewis and his colleagues at The Center for Public Integrity helped form our analysis of abuse of public trust; some of their excellent research is cited in our notes.

Julie Reid lent her wit and criticism to early drafts. Scott Armstrong and Barbara Guss opened their Washington home to us and gave wise counsel. Henry Rossbacher shared his insights and research facilities. Anita Beaty, Jay Coakley, Henning Eichberg, John Hoberman, Maud Leroux, Michael Shapcott and Graham Stringer MP all helped in valuable ways. We're grateful to our editor Helen Simpson who, as we flagged, brought rigour to the final text. And to friends and family who put up with our neglect, thank you.

Andrew Jennings, London, March, 2000.

Notes and Sources

The Great Olympic Swindle is an entirely new book which builds on *The Lords of the Rings: Power Money and Drugs in the Modern Olympics* (Andrew Jennings & Vyv Simson, Simon & Schuster, 1992) and *The New Lords of the Rings: Olympic Corruption and How to Buy Gold Medals* (Andrew Jennings, Simon & Schuster, 1996).

The Lords of the Rings appeared in America as *Dishonored Games*, SPI Books, New York, and in translation in Denmark, the Netherlands, France, Germany, Greece, Japan, Norway, Brazil, Spain, Colombia and Sweden. Pirate Chinese editions were produced in Taiwan and Hong Kong. *The New Lords of the Rings* appeared in Danish, German, Japanese, Norwegian and Spanish.

The themes of *The Great Olympic Swindle* continue at www.ajennings.8m.com.

There are few reliable, factual sources on the IOC. Outstanding is John Hoberman's essay, 'Toward a Theory of Olympic Internationalism', *Journal of Sport History*, Vol. 22, No. 1, spring 1995.

The best study of Samaranch's political and business career in Spain is Jaume Boix and Arcadio Espada, *El Deporte del Poder*, Ediciones Temas De Hoy, Madrid, 1991.

Allen Guttmann, *The Games Must Go On*, Columbia University Press, New York, 1984, is an excellent study of the IOC Samaranch inherited.

The way the IOC likes to see itself is reflected in three books:

David Miller, *Olympic Revolution: The Olympic Biography of Juan Antonio Samaranch*, foreword by H. M. the King of Spain, Pavilion Books, 1992.

Kevan Gosper with Glenda Korporaal, *An Olympic Life*, Allen & Unwin, Australia, 2000.

Rod McGeoch with Glenda Koporaal, *The Bid: How Australia won the 2000 Games*, William Heinemann, Australia, 1994.

The IOC's website, www.olympic.org, holds copious, albeit sanitised, information, including press releases, speeches and biographies.

Among valuable online news sources are the archives and reporting of: *The Salt Lake City Weekly* (www.slweekly.com), *The Salt Lake Tribune* (www.sltrib.com), *Deseret News* (www. desnews.com), *Sydney Morning Herald* (www.smh.com.au), *News Ltd* (www.news.com.au) and *The Atlanta Journal-Constitution* (www.accessatlanta.com/ajc).

1: Anita's Bad Hair Day

1 Anita DeFrantz testified before the Senate Committee on Commerce, Science and Transportation, 14 April 1999.

1 DeFrantz and Harriet Tubman: *Dallas Morning News*, 14 April 1999.

2 Free ski holidays and sleigh rides and shopping trips etc: report by lawyers Hogan & Hartson for the United States Olympic Committee, 26 February 1999.

2   Blaming the Salt Lake City hosts: *Reports of the IOC ad hoc Commission to Investigate the Conduct of Certain IOC Members and to Consider Possible Changes in the Procedures for the Allocation of the Games of the Olympiad and Olympic Winter Games*, presented to the IOC executive board, 24 January 1999 and 11 March 1999.

3   Anita DeFrantz won her bronze medal in a rowing eight at the Montreal Games in 1976.

3   McCain's biographical details: www.senate.gov/~mccain.

4   Ali in Rome: David Remnick, *King of the World: Muhammad Ali and the Rise of an American Hero*, Random House, 1998, p102-103.

6   The *Mitchell Report*: Senator George Mitchell headed the Special Bid Oversight Committee that reported to the United States Olympic Committee, 1 March 1999.

6   The *Toronto Report*: *Report to the IOC by the Toronto Ontario Olympic Council on the Candidature of the City of Toronto to Host the Games of the XXVIth Olympiad*, Lausanne, 9 January 1991. George Mitchell attached the *Toronto Report* to his own report of 1999.

8   The Amateur Athletic Foundation of Los Angeles did not respond to a request for DeFrantz's salary details. According to the foundation's 1998 tax return DeFrantz took $217,744 in salary and $12,800 in benefit contributions.

9   Easton's bicycles: Jere Longman, *New York Times*, 12 February 1999.

10 'people in glass houses': AP, 20 March 1999.

11 Andrew Jennings, *The New Lords of the Rings*, 1996.

11 Samaranch's fascist past is covered in Chapter 10.

16 DeFrantz on rowing: *Women's Sport & Fitness*, April 1991.

16 Deford's interview with Samaranch: *Real Sport with Bryant Gumbel*, HBO cable TV, 15 July 1996.

2: The Raiders Are Coming!

Essential source material for this chapter are the two *Reports of the* IOC *ad hoc Commission*, 1999.

Except where otherwise cited, internal correspondence is from the archive of the Salt Lake Bid Committee and the *Salt Lake Ethics Report*, whose official title is: *Report to the Board of Trustees*, Salt Lake Board of Ethics of the Salt Lake Organising Committee for the Olympic Winter Games of 2002, 8 February 1999.

The history of Salt Lake's early Olympic bids is told, delightfully, in Alexis Kelner, *Utah's Olympic Circus*, Recreational Guidebooks, Salt Lake City, 1989.

19 Pat Rosenbrock's notes were released by New South Wales Olympics minister Michael Knight, 5 May 1999.

20 'This is the place': Wallace Stegner, *Mormon Country*, University of Nebraska Press, 1981, p33.

20 'grease the wheels': AP, 16 January 1999.

21 'too high a cost for the Olympics': *Deseret News*, 3 January 1999.

24 David Sibandze's children: *The New Lords of the Rings*, 1996, Chapter 11.

24–5 Bribes in Birmingham: *Salt Lake Ethics Report*, 1999.

25 Paying for the Lausanne Museum: *The New Lords of the Rings*, 1996, Chapter 6.

29 'They were really nice to me': *Washington Post*, 2 March 1999.

30 'way above and beyond': *Salt Lake Tribune*, 16 January 1999.

31 Mukora's demand for $4,371: *The New Lords of the Rings*, 1996, Chapter 15.

33 Bjarne Haggman: AP, 19 January 1999, *Toronto Sun*, *Toronto Star* and *Globe and Mail* extensively in mid-January 1999.

36 'I really respect their privacy': *Salt Lake Tribune*, 30 January 1999.

3: There's Jim and Earl and Frank and Nick and Spence and Bob and all those Fellows doing Deals down in Salt Lake

38–42 Snowbasin, the SLOC and the US Government: *Wall Street Journal*, 9 July 1998, *Salt Lake Weekly*, 16 July 1998 and *Salt Lake Tribune*, 15 April 1997.

38–42 Sinclair Oil, Snowbasin, Sun Valley and other Holding enterprises: www.sinclairoil.com.

39 Earl Holding biographical detail: *Salt Lake Tribune*, 13 February 2000.

42 Center for Responsive Politics: www.opensecrets.org.

43 Snowboarding, Joklik and MK Gold: *San Jose Mercury News*, 18 February 1999.

45 'bullshit': *Salt Lake Weekly*, 23 October 1997.

45 Mayor Deedee Corradini and Bonneville Pacific Corp: *Salt Lake Weekly*, *Salt Lake Tribune* and *Deseret News*.

46 Alma's home cooking: *Salt Lake Tribune*, 23 April 1997.

47 Bob Garff: *Salt Lake Tribune*, 26 November 1998.

47 'shoddy bribe': *Salt Lake Tribune*, 6 December 1998.

4: The Corruption-Hunter, *or* Blind Man's Buff

49 Howard Berkes's story and its impact: *American Journalism Review*, March 1999.

50 'IOC Official Criticizes SLOC': Mike Carter, AP, 10 December 1998.

52–5 *Toronto Report*, 1991.

57 *Astrid Report*: AP, 2 June 1992. Berlin bid: *The New Lords of the Rings*, Chapter 15.

60 IOC human rights press release: www.olympic.org.

62 Allegations are a surprise: *Deseret News*, 13 December 1998.

62 Gosper on Hodler: Gosper, *An Olympic Life*, 2000, p312.

63 'under the carpet': *USA Today*, 16 December 1999.

5: Detective Dick, Salesman Dick

64 Mr Wandering Hands: Falun municipal archive.

67 'Kenneth Starr': *Toronto Sun*, 22 December 1998.

68 'I'd like to have it out of the way': AP, 14 December 1998.

69 'water bomb': *Toronto Sun*, 19 February 1999.

69 'pond scum': *Toronto Star*, 19 February 1999.

69 Dennis Loeb: *Los Angeles Times*, 5 March 1999.

69–71 Pound in New York, 21 January 1999: www.olympic.org.

71 Attarabulsi resigns: UPI, 1 February 1999.

71 Sibandze resigns: Reuters, 27 January 1999.

71 Pound comments, 24 January 1999: reported world-wide, and www.olympic.org.

72 Pescante's vocation: *La Gazzetta dello Sport*, 23 December 1998.

72 Anchorage: *The New Lords of the Rings*, 1996, Chapter 11.

72 Joan Kirner: AAP, 22 January 1999.

73 Saab car: *Washington Post*, 18 January 1999.

73 Prince Frederik von Sachsen-Lauenberg: AP, 20 January 1999.

76 Kim Warren: Agence France-Press, 17 January 1999.

76 Anita DeFrantz on Samaranch: *Los Angeles Times*, 9 January 1999.

76 Gosper on Samaranch: Reuters, 23 January 1999.

76 'destabilise the situation': AP, 15 February 1999.

77 Plot against Samaranch: UPI, 20 January 1999.

77 Scandal exaggerated: AP, 12 March 1999.

77 'quite unacceptable': AP, 2 March 1999.

78 'not out to compete': *New York Times*, 15 March 1999.

78 Kim squares up to Carrard: AP, 17 March 1999.

79 IOC expenses: Reuters, 18 March 1999, and www. olympic.org.

79 $180 million profit: *Atlanta Journal-Constitution*, 14 March 1999.

79 'whitewash': Reuters, 12 March 1999.

6: Embarrassing Odour? Call Hill and Knowlton

81 Tom Hoog was a general policy adviser to Governor Bill Clinton: *Under the Influence. Presidential Candidates and Their Campaign Advisers*, The Center for Public Integrity, 1991.

81 'the inside must match the outside': address to Albany Chamber of Commerce Executive Symposium, 22 May 1997, www.hillandknowlton.com.

81 'Train key individuals': Albany Symposium, 1997.

82 David Miller: *Private Eye* No. 908, 4 October 1996.

82 They'd left CyberMan in sole charge: *Director of Communications: Report to the 109th IOC Session*, Seoul, June 1999.

83 'As in all crises': Samaranch to Olympic leaders, 23 December 1998.

83 'The crisis brought the attention': *Director of Communications Report*, 1999.

84 Privately, top sponsors: Dick Pound's *Report to the Executive Board*, Lausanne, March 1999.

84 Peter Knight: IOC *Executive Board Minutes*, June 1999.

84 'under pressure': IOC *Executive Board Minutes*, June 1999.

84–5 Dick Hyde's career: *Inside PR*, 17 January 2000.

85 'Hill and Knowlton senior management noted immediately': *Director of Communications Report*, 1999.

85 Dick was there too: www.hillandknowlton.com.

85 Hill and Knowlton achieved world-wide fee income of $189 million in 1997: *Inside PR*, www.hillandknowlton.com.

85 Boeing, Motorola and Barnes & Noble: *Washington Representatives*, Columbia Books, 1999.

86 'Reputation Protection System': www.hillandknowlton. com.

86 *The Torturers' Lobby: How Human Rights Abusing Nations Are Represented in Washington*: The Center for Public Integrity, 1992.

86 States of mind were altered: AP, 26 January 1992.

87 The *Waxman Dossier*'s official title is: *The Hill and Knowlton Documents: How the Tobacco Industry Launched its Disinformation Campaign*: A Staff Report, Majority Staff Subcommittee on Health and the Environment, US House of Representatives, 26 May 1994.

87 'no proof of the claims which link smoking to lung cancer': *Preliminary recommendations for cigarette manufacturers*, 14 December 1953, *Waxman Dossier*.

87 'pro-cigarettes': *Background Material on the Cigarette Industry Client*, 15 December 1953, *Waxman Dossier*.

87 Staff used personal connections: *Confidential Memorandum: Activities, August and September, 1954, Waxman Dossier*.

87 They paid freelance reporters: *Hill and Knowlton Report of Activities through July 31 1954, Waxman Dossier*.

88 'attitudes influenced by radio and television' . . . 'public discussion programs': *Preliminary recommendations*, 1953.

88 'advance information': *Report of Activities*, 1954.

88 'long lived distinguished public leaders' . . . 'up-to-date information': *Preliminary recommendations*, 1953.

88 'Positive stories': *Public Relations Report to the Tobacco Industry Research Committee*, 28 April 1955.

88 *Hill and Knowlton's* IOC *Communication Strategy*, 11 February 1999.

89 'crisis generators or enhancers': presentation at the PRSA National Conference, Boston, Massachusetts, 20 October 1998, www.hillandknowlton.com.

89 'new semiotic technology': 'Summary of the Crisis', IOC *Background Information*, June 1999.

89 'Tap into respect': *Communication Strategy*, 11 February 1999.

91 'It should be no mystery': *International Herald Tribune*, 23 March 1999.

91 Frank Mankiewicz: Henry Kissinger, *Years of Renewal*, Weidenfeld & Nicolson, 1999, p773.

91 Gary Hymel: *Legal Times*, 3 February 1997.

91 $1.5 million: IOC *Executive Board Minutes*, June 1999.

92–4 confidential briefing: *Memorandum to the* IOC *Executive Board*, 15 March 1999.

94–8 Dick Pound: *Report to the* IOC *Executive Board* and *Minutes*, March 1999.

100 'immediate impact': 'Summary of the Crisis', June 1999.

7: A Handmaid of the Sacred Heart Battles the Olympians

102 'inappropriate behaviour': IOC press release, 29 January, 1999.

102 'never heard of such a thing': AP, 13 December 1998.

103 'Japanese friends': Reuters, 6 February 1999.

103 'not for the public': AP, 15 January 1999.

103 'may have been excesses': AP, 15 January 1999.

103 'international row': *Kyodo*, 12 February 1999.

103 'Japanese boosters had paid': Sapporo's bid committee gave $2,800 each to four IOC members in 1964 in an

361

unsuccessful bid for the 1968 winter games. *Yomiuri Shimbun*, 4 February 1999.

103 $17 million missing: AP, 13 December 1998.

103 'We have a big painting': *Washington Post*, 6 February 1999.

104 Tsutsumi and Samaranch's Museum: *The New Lords of the Rings*, 1996, Chapter 13.

106 'I worked for 12,000 yen': *Kyodo*, 7 February 1998.

106 Operation White Snow: *Japan Times*, 4 February 1998.

107 'fifty thousand hostesses': *Daily Yomiuri*, 7 February 1998.

109 'Japanese democracy': *Kyodo*, 12 February 1999.

109 Takakazu Fukushima: *The Sponichi*, 5 February 1998.

111 Quotas: *Yomiuri Shimbun*, 5 February 1998.

112 Bob Verdi, *Chicago Tribune*, 22 February 1998.

112 *60 Minutes*, CBS, 22 February 1998

8: How Atlanta got the Games . . .

The bid committee's internal documents quoted here are among thousands held in the Atlanta History Center. A limited list of gifts and hospitality appears in the report by Griffin Bell of Atlanta law firm King & Spalding. Its official title is *Report to The Honorable Thomas Bliley and The Honorable Fred Upton, US House of Representatives for the Georgia Amateur Athletic Foundation, Inc.*, 16 September, 1999.

Excellent guides to Atlanta politics and business are: Charles Rutheiser, *Imagineering Atlanta*, Verso, 1996, and Clarence Stone, *Régime Politics*, University Press of Kansas, 1989.

115 'nothing untoward, nothing unethical': AP, 21 January 1999.

115 Billy Payne 'proud': Reuters, 15 December 1998.

117 'talented gift givers': *The Lords of the Rings*, 1992, Chapter 19.

117 'true believers': AP, 19 February, 1999.

118 'Miss America pageant': Reuters, 20 June 1996.

124 Ticket rackets: *Griffin Bell Report*, 1999.

9: . . . And how it Hurt the Poor

132 Payne land deals: Melissa Turner, *Atlanta Journal-Constitution*, 30 May 1999.

133 Billy's angle: *Atlanta Journal-Constitution*, 1 May 1999.

133 Billy's legacy: *Atlanta Journal-Constitution*, 12 February 1989.

137 Alberta Mitchell's home: AP, 16 July 1996.

140 'cruel restraints': Reuters, 11 July 1996.

140 Deford and Samaranch: HBO, 1996.

140 *El Mundo*, 4 August 1996.

141 'love and devotion': AP, 14 July 1996.

141 Papua New Guinea: UPI, 16 July 1996.

142 Christian Ruud: UPI, 22 July 1996.

142 Coca-Cola salutes fathers: *PR Newswire*, 13 June 1996.

142 GM's John Middlebrook: AP, 18 July 1996.

142 GM disappointed: *PR Newswire*, 20 July 1996.

142 Nissan sponsors: *PR Newswire*, 26 July 1996.

143 Poor bus service: news agencies from 20 July 1996.

143 Matthew Pinsent: UPI, 21 June 1996.

143 Paralympics: UPI, 19 August 1996.

143 'Most exceptional': news agencies, 4 August 1996.

145 Memorabilia: *Atlanta Journal-Constitution*, 25 February 1999 and 10 March 1999.

146 'extended resource availability program': *Atlanta Journal-Constitution*, 1 April 1999.

146 'I wish they'd just investigate us': AP, 21 January 1999.

146 'heart transplants': *Atlanta Journal-Constitution*, 16 January 1999.

146 Billy's secret memo: *Atlanta Journal-Constitution*, 10 February 1999.

147 No evidence of wrongdoing: AP, 1 March 1999.

10: Samaranch's Beautiful Launderette

149 Reports on Berthold Beitz's two visits to East Berlin: Archive of the Central Committee of the East German Communist Party, Berlin. Also *Der Spiegel*, 15 July 1996.

151 Avery Brundage correspondence: University of Illinois at Urbana-Champaign.

152 Samaranch and secret police reports: archives of the Barcelona civilian governor.

153 Samaranch loyal to Franco: *Diario de Barcelona*, 15 July 1973.

154 Salvador Puig Antich: *The New Lords of The Rings*, 1996, Chapter 14, and *Wall Street Journal*, 7 December 1999.

156 Monique Berlioux: *Minutes of IOC Executive Board*, June 1985.

157 Berlioux interview: *Minutes of IOC Executive Board*, July 1988.

159 Frederick C. Klein: *Wall Street Journal*, 5 February 1999.

161 David Duke: *Marketing Magazine*, 11 June 1992.

161 Marc Hodler on Samaranch's politics: interview with author, January 2000.

161 Gosper on Samaranch, spring 1992.

162 *The Lords of the Rings*, Granada TV, 1 June 1992 (also screened in several dozen other countries that year).

11: The Rainforest Logger, the TV Executive and Boris Yeltsin's Tennis Coach

165 Gilady and NBC: *New York Times*, 28 January 1999.

167-171 Bob Hasan and the fires of 1997: *Kings of the Jungle*, BBC, 5 September 1998.

168 Students cry 'Thief': AFP, 10 December 1998.

169 'monopoly is allowed': *Kyodo*, 16 March 1998

170 Loincloths: *Kings of the Jungle*, 1998.

170 Hasan's East Timor logging venture was located in the Viqueque area and officially opened by Suharto.

171 Hasan's Apkindo plywood cartel regulated $3.7 billion in annual exports.

171 Hasan and Freeport-McMoRan: *The Nation*, New York, 7 September 1998.

173–5 Tarpischev, Fyodorov and the National Sports Fund: *Moscow Times* at www.TheMoscowTimes.com.

174–5 Wife of Lev Chernoy: *Independent on Sunday*, 10 October 1999.

175 Tarpischev's days are numbered: *Sport Intern*, 19 February 1997.

176 Lee Kun Hee and Samsung: www.samsung.com.

176 Korean companies fiddling their books: Reuters, 19 January 1998.

177 Lee Kun Hee in court: Reuters, 25 August 1996.

180 League table of European royal families: *EuroBusiness*, cited by Reuters, 4 June 1999.

12: Just Another Family Man

187 Kim and the Korean intelligence service: Hearings before the House of Representatives Sub-committee on International Relations, 95th Congress, 1977, and *Report of The House of Representatives Investigation of Korean-American Relations*, 31 October 1978.

189 Bell Young review: *American Record Guide*, March-April 1998.

190 Kim Hae-Jung in Melbourne: AAP, 20 January 1999.

190 Philip Hersh and Colin McMahon, *Chicago Tribune*, 25 February 1999.

190 Marc Fisher, *Washington Post*, 28 February 1999.

191–3 John Kim and David Simmons: *Salt Lake Tribune* and *Deseret News* archives.

192 John Kim sues Simmons: AP, 25 August 1999.

193 John Kim's Salt Lake contract: *Salt Lake Ethics Report*, 1999.

193 Taekwondo uniforms: Alan Abrahamson, *Los Angeles Times*, 6 May 1999.

193 Kim Hye-won (Helen): *Griffin Bell Report*, 1999, and *Sydney Morning Herald*, 8 May 1999.

193 'dirty plot': AP, 12 June 1999.

193–4 Reprimands for Kim: *Reports of the IOC ad hoc Commission*, 1999.

194 IOC rejects luxury: AP, 15 June 1999.

195–6 Kim's manifesto: *Korea Times*, 19 June 1999.

197–8 Samaranch speech: www.olympic.org.

200 Executive board letter to Samaranch: AP, 15 June 1999.

200 'Mafia': Reuters, 19 June 1999.

13: Anwar's Boys Fix Fights

205 Hookers: author's confidential source.

207 'Our situation is disastrous': Wehr to Chowdhry, 10 October 1988.

208 'if two Muslims are boxing': Wehr to Chowdhry, 5 October 1992.

208 'people allegedly bribed officials': Wehr to Chowdhry, 31 December 1996.

209 'I am being honoured': Chowdhry to Wehr, 11 October 1995.

210 'plunder the cash-box': Wehr to Chowdhry, 17 July 1995.

210 'Your battle cry': Wehr to Chowdhry, 20 August 1996.

210 'sincerity, honesty and fairness of boxing's leadership': Maurath to Wehr, 25 June 1995.

210 'some of us are not honest': *Minutes*, AIBA executive committee meeting, Seoul, 11 June 1995.

210 'one of the best ever': Caner Doganeli, Seoul executive committee meeting.

211 Chowdhry made a straight approach for cash: *The New Lords of the Rings*, 1996, p120.

211 'furtively jotting the officials' names': Wehr to Chowdhry, 31 December 1996.

213 'misdeeds in Seoul': Wehr to Chowdhry, 20 August 1996.

213 'very insulting for AIBA': Chowdhry to Wehr, 8 December 1996.

213 'worried about the Park-Jones decision': Chowdhry to Wehr, 12 March 1997.

214 'If someone was wronged': AP, 4 March 1997.

214 'no gold medallist in Olympic history': David Wallechinsky, *The Complete Book of the Olympics*, Little, Brown, 1992.

214 'flashy, spectacular style': IOC press conference, Monte Carlo, 20 May 1997.

215 HBO film on Park-Jones decision, 18 July 1998.

216 'foiled by the IOC': Chowdhry, *Minutes* of executive committee meeting in Santo Domingo, 28 June 1997.

216 *New York Times*, 26 September 1997.

14: Here Comes the Mob!

220 'victim of some dubious early refereeing': Reuters, 25 October 1997.

220 'two exhibition bouts': Chagaev affidavit, 27 January 1998.

221 Wehr fax to Uzbeks, 16 January 1998.

221–2 Manatt, Phelps & Phillips, 27 January 1998.

222 'attempts at corrupting officials': Wehr to Chowdhry, 8 December 1997.

222 'submachine gun pointed at his chest': Wehr to Chowdhry, 30 January 1997.

223 Toney to Konnor, 8 May 1997.

223 Konnor to Samaranch, 1 April 1998.

224 'amateur boxing's greatest minds': *Minutes* of executive committee meeting, 3 August 1998.

231 Chowdhry's opponents in European amateur boxing: www.iat.uni-leipzig.de/eurobox/news/newse100.htm.

231 Samaranch to Chowdhry, 13 November 1997.

233 Michael Gillard, *Observer*, 29 November 1998.

15: Masters of the Universe

234 'welcomed back with great ceremony': Geopolitical Drugs Watch (Observatoire Géopolitique des Drogues), www.ogd.org.

234–5 Raid on the Black and White club: *Panorama*, BBC, 6 December 1999.

238 Rakhimov flight, Zurich to Le Bourget, 22 January 1998: French Interior Ministry documents in author's possession.

240 Rakhimov flight, Geneva to Paris, 20 March, 1998: French Interior Ministry documents in author's possession.

241 *Politiken*, 18 March 1998.

241 Samaranch and Rakhimov: Guelfi, *L'Original*, Robert Laffont, Paris, 1999.

242 Rakhimov, Prince Jean de Luxembourg and Georges de

Charette: *Le Vrai Journal*, produced by Pascal Henry and Stefan Ravion, Canal Plus, 18 October 1998.

242 Rakhimov abandons his case: documents filed at Tribunal De Grande Instance de Paris, 9 August 1999.

242–3 Interpol, Tashkent, 11 May 1998.

243 Guelfi, Samaranch, Dassler and Smirnov: Guelfi, *L'Original*, 1999.

243 Guelfi and Olympic politics: Craig Copetas and Roger Thurow, *Wall Street Journal*, 3 March 1999, and Christopher Dickey, *Newsweek*, 29 March 1999.

244 'Every tree in the forest': *Washington Post*, 9 February 2000.

248 Invitation to Chowdhry, 7 February 1996.

249 Samaranch's visit to Tashkent on 31 August 1996: *Olympic Review*, XXVI–II, October–November 1996.

16: Robbery in the Ring

252 Letter from Judge Mbaye, 28 July 1999.

254 'shameful decisions': Reuters, 5 September 1999.

263 African and Asian boxing federation press releases: www.aiba.net.

265 Ali and the Mob: David Remnick, *King of the World*, 1998.

17: Tantrums and Tussles

267–70 *Executive Board Minutes*, June 1999.

270 Jennings profile: 'Olympic Gadfly Gets The Gold Medal For Role Reversal; Salt Lake City Scandal Turns Spurned British Crusader Into Valued Consultant': *Wall Street Journal*, 21 January 1999.

272 Story about judicial murder: 'A Distant Mirror; IOC Scandal Has A Familiar Ring For Mr Samaranch; Olympic

Imbroglio Reflects President's Francoist Past; A Clear Pattern Emerges', *Wall Street Journal*, 7 December 1999.

272–3 Servan-Schreiber to *Suddeutsche Zeitung*, 8 October 1999.

273–4 Servan-Schreiber to *News Limited*, 1 November 1999.

18: A Rebel in the Family

279 'freezing my butt off': *Los Angeles Times Magazine*, June 1996.

280 Architecture, decor and directors: AAF website, www. aafla.org. Board directors' salaries are drawn from their various company websites.

280 Asset growth: Amateur Athletic Foundation of Los Angeles tax returns.

282 OATH: www.theoath.org.

283 'such a marginal group': *Toronto Star*, 27 March 1999.

283 Dawn Fraser: Wallechinsky, 1992.

286–7 DeFrantz appeared before Congressman Upton's Committee, 14 October 1999. Its official title is: US House of Representatives, Committee on Commerce: Subcommittee on Oversight and Investigations.

287 Big Birthday Party: Hogan & Hartson, 1999.

288 'Mrs Igaya wanted to do something nice': *Salt Lake Tribune*, 16 February 2000.

288 Hogshead testified before Senator McCain's Commerce Committee on 20 October 1999.

19: A Real Soldier Joins the War on Doping

292 'China is clean': Reuters, 5 October 1994.

294 Don't call me Excellency, 1 February 1999.

295 replacing 'independent' with 'international': AP, 1 February 1999.

295 McCaffrey calls for institutional reform: Reuters, 2 February 1999.

295 Tony Banks: Reuters, 2 February 1999.

295 Otto Schily: AP, 2 February 1999.

296 IOC opposed anti-doping agency: AP, 2 February 1999.

296 Dick Pound's WADA meetings: IOC press releases, 1999.

297 Dr Andrew Pipe: *Toronto Star*, 17 June 1999.

297 'a former fascist': *Deseret News*, 17 November 1999.

297 IOC stonewalling: USA *Today*, 13 July 1999.

297 Pound to McCaffrey, 22 September 1999.

298 'a unilateral solution': AP, 27 October 1999.

299 'won't have credibility with the world's athletes': AP, 27 October 1999.

302 'never been any question of the IOC controlling the agency': AP, 27 October 1999.

304 'not a friend of the Olympic movement': *Sun Herald*, 14 November 1999.

304 Coates and casino: *Melbourne Age*, 14 October 1998.

304 'United States has not really kept fully in touch': AP, 15 November 1999.

306 'you're part of the solution or part of the problem': *Globe and Mail*, 13 January 2000.

20: Juan the Reformer!

307 McDonalds and UPS: AP, 18 March 1999.

308 New allegations about Kim and Coles: AP, 3 May 1999.

309 'what you could call cases or affairs': Reuters, 3 May 1999.

309 None as serious as to merit a warning: *The Australian*, 7 June 1999.

310 Atlanta investigative report: *Griffin Bell Report*, 1999.

310 'the IOC is serious about reforms': AP, 27 September 1999.

310 Mbaye grateful to Young: Sibley memo, 26 September 1988. Atlanta History Center.

311 'pleased by the progress of the IOC Ethics Commission': IOC press release, 28 October 1999.

311 'just another case of a US "inquiry"': Dick Pound to author, 26 December 1999.

311 'just one honest man': AP, 10 December 1999.

312–3 Gosper's losses: Lloyd's confidential sources.

313 'no documents . . . will be released': *Sydney Morning Herald*, 1 February 1999.

313 Documents released: *Sydney Morning Herald*, 2 February 1999.

314 'as close a friend as I've got in the IOC': *An Olympic Life*, 2000, p252.

314 'ongoing struggle with credibility': AP, 6 March 2000.

314 $4,200 meal at Le Cirque: *Deseret News*, 22 February 2000.

315 IOC 2000 Commission members: www.olympic.org.

317 'a tempest in a teapot': *Salt Lake Tribune*, 13 December 1998.

317 Absence of Oscar Arias Sanchez: confirmed to author by his Costa Rica staff.

319 Hill and Knowlton, China and Air China: *Under the Influence, Presidential Candidates and their Campaign Advisers*, 1991, Center for Public Integrity, and *Washington Representatives*, Columbia Books, 1999.

319 Kissinger and Hill and Knowlton: Kissinger, *Years of Renewal*, Weidenfeld & Nicolson, 1999, p773. Seymour Hersh, *The Price of Power, Kissinger in the Nixon White House*, Summit Books, 1983, p433.

319 Kissinger and Coca-Cola: Kissinger's biographer Walter Isaacson, interview with Brian Lamb, broadcast C-SPAN,

27 September 1992.

319 Kissinger and sanctions: Isaacson interview, 1992.

319 Samaranch rides a bike across Tiananmen Square in 1993: *The New Lords of the Rings*, with picture.

320 Baker's law firm: www.bakerdonelson.com.

320 Mitchell's law firm is Verner, Liipfert, Bernhard, McPherson and Hand.

320 Mitchell's directorships: corporate CV.

321 'cross-eyed': AP, 1 June 1999.

325 'trying to protect members': author's note, 12 December 1999.

325 DeFrantz in Sydney, 1991: *The New Lords of the Rings*, 1996, p203.

325 'It was wrong': *Los Angeles Times*, 31 October 1999.

326 IOC reform proposals and final report: www.olympic.org.

326 'You have faced harsh criticism': AP, 11 December 1999.

327 The IOC appointed the new athlete members by acclamation.

327 'Churchill of the Olympic movement': Reuters, 12 December 1999.

21: Mr Samaranch goes to Washington

328 Samaranch testified before Congressman Upton's Committee, 15 December 1999.

331 'Reforms are in Place': *Washington Post*, 15 December 1999.

332 Henry Waxman is the same congressman named in Chapter 6 as collator of *The Hill and Knowlton Documents: How the Tobacco Industry Launched its Disinformation Campaign*.

332 Waxman's statement introducing the International

Olympic Committee Reform Act of 1999: www.house.gov/waxman.

333 Dr Strangelove: Stanley Kubrick, 1963.

335 'Play up the IOC's history': confidential briefing: *Memorandum to the Executive Board*, 15 March 1999.

345 'occasional humor and unshakeable calm': *Washington Post*, 16 December 1999.

Index

375